ID0982702

Told in Letters

Told in Letters

Epistolary Fiction
Before Richardson

Robert Adams Day

Ann Arbor
The University of Michigan Press

Detur dignissimis:
M. D. *and* M. C. M.

ACKNOWLEDGMENTS

The chapters that follow grew out of an investigation commenced at Harvard under the late Professor George Sherburn and directed jointly by him and by the late Professor Hyder Edward Rollins. It is an honor to join many others in paying tribute to the memory of these two great scholars and in expressing gratitude for their wise guidance. The staffs of the Harvard University libraries, the library of the University of Chicago, the British Museum, the Bodleian Library, the Bibliothèque de l'Arsénal, Paris, the Newberry Library, Chicago, and the library of Trinity College, Dublin, have been courteous and helpful. Part of the work for this study was done on a research grant at the Newberry Library, for which I am grateful to the trustees and to Mr. Lawrence Towner, the director. I wish to thank Professor Emeritus George Parks, Professors Miriam Starkman and James Tobin of Queens College, and Mr. Herbert Cahoon of the Pierpont Morgan Library for assistance in my research, and Dean Sidney Axelrad of Queens College for the help given by his office staff, especially by Mrs. Florence Waldhetter, in typing the manuscript. Mr. Glen Baxter of the Harvard-Yenching Institute gave me valuable advice at an early stage of my work. Mr. Milton Malkin, who generously and patiently tracked down many errors and infelicities, deserves a gratitude which he best can estimate.

R. A. DAY

Queens College, City University of New York

Contents

❧

CHAPTER I

Introduction

...that vast inundation of histories, memoirs, adventures,
&c. &c. &c. &c....

—*The Drury-Lane Journal*

In the history of English prose fiction, the period between the
death of Elizabeth and the writing of *Pamela* may be fittingly
compared to an uncharted waste. Two considerable promi-
nences called Bunyan and Defoe are indicated, while some
writers hesitantly include smaller landmarks—*Oroonoko* and
Incognita. But around these spreads a vast desert of popular
literature, scarcely studied and mostly unremembered. In the
standard one-volume histories of the English novel one can almost hear the author sighing with relief as he approaches the
crucial date of 1740, after which he can proceed in detail and
with confidence. The literary historian, in the words of
Northrop Frye, "postulates a great fictional gap in the seventeenth century, which exactly covers the golden age of
rhetorical prose,"[1] and the reader finds what Swift found in
cartography:

> So Geographers in Afric-Maps
> With Savage-Pictures fill their Gaps;
> And o'er unhabitable Downs
> Place Elephants for want of Towns,

the elephants in this case being the ponderous French romances and the several English imitations of them. It is true

that a certain amount of detailed information covering particular areas can be found in specialized works; but the areas are
far apart and unconnected. Indeed, even with Bunyan and
Defoe, the idea that they somehow blundered into immortal-
ity has not entirely given way in the light of detailed research
into their literary background. The spaces between the "elephants" remain to be filled.

This study is an attempt to follow one track through a
century and a half of subliterature. The track, never entirely
obliterated in the badlands of popular fiction, is the epistolary
technique: the use of imaginary letters as a vehicle for conveying a connected narrative. It is seldom hard to follow, for
letter fiction was usually marked by qualities that set it apart
from other kinds of narrative—qualities that became more
prominent with the passage of time and that have acquired the
highest importance in the fiction of our own day. To alter the
metaphor, this is the history and biography of a literary device during a period when it changed and grew, developed
complexity, and became an organic part of fiction. If we take
"biography" to imply an examination of this device restricted
to literary or artistic considerations, then "history" will en-
compass its ancestry, its social and economic status, its reception by the public, its revelation of public taste, and its influence on what came after. For the study of popular literature
in a primitive stage of development the two approaches are
complementary and should be inseparable, a point exemplified
in such significant contemporary studies of fiction as Ian
Watt's *The Rise of the Novel* and Wayne Booth's *The Rhetoric of Fiction*. Methods that apply to Henry James will not
tell the whole story for Defoe.

Epistolary narratives held no unimportant place in early
English fiction. We may very roughly estimate that a thousand works of fiction, new or revived, appeared in something
like forty-five hundred editions or issues between the Restoration and 1740. Of these, over two hundred works in five
hundred editions or issues were letter fiction. This proportion
compares very favorably with that for the years 1740–1800,
when the English epistolary novel was in its heyday.[2] Some
of the most popular tales of the day were letter fiction; several
of these were widely imitated, and a few were of remarkable
literary merit, at least for their time and their kind.

At this point the reader may wonder why works of such interest have been so strangely neglected; but there is nothing at all astonishing about the neglect of these books. Though they were so popular that some editions have been literally read out of existence, they went largely unnoticed by the men who made, amended, and recorded official taste. They are now very scarce, some surviving in single copies only, and most confined to the rare-book rooms of the great English and American research libraries. Their authors—those who bothered to affix their names—are unknown today except to specialists.

In 1907 Sir Walter Raleigh wrote to Arundell Esdaile, when the latter was preparing his pioneering bibliography of English prose fiction:

> My book on the Novel is hopelessly inadequate, like all its predecessors, on the 1660–1740 period. That, I think, is the crucial period and the output of novels is very large. All the elements of Richardson are there. . . . Many of the books are forgotten or lost.[3]

"Crucial period" is a strong term. But an era whose beginning offered nothing more remarkable than conceit-laden translations of French romances, heavy-handed imitations of them, a few remains of the Elizabethan novel, religious allegories, jest-books, and rogue biographies, and whose end ushered in the age of Richardson, Fielding, and Smollett, must have been a time when significant literary changes occurred.

Precise investigation of this period can supply new facts and can also correct what amounts to misinformation. To illustrate: certain passages in authoritative and detailed modern studies might lead one to assume, for example, that dime-novel palpitating passion existed not at all before the nineteenth century, that no book which could be called a bourgeois letter-novel was written before *Pamela*, that Aphra Behn wrote no sentimental fiction, and that only her *Oroonoko* survived into the eighteenth century.[4] These are not, of course, deliberate misstatements—they are based on a literary picture which excludes subliterature—but they are not true.

Regrettable as this misinformation or lack of information may be, there are good reasons for it. In addition to the scarcity and obscurity of pre-Richardsonian popular fiction, another stumbling block has until very recently been in the way: the bibliography of early English prose fiction has had to wait until the last two decades for anything resembling accuracy and completeness. Previously, the investigator had to rely on random dippings into the catalogues of such libraries as he could reach, guided by the capriciously titled entries in Arber's enormous *Term Catalogues* or by Esdaile's excellent but incomplete list; and this fact has been partly responsible for the inadequacy of several standard works on the subject.[5] At present, however, in addition to the Wing short-title catalogue of English books to 1700, we have excellent bibliographies of English prose fiction from the beginning of printing through 1740.[6] Even these have had to be selective, adhering to fairly strict definitions of "prose fiction" or "novel," and hence have not included fiction in miscellanies or periodicals, fiction shorter than a certain length, or fiction mixed with other forms.[7] But with these aids it is now possible to examine a single genre of early English fiction in confidence that the results will not be distorted by ignorance of important gaps in the materials and will be accurate enough to throw light on the nature and development of the whole body of fiction of the time.

In this early era, when fiction was not firmly established, methods of composition were not dictated by what was thought artistically "right," but rather by what the ill-paid, slapdash authors could perform most easily and by what the booksellers thought would best please the public. Yet elements of technique, choice of subject, and general method of conducting the narrative may be identical in a badly written book and a well-written one, and what is at first popular in a catchpenny novel may gradually influence both writers and readers of superior fiction without violating "highbrow" taste. Thus, what is scorned in contemporary novels about scientists and businessmen may be respected in C. P. Snow, while pathological violence has traveled from the detective thriller to the novels of Faulkner and Camus. Minor works may reveal much about the public taste of their time and perhaps about the origin of certain later movements of taste. Again, there is the puzzling question of why fiction, which had been "bad" up to a certain time, suddenly became "good" with Richardson, Fielding, and Smollett. Did these masters adopt new, different, and better techniques, or did a change take place in the sort of persons who wrote fiction and in the conditions under which they wrote it? To what point had fictional methods, such as the epistolary technique, developed (even as sheer mechanics) in the chaotic period of experimentation before the great novelists wrote? Were *Pamela* and *Clarissa* literary Minervas, sprung full-grown from the head of Richardson? And had authors and public exploited and understood the advantages peculiar to letter fiction before his day? These questions need answering, if only to fill a gap in the history of English literature and provide a satisfactory background against which to see Richardson and his followers in perspective; the answers may also help to elucidate problems in the art of fiction and to indicate "missing links" in the English novel's evolution.

It is not a simple task to produce an acceptable definition of "letter fiction." Indeed, we discover that fiction itself in this era is a slippery and elusive thing. Genres are not established; fact masquerades as fiction and fiction as fact; the two may alternate even from page to page. Titles give little help: "history," "romance," "true relation," "memoirs," "novel" may mean almost anything, and this has led Walter Allen, in *The English Novel,* to compare the period very aptly to a frontier territory, such as Alsace-Lorraine.[8] One must examine a book itself with care to determine precisely what it is, and even then one may be mistaken.[9] Moreover, what is *epistolary* fiction? Needless to say, the period does not afford any *Clarissas, Humphry Clinkers,* or *Evelinas;* nevertheless, it was a rare work indeed at this time that did not contain at least one letter printed in full, set off in italics, and perhaps headed with a band of type ornaments. The following rather loose characterization of epistolary fiction must suffice as a working definition: any prose narrative, long or short, largely or wholly imaginative, in which letters, partly or entirely fictitious, serve as the narrative medium or figure significantly in the conduct of the story. This definition eliminates several categories of literature which are letter fiction only by courtesy: French romances "*de longue haleine*" in translation, and some English imitations; collections of letters by actual persons such as Howell, Balzac, Voiture; most manuals and "complete letter-writers"; stories containing only a few letters, unimportant to the plot; and a few interesting epistolary narratives in verse. What remains is a group of stories in which imaginary letters figure in various quantities—from a page or so to the entire work—and in which the narrative element varies from the slenderest of threads to plots involving intrigue of dizzying intricacy. The letters are presented and related to one another with an amazingly wide variation in subtlety and complexity.

What the use of letters achieves for narrative art may seem fairly obvious, but this achievement meant much to primitive fiction. Epistolary narrative occupies a historical place between the simple objective recounting of events and actions, with its refinements in the autobiographical novels of such writers as Nashe and Defoe, and the more complex, analytical, subjective novel of the nineteenth century, which progresses to the "psychological" novel of Proust, James, Virginia Woolf, Mann, Gide, and Joyce. It represents a stage in the development of technique for depicting and analyzing emotion, thought, motive, character, and reaction to events —the background and climate before and in which events take place—rather than the events themselves. The medieval definition of the letter—*"sermo absentis ad absentem"*—is highly relevant to fiction: the lonely writer of a letter may deliver himself at length and with an intimacy which the exigencies of speech seldom permit; he may pour out his heart, or the author may choose to make him reveal his character in spite of himself. The reader need not be told directly what a character thinks or why he does something, but may be invited to participate in the creative work of the story by finding out for himself, so that the fictional impact on him gains in vividness and comprehensiveness. There is a simultaneous triple action: that of the story, that of the letter writer who renders it, and that of the reader who grasps it and takes his individual sight both upon it and upon the rendition.

The use of letters in fiction at a time when author and public scarcely recognized the possibility of departing from the logical, retrospective, organized presentation of thought— as Faulkner and Joyce do—was of revolutionary importance both to those who wrote and those who read. The epistolary method allowed subjective narrative, which had expired successively with the medieval romance, the Renaissance love-tale, and the *"roman de longue haleine,"* to live again, and to live with enough vigor to survive and grow to the present day. Whether art which emphasizes action or feeling—Sophocles versus Euripides—is more worthy may still be a moot point; but the latter has always found public favor because it satisfies the reader's fundamental craving to know why as well as what.

The advantages and improvements which the epistolary method added to fictional technique may be summarized under the following heads:

Revelation rather than description in depicting character and motive.

The opportunity to analyze and portray emotion and feeling at length without exceeding the privileges of the "omniscient author."

The ability to color the whole narrative with subjectivity, personality, and intimacy, since the letter writer will usually be writing to trusted friends, and will tell the story in his own characteristic way.

The ability to present a rounded picture of an event by recording it from several contrasting points of view—the method of *The Ring and the Book.*

Two other advantages were particularly important, especially if we see them in the light of twentieth-century developments in fiction. The first of these is immediacy. The author may give his story vividness and at the same time artistically disrupt an organized relation in which everything is properly subordinated and arranged (the method of autobiographical narrative), in order to present action in the chaotic and unfinished manner in which we ordinarily see it in life. Richardson was highly conscious of this advantage when he wrote in the preface to *Clarissa:*

All the Letters are written while the hearts of the writers must be supposed to be wholly engaged in their subjects (The events at the time generally dubious): So that they abound not only with critical Situations, but with what may be called *instantaneous* Descriptions and Reflections (proper to be brought home to the breast of the youthful reader); as also with affecting Conversations; many of them written in the dialogue or the dramatic way.

"*Much more* lively and affecting, says one of the principal characters (Vol. VII, Let. 22.) must be the Style of those who write in the height of a *present* distress; the mind tortured by the pangs of uncertainty (the Events then hidden in the womb of Fate); than the dry, narrative, unanimated Style of a person relating difficulties and dangers surmounted, can be; the relater perfectly at ease; and if himself unmoved by his own Story, not likely greatly to affect the Reader." [10]

The second of these advantages—used and appreciated surprisingly often in the fiction of this early period—is that the author may let his characters think on paper; he may try to show the actual motions of the mind, its veerings and incoherences, the shape which thoughts take before they are arranged for formal presentation: inchoate ideas, when the mind is tugged this way and that from its intended course by emotions and small happenings, or is wholly carried away on a new track in spite of itself. This method, now removed from the less "realistic" convention of the letter, is called interior monologue or stream-of-consciousness technique.

All of these technical contributions of the letter to fiction tend in the same direction—toward vivifying the static, formal nature of composed, objective, third-person narrative in the past tense and bringing it into closer contact with the reader. The novel, while retaining its form of words on paper, addressed to the single reader, and requiring no additional medium for presenting its artistic effects, attempts to engross the qualities of the spoken drama. [11]

Samuel Richardson, consciously or unconsciously, made masterly use of these devices, and his contributions to fictional technique have been thoroughly studied. [12] How far his predecessors anticipated him is largely unrecognized. It appears, however, that what they lacked in artistic depth and intuition they made up in inventiveness, and, indeed, in mechanical matters Richardson occasionally fell short of his literary ancestors. But aside from mere mechanics, they produced a large amount of what may properly be called subjective or psychological fiction. The amount of subjective narrative produced and read in the years before *Pamela* is strikingly large, considering our prevalent opinions on the nature of fiction in this period. If it was the age of Defoe, it was also the age of Mrs. Eliza Haywood and other writers who were sometimes preoccupied with the passions and the heart almost to the point of excluding plot and action. The "psychological novel" had a vigorous infancy before it reached maturity.

The question of how much Richardson may have known of this earlier fiction and of how much it influenced him is still unsolved, but it is clear that pre-Richardsonian epistolary fiction developed by fits and starts to a point where Richardson's work may be viewed historically as the culmination of a process or development rather than as a literary eruption. No one would deny that it was so striking a phenomenon as to obliterate the memory of what had gone before. Yet the earlier writers pleased their public; to evaluate their work and to afford information on how much they had accomplished before Richardson's time will place him in proper historical perspective, correct our views on the nature of his achievement in fiction, and emphasize the strength of what remains —his just claims to be a master of narrative and the creator of something new in the realm of the novel.

CHAPTER II

Letters as Ornament[1]

Pythie Epistles, learned Letters, and feruent Complayntes.
—*The Treasurie of Amadis of Fraunce*

Samuel Richardson did not invent the novel in letters. While this statement does not sound as astonishing as it would have fifty years ago, few are familiar with the extent and antiquity of the use of letters in fiction before Richardson's day. From Roman times onward, there was no period when some liaison between the letter and the narrative did not occur. The late Greek romances frequently employed letters in quantity, the romances of the Middle Ages contained them, and a group of letters forming a narrative sequence exists in a French manuscript collection of the early thirteenth century.[2] The early prose tales (or late romances) of Italy, France, and Spain often used the letter lavishly as a narrative device, and the *Processo de cartas* of Juan de Segura, which can be called a true epistolary novel since it consists of forty-four prose letters, appeared in Spain as early as 1548. English fiction of the sixteenth century and after, both native and translated, was filled with letters.

Although our present concern is chiefly with English fiction after 1660, a literary form evolves continuously, and even though much is added to it or altered in the course of time much also remains. The period loosely designated as "the Restoration" produced significant changes in the methods and content of English fiction and saw the establishment of letter fiction for the first time as a genre of real importance, but these changes occurred in varieties of fiction that had been developing for a century and a half.

English fiction in its early stages owed much to translations of Continental works, and not until the eighteenth century did the stream of influence begin to swing the other way. Two of the forms which made up this influx are particularly important: the "Ovidian wooing-story" and the French heroic romance. Ovidian tales appeared in England in the early sixteenth century, and while Ovidian influence fluctuated in the next two hundred years, it never died out. The romance dominated English fiction (at least among the upper classes) without a rival through Caroline and Commonwealth times, the peak of its vogue ending with the Restoration, but its conventions for many decades kept a tenacious grip on writers of fiction.

"Ovidian wooing-story" is a flexible term which characterizes much Renaissance fiction and includes elements present in even more of it. Ovid, in fact, from the vast influence of his *Amores, Ars amatoria, Remedia amoris,* and *Heroidum epistulae* or *Heroides,* may be considered the father of epistolary, sentimental, and psychological fiction. The wooing-story, in its essentials of plot, tone, and setting, derives largely from suggestions in Ovid's treatises on love. It is a tale of amorous intrigue, and in its most characteristic form, realistic and urban. The hero sees and falls in love with the heroine, and lays siege to her affections by means of letters, presents, and go-betweens. The two usually meet and exchange vows, but often complications such as false friends, jealous husbands, or enforced absence prevent the consummation of the affair. Great prominence is given to exchanges of letters at the inception of the wooing and to the role of the servant or friend who carries them. We shall see this pattern repeated endlessly in English fiction, with variations in tone and emphasis, but always the same in basic structure and always involving amorous correspondence.

The mere use of letters as a means of communication between lovers, however essential to the plot the author may make it, does not constitute a letter novel. But if the letters tell us much about the emotions and reactions of the sender, the story gains a new dimension. This, too, may be traced to Ovid—to his *Heroides*. These poetic epistles are one of the most important sources or models for the emotional layer in the structure of modern fiction, not alone because of their literary quality, but because of the immense popularity and prestige which Ovid has always enjoyed. Here are letters which express changing and wavering emotions or outbursts of passion, written in the crises of love; further, in the epistles of Helen and Paris, Hero and Leander, and Acontius and Cydippe (*Heroides* XVI-XXI) the technique is carried a step beyond; we find exchanges of letters which carry the burden of a dialogue. The elements of letter fiction are all here, requiring only to be combined and properly developed, though they had to wait centuries for the process to take place. Furthermore, the *Heroides* carry depiction of the writer's feelings to a high pitch:

> How thin and wasted am I now, think you, scarce able to write this answer to you? and how pale the body I scarce can raise upon my arm? And now I feel an added fear, lest someone besides the nurse who shares my secret may see that we are interchanging words. She sits beside the door, and when they ask how I do within, answers, "She sleeps," that I may write in safety. Presently, when sleep, the excellent excuse for my long retreat, no longer wins belief because I tarry so, and now she sees those coming whom not to admit is hard, she clears her throat and thus gives me the sign agreed upon. Just as they are, in haste I leave my words unfinished, and the letter I have begun is hid in my trembling bosom. Taken thence, a second time it fatigues my fingers; how great the toil to me, yourself can see. May I perish if, to speak truth, you were worthy of it; but I am kinder than is just or you deserve. (Cydippe to Acontius)

Might not this be Clarissa writing to Miss Howe or Lovelace?

> That you are alive, that you take to wife one who, with the father she brings you, is of kingly station, that you have the very power of being ingrate—you owe to me. Whom, hark you, I will straight—but what boots it to foretell your penalty? My ire is in travail with mighty threats. Whither my ire leads, I will follow. Mayhap I

shall repent me of what I do—but I repent me, too, of regard for a faithless husband's good. Be that the concern of the god who now embroils my heart! Something portentous, surely, is working in my soul! (Medea to Jason)

Is this not written as much "to the moment" as Richardson could have wished, and with as much passion as he could command?

I will endure all; my only fear perhaps will be lest that hand of yours be bruised on me. . . . You will say to yourself, when you have seen me bearing all: "He who is a slave so well, let him be a slave to me!" (Acontius to Cydippe)[3]

Here to perfection is the "whining lover" of Restoration drama and heroic romance. The art of Ovid did not have to go far before it became the art of Richardson, and when the form of the epistolary novel began to crystallize in England the process was rapid.

In addition to Ovid's indirect influence through the wooing-story, it is highly probable that the *Heroides* exerted considerable direct influence on authors of fiction who wished to exert their talents in writing passionate complaints. Naturally a part of the educated man's Latinity, they were bound to be more popular and more readily perused for pleasure than drier works. In England they became available in the vernacular through the translations of Turberville in the sixteenth century and of Wye Saltonstall in the seventeenth; Dryden's edition of the *Heroides*, translated by several hands, in 1680, was very popular. Drayton's *England's Heroical Epistles* (1597) is a tribute to the vogue and high favor of the heroid; these were republished throughout the seventeenth century. When Lyly began to portray the divided mind of Lucilla in *Euphues* he went to Ovid (via Turberville) for assistance;[4] and the technique of the famous *Portuguese Letters* (1669) was Ovidian. When they were versified in 1709 as *Love Without Affectation*, the poet, quite conscious that they were "heroic epistles," compared them with the *Heroides* to Ovid's disadvantage.[5] Steele recommended a knowledge of the *Heroides* for the lady's man.

The Ovidian tale first reached England in printed form

in 1540, with *The Castell of Loue*—Lord Berners' translation of Diego de San Pedro's *Cárcel de amor* (1492). The story, a chivalric romance, ends with the hero, Leriano, pining away when his beloved Laureola, daughter of the king of Macedonia, refuses to grant his suit. Its character is conventional enough; but its structure is of great importance, considering its early appearance, in the history of English fiction in letters. Although it is short (fourteen gatherings in octavo) it contains no less than ten long letters, and these include not only the correspondence of the lovers, but a challenge and acceptance and a piteous plea from Laureola to her father, who is about to have her executed for treason. The narrator acts as messenger between the lovers, and the important and organic connection of the letters with the plot is clear from such a passage as the following:

> Ryght doubteous I was when I had receyued and redde the letter sent fro Laureola to Leriano, whether I shulde send it to Leriano, or els kepe it styll tyll I went my selfe.... I feared to put our secretes in peryll of discouerynge by reason of puttynge truste of any meane messanger [or lest the letter] shulde cause hym to execute his purpose in hast, before the tyme agreed.[6]

The entire narrative is divided into sections set off with descriptive titles; the sections include passages labeled "Auctor," long speeches or more properly discourses, and the letters. Thus, the letter is equated with the speech, as one of the bricks which are laid end to end to make up the tale, and has at least equal importance. It plays the same part as the speeches in conveying the characters' feelings and enables the author to let the lovers converse when they are parted, or when, as at the beginning, the lover dares not avow his feelings in the presence of his lady.

Another novel of San Pedro, the *Tractado de amores de Arnalte y Lucenda*, was translated in 1543, and again in 1575 as *The Pretie and Wittie Historie of Arnalt & Lucenda*. This short sentimental novel contains seven letters in which the progress of a tragic wooing and the emotions of the characters are displayed. The story is somewhat closer than *The Castell of Loue* to the Ovidian type, for it does away with medieval trappings and might almost be called a domestic

novel. There is a false friend (as in the later *Euphues*), and
the story ends tragically with both lovers disappointed and
plunged in grief. The letters are executed in a style which
permits the display of strong emotion with some power, in
spite of the rhetorical figures:

> I am become thine, more by unability to resist, then of my
> proper accorde: for if I could, I woulde willinglye eschue
> thee, whereas now I sue vnto thee. ...when I haue
> willed no longer to loue thee, I could not: for mine
> afflicted harte is (thorough mine owne steadfastnes & thy
> good grace) ioyned & linked with thee.

> O how manye times haue I drawen backe my hande from
> this paper, to th' end not to write vnto thee. But ahlas,
> what might she be, that coulde be able to defend hir self
> from such importunity? [7]

The next work of letter fiction to appear in England was
dominated rather more by the spirit of the Renaissance than
by that of the Middle Ages. The *Historia de duobus amanti-
bus* of Aeneas Sylvius Piccolomini, later Pope Pius II, rendered into English as *The Goodli History of the Moste Noble
& Beautiful Ladye Lucres of Scene in Tuskan, and of Her
Louer Eurialus*, first appeared in 1550.[8] *Lucres and Eurialus* is
a landmark in the development of English fiction, for apparently it was the first novella translated into English purely for
entertainment rather than moral instruction, and it marks the
beginning of what we would call the truly realistic, com-
petently plotted, domestic love story. But for us it has additional importance, particularly in view of its early date and
long-lived popularity. The ten letters between the lovers,
which are printed in full, take up a large portion of the narrative and have such a close connection with events that, although the plot is fairly complicated and contains a number
of ingenious intrigues, the story's progress can be traced
through the letters alone. Letters perform almost the entire
task of depicting the emotions of Eurialus and Lucretia and
their reactions to events. We see Eurialus pleading, Lucretia
at first scornfully tearing up his letter, then tolerant, then
capitulating, and finally passionately begging to be allowed to
elope with him to Rome, while he sorrowfully argues that

they must separate to preserve their honor and happiness. The letters create an emotional climate with which we shall become increasingly familiar in later epistolary fiction: the heroine's emotions slowly rise to a crescendo of passion while the hero's, in contrast, begin with violence and decrease to cool reasonableness after the fruition of his love. The vehemence of the letters is emphasized all the more by the rather dry and objective manner in which the straight narrative is written and by the comparatively unemotional dialogue. It would appear that the learned author felt the need of adding a subjective dimension to his story and used the most realistic and pliable means at his disposal.

While these works were enjoying a certain popularity, the English reading public was showing other signs of interest in the fictional or semifictional letter. Lord Berners' translation of Guevara, *The Golden Boke of Marcus Aurelius*, a romanticized biography with twenty moralizing and amatory epistles, had a steady run of editions from its first printing in 1535 until the appearance of Sir Thomas North's translation of a revised version as *The Diall of Princes* in 1557. A tendency to prefer the ornaments of a story to the story itself was manifested with the publication in 1567 of a book called *The Treasurie of Amadis of Fraunce*, "conteyning eloquente orations, pythie Epistles, learned Letters, and feruent Complayntes." This was a translation of a French work which was simply a compilation of all the complaints, letters, discourses, and challenges in the romance of *Amadis de Gaule*. Apparently, a profitably large segment of the public preferred discourse to knightly deeds, like the innkeeper's daughter in *Don Quixote*:

> I do not like those blows that my father speaks of; I prefer the laments which the knights utter when absent from their lady loves and which sometimes make me weep from sympathy.[9]

The Castell of Loue and *Lucres and Eurialus*, to indicate the popularity of these early novels containing letters, were among the books which the bibliophile mason, Captain Cox of Coventry, had "at hiz fingerz endz" in 1575.[10] But in spite of such isolated facts, we could hardly claim that letter fiction made an important figure in the England of Elizabeth had not a host of similar works filled the latter half of the sixteenth century.

The fictional output in England between 1560 and 1580 was dominated by the famous Elizabethan translations of classical, French, and Italian stories, and by original English works which copied their technique. Painter's *Palace of Pleasure*, Fenton's *Certain Tragical Discourses*, Gascoigne's *Master F. J.*, Pettie's *Petite Palace*, Whetstone's *Rocke of Regard*, Grange's *Golden Aphroditis*, the two parts of Lyly's *Euphues*, and the first part of Greene's *Mamillia* belong to this period. All these works—and all of them use letters to further their ends—usher in a new and important phase of fictional technique: the subjective or psychological narrative, in which the speeches, sentiments, and reactions of the characters vie with or surpass the action in importance, detail, and extent.

Though this "subjective" or "psychological" technique was widely popular in Elizabethan England and had been anticipated in the translated works mentioned earlier, in the main it probably owed its origin to certain literary tendencies in France, notably the strong influence of the *Amadis* romances. For while the English were producing "translations" of Italian *novelle*, particularly those of Bandello, they preferred to go to the versions of Boaistuau and Belleforest for the most part, rather than to the originals, being more at ease in French than in Italian. These French versions were executed with a technique which strikingly altered Bandello's tone and conduct of the tale. The typical *novella* of Bandello is short, has a fairly complicated plot, and is narrated in a brisk, spare, objective fashion; Bandello does not dwell on the feelings of his characters, and often gives little indication of them. But in the Boaistuau-Belleforest versions the tale is lengthened, sometimes enormously, and deliberately padded with ornaments which included soliloquies, letters, debates, and long moralizing comments by the translator. The new matter overwhelmed the old, and the intrigue shrank into insignificance beside the sentimental rhetoric.

That this technique proved congenial to English tastes is shown by such writers as Fenton, who, not content with mere literal renditions, repeated the process of inflation with yet more discourses and digressions. Writers of "original" fiction were quick to take up this ornamental mode, so that in Pettie, Grange, and Lyly almost nothing happens in the tale, and even that modicum of action is cavalierly treated, with a tacked-on catastrophe of hastily improvised incidents.

If all this rhetorical ornament were mere decoration, it might be dismissed as a literary curiosity not to the purpose. But it has been argued very persuasively that sentimental rhetoric, within the bounds dictated by the considerations of formal discourse, was used to create a true "psychological novel" and that the authors of these early stories were consciously attempting not only to depict their characters' emotions, but also to analyze them and to portray the processes by which thought takes shape in the mind. An examination of the texts leads to the discovery that surpisingly high percentages of the total wordage, even in comparison with modern fiction, are devoted to emotions and thoughts or to expression tinged with personality and that the plots focus upon internal conflicts—love versus duty, conscience, or fidelity.[11]

The pattern, or loose design, established in these stories is seen to be that of the Ovidian wooing-story, with an elaborate embroidery of rhetoric, sentiments, and psychology heavily draped over the bare bones of the slight tale. It consists, in its essentials, of a declaration by the hero and its modest rejection, an analytical "passion" or soliloquy by both hero and heroine, and exchanges of letters, speeches, and poems, all revolving about the main conflict between love and honor or love and duty. As one of Lyly's editors points out, the object here is not to tell a story but to illustrate themes, with the stress not upon action but upon subjectivity and the analysis of passion.[12]

A few general observations need to be made concerning the permutations of sentimental rhetoric in these stories of Tudor times. While letters are an important factor in the sentimental machinery and are almost never omitted, they do not outrank other set pieces, but are merely one of several devices; a soliloquy or a sermon may be used just as well to amplify the subject. Nevertheless, letters are often given a close connection with the plot. As early as *Lucres and Eurialus*, for example, we find letters being smuggled to their recipient in the stalk of an artificial violet and in a snowball; just so in *Euphues and His England* the correspondence of Philautus and

Camilla makes use of a pomegranate and a copy of Petrarch.[13]
The reactions of the recipient to the letter are not forgotten;
Lucres, Lucenda, and Pharicles in *Mamillia* tear up or throw
away the first letter they receive, but later think better of it;
and, *ceteris paribus*, Lyly describes the passion into which
Philautus is thrown on receiving Camilla's scornful letter
much in the manner which Mrs. Eliza Haywood was to use in
similar situations one hundred and fifty years later.[14] Letters
are also made to play a part in the development of the plot.
An accusing letter concerning the lady A. O. precipitates a
duel in *The Golden Aphroditis*; Pettie's Iphis is banished from
the court of Scilla's father when his letter, rejected by Scilla,
is discovered; and his Pasiphae, to prove her chastity, shows
Minos her letter from Verecundus, but is caught in her own
trap when the jealous king begins to keep a close watch over
her actions.

The conventions which classical rhetoric and euphuism
forced on the Elizabethan fictional letter did not preclude
realism in portraying emotions. Vehement feelings and plain
language may often be seen peeping through the gorgeous
trappings:

> Fayre Mistresse, if I enjoyed any health, I would wishe
> you parte: but what I do possesse, I acknowledge to be
> yours, and my selfe to be, but your steward. And for this
> service, because it is duty, I crave nothing, but leave my
> meritt wholly to your consideration. Yet, least my scy-
> lence, shuld rob the glory of your pitty, and my death,
> reave you of a faythfull Servant: more of zeale, to do you
> long service: then of any desyre I have to live I heare
> present you my consumed selfe, only kept alive, by the
> lyfe of fayre Felice, who sitteth crowned, in the Pallace
> of my heart: whych bleeding at her feete, showeth the
> meanes of my cure: which if you witsafe, I live: if not,
> you see my death. And thus, doubtfull betweene both,
> untill I kisse your sweete aunswere, I remayne,
>
> Unto my latter Gaspe
Your faithfull
MARINO GEORGIO.[15]

Brian Melbancke's *Philotimus* (1583) contains a long
expostulation in letters with a jilt. Austen Saker's *Narbonus*
(1580) offers an interesting example of early experimentation

with the letter to enlarge the psychological dimensions of fiction; it contains three rough drafts of a letter which, after all, is never sent.[16]

In the last twenty years of the sixteenth century English fiction acquired adventurous episodes, greater narrative objectivity, and longer and more complicated plots. These changes came partly from the powerful influence of the Greek romances and Sidney's *Arcadia;* but the Greek romances too contained epistles among their set pieces, and the euphuistic narrative did not decline abruptly. For example, though the romantic tales of Robert Greene varied in plot from static to violently active, no less than twelve of them contain one or several epistles, often in the form of a sugary love exchange. Somewhat later, Emmanuel Forde's *Ornatus and Artesia* (1607), popular until well after the Restoration, contained five letters, two of which were forged to deceive the lovers. *Fragosa, King of Aragon,* appearing steadily from 1618 to 1663, contains a number of letters important to the plot; a romance of adventure and action, it nevertheless inherits the euphuistic pattern and tone, blending the traditions of Lyly and Sidney.

So far the letter had been used with considerable virtuosity in fiction for motivation, plotting, and characterization. But it was still only an auxiliary device, and no English work had yet appeared in which letters carried the narrative forward unassisted. Such a work came in 1602, when Nicholas Breton's *Poste with a Packet of Madde Letters* was published. Breton's book consisted entirely of letters, lively and realistic, and the realism was perhaps even more important than the innovation in form. It performed valuable services for letter fiction, and these were maintained by its great popularity throughout the seventeenth century. Breton discarded formal rhetoric in letters for the first time; his characters wrote pithy, colloquial English, had believable names (or initials), and corresponded for reasons that might credibly be those of ordinary people. Such narrative as *A Poste* contained was largely in the form of brief sketches, which presented with vivid detail a single character or situation in a domestic setting. *A Poste*, whatever its defects as letter fiction, introduced the truly "familiar" letter into English literature; and its language, as well as many of the fictional situations it originated, became the stock-in-trade both of manuals of letter writing and works of epistolary fiction for many years to come.

Although English fiction in the earlier years of the seventeenth century is an arid expanse, consisting principally of reprints of the more popular books from the age of Elizabeth, two new works of this period claim attention. The first, *Amanda: or, The Reformed Whore*, by Thomas Cranley (1635 and 1639) is interesting because it uses letters in a story which is not romantic or Ovidian, but realistic, moralizing, and sentimental. The author relates that while in prison he caught sight of the fair but wicked Amanda, was seized with a pious desire for her reformation, and admonished her in a series of verse epistles (since he was denied other means of communication) until she repented. That the epistles are in verse does not remove the tale from the category of prose fiction, since at the time verse as a matter of course was accorded a place as a medium for narrative.

The second of these Caroline works is of far greater importance in every way to the history of letter fiction. *The Triumphs of Gods Revenge Against the Crying and Execrable Sinne of Murther*, by John Reynolds, merchant of Exeter, was eagerly bought for nearly a century after its appearance in 1621. For survival through the turbulent seventeenth century it had the advantage of combining sensational crime stories with a specious appeal to the pious, who might be titillated and edified at the same time by reading of the hideous fates of murderers. So great was its popularity with the mass of English readers that the minor critic Charles Gildon, attacking *Robinson Crusoe* in 1719, sneered:

> There is not an old Woman that can go to the Price of it, but buys thy Life and Adventures, and leaves it as a Legacy, with the *Pilgrims Progress*, the *Practice of Piety*, and *God's Revenge against Murther*, to her Posterity.[17]

Although *Gods Revenge* has almost escaped the notice of scholars,[18] it merits detailed comment as letter fiction. Its thirty "tragical histories," though they are short and are related in a manner almost devoid of art, are heavily embellished with epistles. These not only perform the function of enabling the characters to communicate, but perform it almost without assistance, since what little "dialogue" exists is rendered in indirect discourse, and Reynolds makes no attempt to fathom the minds of his personages except to reflect piously on the depravity of their passions or the craftiness of their plots. Many of the stories involve criminal amours, and therefore repeat to some extent the wooing formula of the euphuistic novel. Challenges in writing likewise are frequent, as are letters of advice and letters containing instructions for performing a murder or pleas for release by misunderstood wives. Another interesting use of the letter occurs when a dying priest thus reveals the secret of a murder confided to him in the confessional.[19] Reynolds discarded most of the euphuistic trappings of the letter: his letters are short—ten to fifteen lines—and are written in direct and idiomatic English.

With Reynolds the letter attained a higher status as an instrument of fiction than it had with the Elizabethans, since whether from ineptitude or a desire for realism he eschewed the "passion," the soliloquy, and other aids to fictional discourse used by earlier writers, and retained the letter alone to leaven his dry and objective stories. That it succeeded is evident, for Reynolds' letters showed a tendency to detach themselves from their trammels and assume an independent existence. In the edition of 1670, for example, the letters are printed in italics and set off from the body of the text with a heading and conclusion in large bold-face type. The table of contents is followed by "A TABLE, Of all the Letters (and Challenges) contained in the whole Six BOOKS; with the *Pages* where to find them." As we have already seen with the *Treasurie of Amadis*, there were pre-Restoration readers (and those not of the higher social classes) who so craved the subjective element in fiction that they viewed it in isolation with a pleasure equal to what they got from reading stories of intrigue. Moreover, exclusive of challenges, there are 136 letters, which means on the average one letter to every four pages of narrative. Apparently, the bookseller expected the public to be genuinely appreciative of the distinctive qualities of these letters, for the preface speaks of "the sublimeness of some parts, where suitable passions were to be expressed." [20]

The best means of conveying the importance of letters to Reynolds' technique is to analyze one of his stories in detail. History XVIII, in Book IV, contains seven letters, all of which have an intimate connection with the plot. Borlary, "crook-backed and Camber-legged," and the good Lord Planeze woo Felisanna by means of letters (not printed) conveyed by her maid Radegonda. The maid, however, allows Planeze to see his rival's letters, and Borlary, enraged by her perfidy, cuts off her hair. Planeze, irked at this indirect insult to his lady, accepts a challenge from Borlary, and they duel, but are parted by a passing nobleman. Planeze marries Felisanna, and Borlary attempts to seduce her by means of letters, which she rejects in an indignant epistle. Planeze sees the letters of Borlary and challenges him. In the resulting duel Planeze vanquishes but spares his rival, who promptly has him poisoned. Castruchio, the poisoner, in prison for debt, sends a blackmailing letter to Borlary, but the drunken bawd to whom he entrusts it mistakenly delivers it to the widowed Felisanna and all is discovered. Thus, with Reynolds (for extensive use of letters is the rule in nearly all of his tales) the letter has the important triple function of revealing emotions and character, furnishing motivation, and complicating and resolving the plot; though not so ornamentally impressive as it had been in earlier narratives of psychological conflict, the letter is far more readable and of far greater organic importance in its new objective sphere of action.

Three other important early influences on the form and technique of English letter fiction remain to be mentioned: the enormous French romance, the letters of the French *précieux* writers, and the brief novella, or "novel," as it was coming to be called. The latter two will be discussed in the following chapters.

Without entering into a detailed discussion of the technique and influence of the French romance, we need to keep a few points in mind. This unwieldy dinosaur of fiction, both in French and in translation, has to be reckoned an important influence on the English reading public from the beginning of the seventeenth century until well past the middle of the eighteenth. Romances were read or skimmed by nearly everyone of good taste, particularly by women, and read with unabated ardor up to the time of Richardson. The comments of Dorothy Osborne, Pepys, and Addison attest their early and late popularity, as do even the writings of Scott; in the youth of Mrs. Chapone, who was born in 1727, they were "the favorite reading of females." [21] Their influence on writers was not less pervasive; for example, the student of English fiction between the Restoration and Fielding can almost count on his fingers the number of characters who do not have romance-derived names such as Berontes and Parthenissa. (Defoe himself had his Roxana.) Again, the digressive and structurally inartistic "history" which brings the story to a standstill survives even in Fielding, Smollett, and the Gothic novelists; it is a trademark of the French romance.

More important, such "histories" could be and were considered separately from the rest of the story. Cultivated readers discussed and recommended particular histories to one another as though they were distinct works, and they were sometimes called "novels" and on occasion independently translated and printed. Together with the comparative ease of the task of writing short narratives, the presence in the romances of these frequent interpolated histories undoubtedly contributed to the development of the short "novel" written by Richardson's immediate predecessors. [22] Again, the romance gave no less importance than had the euphuistic novel to love-casuistry and to the often painfully prolonged and elaborate analysis of the characters' emotions. Such stereotypes of preciosity and Platonism as the abject lover and the impossibly idealized heroine—derived from the romance and commonplace in "Restoration" and sentimental drama—were no less frequent in popular fiction. In short, if the source of any technical device in post-Restoration fiction cannot be precisely identified, it is safe to say that we may look to the *roman de longue haleine* for it.

The French romance used letters copiously. They might vary from twenty-odd to well over a hundred, and at least once the letters were accorded the distinction of a separate index. [23] As might be expected with a form produced by highly conscious literary artists, the letters served the plot by being lost, found, forged, misdirected, sent as accusations or acquittals, and so on; they likewise were a principal vehicle for the tortuous analysis of delicate sentiments. Thus, the romance was not an interruption in the development of imaginary letters as a fictional vehicle. On the one hand, the "histories" of the romances prepared readers to accept the essential form in which the fictional letter was to flourish from 1660 to 1740—the "novel," with its various conventions of length, plot, character, situation, and so forth. On the other hand the romance preserved and expanded the mode of fictional expression for which the letter had been found most congenial in the sixteenth century—the Ovidian wooing-story with its subjective and psychological overtones.

From this brief sketch it is clear that almost from the beginning of printing there was a continuous tradition in English, though not consciously formulated, of sentimental-epistolary fiction. Several invectives against idle and wicked books mention such works by name, and many of them were specifically dedicated to an audience of women.[24] But besides their general influence in preparing authors and public for the flowering of the novel in letters, their character, as several instances show, made them acceptable to "the taste of the age" after 1700. *Lucres and Eurialus* appeared in 1708 as *The Amours of Count Schlick; Euphues* was reprinted in 1716 and later as *The False Friend and Inconstant Mistress; Arnalte and Lucenda* and *Fragosa* both appeared after the Restoration, and Mrs. Mary Manley adapted stories from Painter (or a French version of Bandello) as *The Power of Love* in 1720. That these stories could achieve moderate popularity after years of neglect is a striking testimony to the continuity both of some fictional forms and of readers' tastes in the two periods. The popular novel just after 1700, as written by Mrs. Manley, the prolific Mrs. Eliza Haywood, and numerous lesser and anonymous authors, was not strikingly new. A large proportion of the sentimental "novels" of the late seventeenth and early eighteenth centuries were simply euphuistic tales with seventeenth-century accretions—*précieux* and Platonic modes of conduct from the French romance, a modicum of modern setting, a complicated plot derived from contemporary drama, and a degree of mild realism suitable to the temper of the times. With this realism and with more complicated intrigue in plotting, the ingenious use of letters in the mechanics of fiction increased, and it was a rare novel indeed that did not contain a forged or lost letter. But the letter in fiction had not yet become a unique means of narration; it was but one of several possibilities. Nor had it in general become realistic by escaping from the inherited formulas of classical rhetoric and stilted convention. These developments began during the reigns of the later Stuarts, but they were not of native growth.[25] They received their impetus and direction through a flood of translations of contemporary and modish fiction from the Continent.

CHAPTER III

The Importance of Translations

I have given him an *English* Garb, such as few *French* Authors wear.

—*The Amours of Count Schlick*

...those monstrous productions, which, under the name of Trips, Spies, Amusements, and other conceited appellations, have overrun us for some years past.

—Jonathan Swift, *A Proposal for Correcting...*
the English Tongue

It could be said that between 1660 and 1740 little was done in English letter fiction which the French had not done before and done better.[1] Such a statement is partly a tribute to the dominance of imported fiction over the native product in this period and partly a comparison of the status and caliber of novelists in the two countries. There is no question that the French modes imported with the court of Charles II took a firm hold on English fashionable life; one need only think of the array of fops in Restoration comedy, the invectives of satirists against French affectations, and the necessity of the "Grand Tour" to perfect the English gentleman. A parallel might be drawn with the Elizabethan estimate of Italy: degenerate, wicked (and a threat to England's position), but at the same time fascinating because wicked, and the grudgingly acknowledged source of gallantry and good taste. It was logical that with the acceptance of French cultural domination in the world of fashion, French novels should meet with ready acceptance as both titillatingly evil and full of polished gallantry and *bel esprit*.

But there was another factor to encourage a great volume of translations in this period: the economic reality that with no laws against international piracy it was far cheaper for the bookseller to secure a copy of the latest French novel and pay a hack translator (the lowest class of literary worker), than it was to pay for the rights to an original work of fiction. The bookseller might also speculate more safely on a good market for an already successful and modish French story than on an untried original manuscript. Another form of competition, though its importance is hard to estimate, was that of translations by amateurs, often women, who may have been willing to accept nothing or even to pay for the pleasure of seeing their work in print, like Ned Ward's "London Lady," who "has perhaps presented us with a French novel, translated into English by a Lady of Quality." [2] Original English works (particularly before 1700) had an extremely hard struggle in competing with importations.

Occasional protests were heard. "J. B.," in the preface to his translation of Le Pays's *The Drudge* (1673), spoke scornfully of "a Translation; that word that sounds so gloriously in this pretty Frenchyfi'd Generation," [3] and "L. L." complained in the preface to *Evagoras* (1677):

> He [the English author] hath not that *gaity, briskness, bel humeur*, which has *Messeurs les beaux, Esprits de France* [sic]. . . . Booksellers are grown men of mode too, they scorn any thing of this kind below an *Originally in F*—in the Title Page, with a *Made English*. . . . [4]

Such complaints could not better the lot of the English author, but they testify to the dominance of French fiction and the coldness of booksellers toward original works.

The French had begun about the middle of the seventeenth century to experiment with the shorter and more realistic form of fiction known as the *nouvelle* in contrast to the longer and more stilted *roman*. Before the end of the seventeenth century the *nouvelle* had developed a number of variant forms: short stories of intrigue, influenced by the popular *novelas* or *novelle* of Spain and Italy; "historical" novelettes, with their principal interest focused either on history as influenced by the amours of the nobility, or on the delicate psychological conflicts of semihistorical characters (like the famous *Princess de Clèves* and a host of imitations); *chroniques scandaleuses*, or thinly veiled stories of contemporary figures; and brisk anecdotal *jeux d'esprit*. Other forms of fiction which sprang up in France about this time, but which we can scarcely class as *nouvelles* because they lacked the necessary unity and tightness of plot, included collections of fictional letters—of satire, of travel, and those which told a rather poorly defined tale, usually of love. At least four narratives which may be called true letter novels were produced in France by the 1690's.[5] Many of the *nouvelles*, too, made use of the older device of prose narrative thickly interspersed with letters.

Nouvelles of all these kinds were translated into English (sometimes in the very year in which they appeared) and met with varying success; but most were fairly popular. Some had only one English edition; but a few had enormous popularity, being reprinted many times, pirated, and imitated. Several were so popular as to establish minor genres of their own, and these few cut the principal channels in which English epistolary fiction flowed until Richardson's time.

Of the 203 works of letter fiction considered here, at least fifty-seven are certainly translations; this proportion corresponds fairly closely to that found for all types of fiction in the years 1700–1740.[6] These figures are probably too small, however, and no doubt numerous obscure French novels translated into English remain to be identified as sources. Of the approximately five hundred editions and issues of letter fiction produced in England from 1660 to 1740, about 150, almost a third, are of translated works. It might seem that this proportion of translations is small enough to indicate that native letter fiction was holding its own, but the remaining two-thirds consists almost exclusively of works closely imitative of some earlier translation, and several of the French novels reappeared from ten to twenty times before 1740—a success seldom accorded English productions.

Before considering these novels and the influence they exerted, it will be well to examine the form in which they reached the English public. Booksellers were quick to capitalize on the popularity of a new work from France, and the hacks who kept them supplied were sometimes hard pressed. The "Eminent Hands" and "Persons of Quality" who appeared on title pages were largely fictitious, the translations being often executed by impecunious persons of small learning and less ability. The anonymous translator of *The Amorous History of the Gauls* (1725) remarked bitterly in his preface (though it was probably a case of the pot calling the kettle black, and his remarks were intended to enhance the salability of his own work):

> [Translation] is now become the Companion and Prostitute of every miserable Creature that wants a meal, and has the least smattering of Language. By the help of *Littleton, Boyer,* or some other Dictionary, he gives you the words of an Author, as far as he understands, or thinks he understands them, and adds, diminishes, transposes, and does any thing else but translate the rest . . . doing a double Injury both to his Reader and his Author, at the same time imposing upon them both, by making the one say what he never thought, and the other believe it.[7]

Among translators of letter fiction, however, were some who could hardly be called "miserable Creatures;" such were Aphra Behn, Mrs. Eliza Haywood, Sir Roger L'Estrange, John Hughes, Tom Brown, and John Ozell. This is not to say that their translations of fiction were faithful either to the words or to the tone of the author. But the inaccuracy of their translations owed less to their faulty knowledge of French and other languages (although they all made occasional slips) than to their conception of what a good translation should be. The translator of *The Amours of Count Schlick* (1708), after boasting that he had given Aeneas Sylvius "an English garb" such as few French authors wore, went on to remark jauntily:

> I shall only add for the Translation, that I have kept as near to the Author's Diction as was agreeable to the Difference of the Languages; that I have never made any Scruple to add, where the Author gave a Hint worth the improving; and have ventured to leave out what I thought might prove tedious to an *English* Reader.[8]

The preface to the sixth volume of the *Turkish Spy* contains this significant comment:

> I have often heard *Translations* blam'd for keeping too close to the Original Phrase; but never any, before this, for a Negligence that is absolutely necessary to retain the Sense of a *Foreign Author* . . . . nothing sounds well in any Language, which is not deliver'd in the *Natural Idiom*.[9]

Mrs. Haywood, who certainly knew her French, explained her method of translating in the preface to *Letters from a Lady of Quality to a Chevalier* (1721). She spoke of

> the liberty I have taken, in many Places, of *adding*, and in others of *diminishing* (where I thought so doing would render the whole more entertaining). . . . I am very sensible, that, to those who consult the *French*, what I have done will appear to be more properly call'd a Paraphrase than a Translation; and perhaps, may be judg'd rather to proceed from a want of a true Knowledge of my Author, than any Amendment I could propose by making Alterations: but I hope that Curiosity, which leads them to such an Examination, will be accompany'd with an impartial Consideration, that I have, in every Letter, kept close to the Business of the Original, and that I have made it my Care not to exceed the *Meaning*, wherever I have heighten'd the *Expression*, as well as not to retrench any thing but what was entirely *superfluous*.[10]

She gave the general though unwritten theory of her fellow translators of fiction in a nutshell.

The learned and scholarly, occupied with translations of established classics, might speculate on the virtues of metaphrase, paraphrase, and imitation, giving the preference to paraphrase;[11] but these humbler and less scrupulous translators were interested only in gratifying a public eager for sensation and not overeducated. They therefore removed passages which seemed tedious or required explanation, amplified whatever "hints" contained potential sensationalism, and accommodated the author's expressions to "the Taste of the Town"—that is, to current British manners and modes of ex-

pression. This process often resulted in the enlivening and
coarsening of French *délicatesse*—as when Tom Brown translated Voiture's "je vis encore" as "I am alive and lusty" [12]—
and in other more important changes, such as interpolated
incidents, descriptions, or free elaborations by the translator
(Brown freely admitted that he had "inserted a deal of my
own, as I saw occasion").[13] The French novels that were
given "an English dress" in Grub Street have a right to be
considered as far more than mere translations and to claim
status as original work. But their basic structure, many of
their technical devices, and others of their most important
characteristics were preserved and largely accounted for their
popularity as well as their literary influence.

Four kinds of letter fiction of French origin became established in England during the eighty years before *Pamela*,
largely as a result of the great popularity of a few translated
works. These were letters telling a story of love, letters relating a journey or similar adventure, "spy" letters, and scandal-
chronicles consisting largely or wholly of letters. The important works which chiefly influenced the development of these
varieties were the *Lettres portugaises* (1669) and its imitations; the letters of Abelard and Heloise; Marana's *L'Espion
turc* (1684–86); Madame d'Aulnoy's *Relation du voyage
d'Espagne* (1691); Bussy-Rabutin's *Histoire amoureuse des
Gaules* (1665); and the *Lettres historiques et galantes* of
Madame du Noyer (1704). To be sure, these works were not
exclusively responsible for the vogue of the kinds of fiction
they represented. Better works of the same varieties could be
procured in the original or in translation; but these are representative, and they alone were significantly popular.

Before 1740 the translation of the *Lettres portugaises*
alone had appeared ten times, the imitative *Seven Portuguese
Letters* twice, and the *Five Love-Letters Written by a Cavalier* (an imitative sequel) five times.[14] The letters had also
appeared in a bilingual edition (1702), and had been versified
under the title of *Love Without Affectation*, the poetic version appearing in 1709 and five times subsequently, while a
versified version of the Cavalier's answers appeared at least
three times.[15] The *Turkish Spy* had an enormous sale in the
early years of its appearance, and in all probability some of its
early editions were literally read out of existence. It was

eagerly pirated, and its bibliography is complex and confusing; but besides the various issues, and editions of single volumes, the complete eight-volume work had appeared at least six times by 1740. The *Ingenious and Diverting Letters* of Madame d'Aulnoy made at least sixteen appearances in the same period, the letters of Abelard and Heloise nine (in English and Latin).[16] The other works mentioned did not have such spectacular success; but many references indicate their popularity in the original or in translation.

Without doubt the most celebrated of these letter-stories was the famous *Lettres portugaises*. The letters purported to be five actual epistles written by a Portuguese nun, Marianna Alcoforado, to a French officer, the comte de Chamilly, who had loved and deserted her, and it has been definitely proved only in the present century that they are a literary fabrication. Recent commentators, too, have tended to discount the originality of the letters in matters of expression.[17] In their own day, however, their authenticity was generally credited, and they were almost universally regarded as containing the accents of genuine and heartrending passion. The multitude of references to the letters, both in French and English, leaves no room for doubt of the enthusiasm which they generated. One of the short tales in Mrs. Jane Barker's *The Lining of the Patch-Work Screen* (1726), for example, was a sequel in which the Nun was reported to have put a corpse in her bed, fired the convent, and escaped to join her Cavalier, who was killed by "an unfortunate Shot." The introductory comment is significant.

> It is something of the *Portugueze Nun* [said the lawyer], whose amorous Letters have been the Entertainment of all the World. Her Story must needs be acceptable, replied the Ladies.[18]

Nuns who carried on intrigues with cavaliers became valuable literary property to such popular novelists as Mrs. Behn, Mrs. Eliza Haywood, and Mrs. Barker; Mrs. Haywood was particularly fond of them. But the most pervasive influence of all was the tone and method of the letters themselves; for whatever we may think of the originality of Guilleraques, their creator, they unquestionably set a fashion. The correspondence of actual persons, as well as epistolary fiction and semifictional letters intended for publication, began to be couched in the "Portuguese" tone of passion.

What were the peculiar qualities of the letters which made so vigorous an onslaught upon European sensibility? One striking characteristic was that in contrast to prevailing modes in fiction, the focus of the story was intense. There was no narrative whatever in the conventional sense, almost no *mise-en-scène* or suggestion of the antecedent action. The reader was presented with page after page of the most rarefied subjectivity. The suffering mind of the Nun occupied the entire picture; the text was restricted to the interminable monologues in which she poured out her emotions. Thus, fiction had reached the technique of the drama at its most refined level—the tirade—but without the steps which the drama always provides to lead up to the tirade. Another striking feature of the letters was the Nun's absence of control—an absence so artfully contrived that its artifice went unnoticed until recently. The style was carefully calculated to give the impression that the Nun was dashing her unpremeditated thoughts down on paper as fast as they came, an effect which was enhanced by the use of dashes and sudden exclamations, the absence of rhetorical subordination or periodic sentence structure, and a jerky, nervous style. Both the author and his public apparently forgot to observe that the time-consuming physical and mental effort of putting ideas on paper offers an almost insuperable barrier to rendering them exactly as they first occur in the mind in a state of relative chaos and that what was being presented was really a transcript of broken speech or a stream of disconnected thoughts, rather arbitrarily called letters. The absence of control extended to the depicted emotions of the Nun. In the space of a few pages she denounced her lover, begged his forgiveness, threatened vengeance, avowed her passion, upbraided her own folly; and what is more, she described the departure of one emotion and the arrival of another:

> If it had not been for this Trial to get the Mastery of my Passion, I should never have understood the force of it; and if I could have foreseen the Pains and Hazards of the Encounter, I am afraid that I should never have ventur'd upon the Attempt; for I am verily perswaded, that I could much better have Supported your Ingratitude it self, tho'

never so Foul and Odious, than the deadly deadly
Thought of this irrevocable Separation. . . . My Soul is
strangely divided: Your Falseness makes me abhor you,
and yet at the same time my Love, my Obstinate, and
Invincible Love, will not consent to part with you. . . .
Alas! Your Contempt I have born already: Nay, had it
been your Hatred, or the most Raging Jealousie; all this,
compar'd with your Indifference, had been a Mercy to
me. . . . Sot that I am, to lie thus at the Mercy of an In-
sensible and Ungrateful Creature . . . Miserable Woman
that I am! Methinks after so much pains taken already to
delude me to my Ruin, you might have strain'd one point
more in this Extremity, to deceive me to my Advantage,
without pretending to excuse your self.

  If ever you set foot in *Portugal* again; I do declare
it to you, that I'll deliver you up to the Revenge of my
Parents. It is a long time that I have now liv'd in a kind
of Licentious Idolatry . . . I am confounded with shame
. . . shall this tormented Heart of mine never find ease? . . .
And yet after all this, I cannot find it in my heart to wish
you any sort of Harm?

  Now do I begin to fancy that I shall not write to you
again for all this, for what necessity is there, that I must
be telling of you at every turn, how my Pulse beats? [19]

This continual wavering of the emotions was recognized as a
step toward realism by many subsequent writers, as their
comments revealed; [20] and the extent to which it was stressed
may be seen in the following synopsis of the five letters:

  Letter I: The Nun reflects on her folly and tries to reason herself out of her passion, but has not the power.

  Letter II: She begins scornfully, but soon is pleading ab-
jectly; she tells her lover how she adores his picture and begs
him to have pity on her.

  Letter III: Again she begins with reproaches, but soon is
apologizing for the length of her letters and thanking the absent lover for the torments he has caused her, which she prefers to stupid tranquility.

  Letter IV: She has seen his lieutenant, who waits for her
letter, but she is unable to stop the torrent of her reproaches
and luxuriates in her misery.

  Letter V: She says that she has determined to renounce

him, has destroyed all his gifts, and will have nothing more to do with him; she threatens him with revenge; then she weakens and ends her letter feebly by saying that she thinks she will write him no more.

Here the story, if such it can be called, is subordinated to a remarkable degree. We get nothing but silence from the absent lover; everything we know of the affair preceding the letters must be picked out from hints and vague allusions. The letters are a series of emotional complaints, strikingly like the *Heroides* in tone and method, and it would be strange indeed if the parallel had not entered the author's mind and directed his efforts, for he was a man of education. The total effect, even for a modern reader, unless he examines the letters bit by bit with a critical eye, is remarkably like that of trying to piece together a story from some actual letters; indeed, the theory has been advanced that some such process actually occurred.[21] Moreover, stilted as some of the sentences seem to the modern eye, and obviously as apostrophe, repetition, and climax appear in them, we must remember that in comparison with the conceited and periphrastic style of fictional letters at the time, the *Portuguese Letters* seemed to be written quite artlessly and with an absence of rhetoric which could result only from their being what they were said to be. One might compare their impact with that of Ernest Hemingway, who is only now being discovered to have a rhetoric of his own. The letters were also an important early manifestation of the "sensibility" which was so marked a characteristic of the epistolary novel in the next century: for the Nun was made to enjoy her misery and to prefer a turmoil of feeling to tranquility (though unlike some of her successors she had something about which to be in turmoil).

Seven additional letters of the Nun, the answers of the Cavalier to her first five, and his answers to the seven, all of which appeared soon after the original letters, were poor imitations, but their inferior quality was apparently little recognized at the time, for they were printed together with the originals in various combinations. The seven additional letters were also translated into English, as were the Cavalier's five, the latter probably by L'Estrange. Whether from the author's ineptitude or design, the answers of the Cavalier (which are given a happy ending with his return to Portugal) are cold and formal; they offer an excellent contrast to the Nun's passion and succeed in creating the impression that the Cavalier, although he protests his devotion, is a cold and designing hypocrite:

> You tell me you have not heard from me this six Months; you shou'd rather accuse the Infidelity of the Messenger, since I have written twice to you in that time, and not the easy blind Fondness you believe you were guilty of in Loving me. Chear then yourself (*Madam*) with this happy hope of enjoying more than ever the most gustful and delicious Effects of our Love.

> You are pleased to say, that at some Seasons, you think you cou'd have Humility enough to attend as Servant to the Woman I love, That thought is extreamly obliging, but since you have so much kindness for me, I conjure you to employ that good Service for your self, for you are the only Person I ever will adore and serve as long as I live.[22]

The seven letters of the sequel, admittedly written by "Une Femme du Monde," are markedly inferior. They are written in an affected vein of preciosity, with frequent references to "ma délicatesse," and the author's efforts to approximate the style of the original are largely confined to the frequent insertion of "Ha!," "Quoi!," "Hé!," and "Hélas!" They (and the answers to them) record the jealousies and torments of the Nun and the progress of her love up to the time of the Cavalier's desertion.

The letters of the Nun with their sequels offered English authors and the public a strikingly popular example of a story told entirely in letters, with narrative almost completely suppressed in the interest of emotion and merely suggested, not related. They also offered a comparatively unfettered and highly sensational mode of writing the love letter, whether fictional or personal and semiliterary. Imitations soon followed. The six love letters of Otway to Mrs. Barry, which were often reprinted, are in the "Portuguese" mode; many others follow it to a lesser degree. Five years after the English translation of the letters Mrs. Behn wrote *Love-Letters Between a Nobleman and His Sister*, which was highly successful, and which took over the Nun's method wholesale; her success produced a host of imitations. Novels tended more than ever to be filled with extravagant, languishing epistles, often to no purpose in advancing the plot; this tendency was particularly marked with Mrs. Eliza Haywood and the lesser female novelists of her day who specialized in short romances of sentiment and passion.

The letters of Abelard and Heloise, which were first translated into English by John Hughes in 1713, seemed an echo and reinforcement of the passionate letters of the Nun. Although it might appear strange that these letters, bristling with medieval learning, should "take" as they did in the age of Pope, their popularity is partly explained by the fact that the actual letters were not what reached the English public. The Latin letters had first been published in 1616, but what Hughes rendered into English was the *Histoire des amours et infortunes d'Abelard et d'Éloise*, compiled by one DuBois. This in turn consisted of various materials: part of a novel, some articles from Bayle's *Dictionary*, and the letters, three of which had been translated into French by Bussy-Rabutin and plagiarized and altered by yet another author.[23] The result bore small resemblance to the original. There is little doubt that Bussy was influenced in his treatment of the letters by the "Portuguese" manner. He made many adaptations large and small, ranging from the suppression of phrases to the insertion of scenes. Thus, where Heloise had quoted Seneca at length, she was made merely to mention him; the disaster of the lovers now resulted from the revenge of Heloise's maid "Agathon" when her love was rejected by Abelard; Abelard was converted into a witty gallant, and Heloise into a *précieuse* coquette. The similarity between the resulting book in English (which was more like a work of epistolary fiction than anything else) and the *Portuguese Letters* is remarkable. The story is largely told by indirection, except in the "Historia calamitatum" of Abelard, which precipitates the correspondence; the vacillating emotions and frantic accents of passion, the disjointed utterances, are much the same as the Nun's:

> I would have guarded you from violence at the expense of my life. Oh! whither does this excess of passion hurry me? Here love is shocked and modesty deprives me of words.

I see nothing here but marks of the Deity, and I speak of nothing but man! You have been the cruel occasion of this by your conduct, Unfaithful One! Ought you at once to break off loving me! Why did you not deceive me for a while rather than immediately abandon me? If you had given me at least some faint signs of a dying passion I would have favoured the deception. But in vain do I flatter myself that you could be constant; you have left no vestige of an excuse for you.

Good God! What is all this? I reproach myself for my own faults, I accuse you for yours, and to what purpose? Veiled as I am, behold in what a disorder you have plunged me! How difficult it is to fight for duty against inclination.

But how ingenious are lovers in tormenting themselves. Judge of the exquisite sensibility and force of my love by that which causes the grief of my soul. I was disturbed at the superscription of your letter; why did you place the name of Heloise before that of Abelard? What means this cruel and unjust distinction? It was your name only—the name of a father and a husband—which my eager eyes sought for. Did you address me thus before cruel fortune had ruined my happiness? I see your heart has forsaken me, and you have made greater advances in the way of devotion than I could wish.

You could not foresee that Heloise would conquer so reigning a passion; but you were mistaken, Abelard, my weakness, when supported by grace, has not hindered me from winning a complete victory.... But what secret trouble rises in my soul—what unthought-of emotion now rises to oppose the resolution I have formed to sigh no more for Abelard? Just Heaven! have I not triumphed over my love? ... Weep, unfortunate wretch, for thou never hadst a more just occasion. I ought to die of grief; grace had overtaken me and I had promised to be faithful to it, but now am I perjured once more, and even grace is sacrificed to Abelard.[24]

Moreover, Heloise as abbess relates that "a young nun who had been forced to enter the convent without a vocation therefor, is by a stratagem I know nothing of escaped and fled to England with a gentleman." [25] The transition from the authentic Heloise into the heroine of a popular novel is almost complete.

The great popularity of this literary patchwork was much enhanced by Pope's *Eloisa to Abelard* (which is indebted to Hughes's version rather than to the Latin). William Duncombe remarked in 1735 that although this translation had at first been anonymous, it had met with a very warm reception.[26]

The enormously popular *Letters Writ by a Turkish Spy* inaugurated a literary genre which lasted a full century with undiminished favor. The first volume of the English version is certainly a translation from the *Espion turc* (1684–86) of the picturesque adventurer Giovanni Paolo Marana, but the history and origin of the remaining volumes is still obscure, though they were in some way connected with Robert Midgley, who was at one time licenser of the press, and with one William Bradshaw. The work's early popularity can be judged from the way in which booksellers scrambled to pirate it.[27] An intelligent reader would not be long deceived by the elaborate prefatory account of finding a heap of manuscripts in Arabic left by the mysterious "Titus of Moldavia," secret agent of the Divan of Constantinople;[28] but the "Turk's" pseudo-secret revelations of the intrigues of European courts and his satirical reflections on the customs and prejudices of France and England were well calculated to appeal to an audience which was assimilating a steady diet of "secret histories."

Imitations were many. Charles Gildon included a series of letters by an Oriental spy in his *Post-Boy Rob'd of His Mail* (1692–93). At the turn of the century Tom Brown had a visiting Frenchman comment on London's follies, and Addison and Steele frequently used the "spy" device. Defoe, who had evidently read the *Spy* with some care, produced an imitative letter of topical satire by "Kora Selyn Oglan" in 1717 and a *Continuation* in 1718.[29] Lyttelton's *Letters from a Persian* were inspired by the *Lettres persanes* of Montesquieu, which in their turn were a series of "spy" letters modeled on those of Marana; the *Chinese Letters* and the *Jewish Spy* of the marquis d'Argens employed the same method. Walpole's *Letter from Xo-Ho* (1757) and Goldsmith's famous *Citizen of the World* (1762) are examples of the persistence of the genre and the appropriateness of the device of a foreign observer to the aims of satirical fiction in the Age of Reason.[30]

The *Turkish Spy*, however, was not merely a series of disjointed satirical sketches; its letters are connected by means of a narrative thread, tenuous indeed, but carried through the whole eight volumes of the work. Thus, "Mahmut" describes his arrival in Paris, establishes contact with other Turkish agents by courier, tells of his love for a fair Greek girl, recounts how he was recognized, suspected, jailed, and released, expresses fear for the fate of his correspondence in transit, arranges for his mother to come to Paris and live in disguise, and so on. In the last volume he confides to a friend his fears that another spy in Vienna has been secretly murdered by agents of the Divan and apprehends the same fate for himself, and he breaks off suddenly and mysteriously as he asks for help to escape. The correspondence is ingeniously varied in style and tone. Mahmut addresses the Grand Mufti with Oriental hyperbole and asks his advice on religious matters; he writes to his friend "Dgnet Oglou" in a more intimate and easy manner, recounting his personal adventures, fears, and feelings; he rebukes his ne'er-do-well brother in lofty tones and reports to the Grand Vizier with abject compliments. Still another dimension is added to the epistolary technique when Mahmut tells one of his correspondents with indignation, pity, or fear what another is doing. Though the narrative elements, seen as a whole, do not form a dominant part of the work, they play a part in helping to tie it together. The author (or translators) probably felt the need of some such unifying device, and by reminding the reader from time to time that it was "Mahmut" writing (and thus introducing an element of fiction) made the letters more interesting and readable than they might otherwise have been.

The "spy" technique as originated in the *Turkish Spy* is fluid and potentially protean; its imitations varied greatly according to the abilities and inclinations of their authors. Thus, David Jones's *Secret History of White-Hall* (1697), though told in letters, is a series of spicy "secret" reports on political intrigue and not much else; Montesquieu's *Lettres persanes* (translated in 1722 by Ozell) almost amounts to a psychological novel; Lyttelton's imitative *Letters from a Persian* (1735) is a hodgepodge of essays on British history, laws, and customs, and bits of fiction, with little binding material;

D'Argens' *Jewish Spy* and *Chinese Letters* (translated in 1739) consists mostly of essays on various religions and their follies in all their manifestations, with little said about the Chinese and Jewish observers. Lesser imitations were numerous but undistinguished.

The Ingenious and Diverting Letters of the Lady— Travels into Spain (1691) by Madame d'Aulnoy, initiated a type of fiction in which the author tells a loosely organized and rambling story of a journey or similar adventure in a series of letters to a friend. It went through edition after edition, though probably the wonders and curiosities of such a currently fascinating country as Spain, as described in the letters, played the greatest part in its popularity. The talented Frenchwoman, in spite of her protestations of authenticity, had constructed her account out of various travel books, personal correspondence, and miscellaneous information, to which she added sensationalism, exaggeration, and personal comment. The story is actually an autobiographical account of the journey, which has been rather arbitrarily chopped into fifteen journal-letters of excessive length. Madame d'Aulnoy was not so clumsy, however, as to forget to insert frequent addresses to her "dear Cousin," and she maintained the illusion of a personal account by recording her reactions to events or to the frequently interpolated "novels."

> I not being able to forbear weeping at so tragical a relation, Don Fernand de Toledo, who had observed it and would not take notice of it for fear of interrupting the relation, rallied me about my tenderness, telling me how well he was pleased to find me so compassionate and that I should not be long before I met with objects fit to exercise it on. I did not so much mind the returning an answer to him, as the thanking this gentleman. . . .
>
> I was pleased in the recital of this story, of which I omit a thousand particulars for fear of tiring you by its length. My waiting-woman was so affected with this relation that she was for having us return back again, to set at the mouth of the cave some red partridges which my people had bought. She imagined the Princess's ghost would be mightily comforted in receiving this testimony of our good will, but for my part I thought I should be more content than her in having those partridges for supper.[31]

Madame d'Aulnoy was fortunate in her translator; the English version is sprightly, witty, and idiomatic. The whole narrative manages to create the impression of a real personality commenting upon interesting incidents, more particularly when the author reports imaginary meetings and conversations with Spanish dignitaries or salts her narrative with portraits of amusing people met on the road or with circumstantial and detailed accounts of the annoyances of travel.

The pattern was a pleasing one, and loose enough not to tax an author with the requirements of sustained narrative. Mrs. Mary Manley indubitably imitated the *Ingenious Letters* in her popular *Letters* of 1696, in which she gave a witty personalized account of a journey from London to Exeter by coach. Like Madame d'Aulnoy, she included descriptions of inns and impertinent fellow-travelers, inserted a couple of "novels" which were supposed to be related by acquaintances on the road, described the sights of the towns she passed through, and expressed her feelings about events and people. The effect of realism was improved by the fact that her published letters were at least partly based upon her actual correspondence, written during a journey in 1694, and were short enough to appear authentic.[32] Numerous cryptic references to personal matters added to the illusion. That Mrs. Manley had Madame d'Aulnoy in mind is borne out by a reference to her book in one of the letters.[33]

Mrs. Manley was promptly imitated by Mrs. Susannah Centlivre in her "Journey to Exon" (1700), a letter filled with satirical portraits of provincial types, by Mrs. Haywood in her *Bath-Intrigues*, and by others, notably in short accounts in periodical fiction. The form required a light touch, with plenty of amusing personal comment, but afforded an admirable frame-story for whatever portraits, descriptions, or brief stories of intrigue the author might wish to bring together; and the letter-device provided a means for asserting the complete veracity of the narrative.

The *Histoire amoureuse des Gaules* (1665) of Roger de Rabutin, comte de Bussy, has been recognized as the *locus classicus* of the *chronique scandaleuse* or "key-novel" because it discarded the circumlocutions, disguises, and ornaments of the romance and related the intimate history of living persons in fictional form, but in a direct and vivid manner with no attempt at concealment. Bussy told of his complicated intrigues in a dry, rapid, concise fashion, but made use of frequent passages of dialogue and of passionate letters to give life to his personages. Each intrigue gives occasion for a few love letters of a revealing nature, sometimes cleverly introduced, sometimes not: thus a series of the luscious letters of Mme d'Olonne is discovered in the trunk of a dead nobleman and read and commented upon by a pair of gossips.[34] The narrative is divided into three loosely defined parts: the intrigues of Mme d'Olonne, those of Mme de Chastillon, and those of the duc de Vivonne with Mme de Sévigné and of Bussy with Mme de Monglas. The looseness of structure which characterizes such famous English scandal-chronicles as the *New Atalantis* and the *Memoirs of Utopia* is just as pronounced here; the work is a mere string of gossipy anecdotes, tied together through being related by the same person or called to mind by one or another. The function of such letters as were given in the narrative is made clear by the comment on some that were not:

> They wrote to one another very often...I shall not mention their letters, which spoke of their love, and of their impatience to see one another again, but in a very common manner.[35]

The letters were occasionally tricked out with dates for the sake of authenticity, and one was given an added piquancy by a declaration that it had been written in cipher.

The frequent use of letters being established in the scandal-chronicle, it was adopted by Mrs. Manley and Mrs. Haywood. Letters might serve to further an intrigue or might lend spice to a tale by purporting to be the actual correspondence of the famous contemporaries being slandered, while the reader might amuse himself by attempting to discover what actual persons were concealed behind the conventional "Mirtamenes" and "Alcanders" signed to them. The scandal-story entirely in letters was also popular. Its most notable French example was the *Lettres historiques et galantes* (1704) of Mme du Noyer, which Lady Mary Wortley Montagu was devouring long before they were translated in 1716 as *Letters from a Lady at Paris to a Lady at Avignon*.[36] Richard Steele also was familiar with the *Lettres* and borrowed from them, as their translator noted.[37] They present the correspondence of two witty ladies, who exchange the latest scandals, including much comment on Mme de Maintenon and the English Pretender, whose court was then at Avignon. The translation is in a sprightly, malicious style, and the preface is full of compliments to the naturalness, wit, and unstudied charm of the female pen. Mrs. Manley's *Lady's Pacquet of Letters* (later *Court Intrigues*) is somewhat in the same form, although the letters approach their scandalous quarry in several ways instead of one, and the work was evidently composed in a different fashion. Mrs. Haywood's *Bath-Intrigues* (1725) is closer in method to its French predecessor. In it "J. B." writes four witty letters from Bath to his friend "Will," calming Will's fears about the fidelity of the beautiful Cloe while he retails anecdotes of the latest fashionable adulteries and satirically portrays the various notables who are taking the waters.

After 1720 several important works which deserve to be called epistolary novels rather than letter-stories were translated from the French. Comparatively long, they were written with a high degree of literary competence, and though they might be said to have merely developed the technique of the *Portuguese Letters* to a higher level, they nevertheless represented something new to the English reader, something very close to the mature epistolary novel which Richardson created. The earliest of these was Mrs. Haywood's translation of a novel by Edmé Boursault as *Letters from a Lady of Quality to a Chevalier* (1721). The story consists of thirteen letters from the heroine to her lover. She begins with playful badinage and Platonic affection, but by Letter V she is raving with the torments of the conflict between virtue and inclination. Virtue eventually loses, and she begins to be consumed with jealousy and tremulous fears (later proved false) that her husband has discovered the affair. Her lover is forced to go to England, and she gradually calms herself in her apprehensions and bereavement with thoughts of future happiness. The importance of this work lies not in the story, but in the competence with which the author portrays the alteration and gradual intensification of the heroine's feelings, and in the great length at which he develops a tale which might have been told very briefly and simply. The story apparently sold well, and its translator often tried to imitate its method, as in her letter-sequence "Theano and Elismonda" in *Love Letters on All Occasions* (1730), but with indifferent success.

The *Persian Letters* of Montesquieu were an outgrowth of the "spy" letter, but they elevated its fictional status. The subplot concerning the increasing disorder of the eunuchs and wives in Usbek's harem in Persia is continually kept in the reader's mind, in spite of the predominance of the satiric material; and although in Montesquieu's hands the story remained in a hybrid form, he was quite conscious of the value of letters in presenting a picture of the altering and developing mental states of his personages. He made them analyze their feelings in their letters to one another; and the plot line dealing with the wives increases in importance and interest until the catastrophe, when Usbek's favorite and most trusted wife reveals her triumphant infidelity. The thread of personal relations is made to tie all the letters together into a more organic unity than had been afforded by the random adventures of Mahmut in the *Turkish Spy*.

The *Letters of the Marchioness de M*** to the Count de R****, translated by Samuel Humphreys from the French of Crébillon *fils* in 1735, presented an even more intense development of the psychological novel than Boursault's tale, which it resembled. It consists of seventy long letters and numerous "billets," written by the marchioness to her lover. The reader is treated to a crescendo of emotions which consumes one hundred and eleven pages before the lady grants the "final favor," and an equally long decrescendo as she goes into a decline, repents, and dies. She agonizes over her states of feeling with unbearable prolixity; that such a novel could be produced and eagerly read a decade before *Clarissa* shows how well the public was prepared for Richardson's novels. Action is at an almost irreducible minimum in the story, which takes place exclusively in the present and in the marchioness' mind. Her death is presented in a manner which was to become a cliché in later epistolary novels, with her travail and hurrying thoughts carefully indicated:

> My Tears, and the Pangs of Death, render me incapable of writing more. Pity me, I beseech you; but be careful of your own Welfare! Perhaps I shall be no more, when you receive this Letter. Adieu. I must endeavor to improve my few remaining Moments. I am now come to the last Period of my Days, and am preparing to end them with Fortitude. Adieu! Adieu! Adieu! for ever! [38]

In comparison with the marchioness' letters, the first three parts of Marivaux's *Vie de Marianne*, translated as a novel in the following year, present a story full of lively action. The much-discussed question of this novel's similarity to *Pamela* need not detain us here; but the fact of the similarity indicates a degree of *de facto* continuity between Richardson's work and novels available in the previous decade. The story of Marianne might be called an autobiographical account as well as a series of letters, were it not for its occasional references to the imaginary recipient; but its literary quality raises it above the majority of these early translations, although their epistolary technique is more highly developed and interesting.

This brief survey has attempted to convey some idea of the range of technical devices exhibited by the narratives in letters which came to England from France in the years just before Richardson wrote his novels. The quality of these tales improved, and they grew in complexity and effectiveness as time passed; and, in common with other translated fiction, they had a considerable advantage in popular appeal over most works by English authors. Besides, these translations were so well adapted to current British tastes that their foreignness was less felt than it might have been, and an original epistolary tale with an excellent plot and a domestic setting, such as *The Perfidious P—* or *Lindamira*, both of which appeared in 1702, might have little to recommend it over the well-established and popular translations. Such factors account for the lack of initiative in English authors and the great extent to which translations both stimulated and controlled the writing of early English letter fiction. Native tendencies might be encouraged, as happened with the influence of French scandal-novels and *nouvelles historiques* on the already existing English technique of narrative with inserted letters; but even if authors in this early period were willing and able to experiment with new fictional forms, they had little incentive to do so. English writers of epistolary fiction allowed themselves to be confined to the paths marked out for them by Continental novels until the conditions affecting their work began to alter toward the middle of the eighteenth century.

CHAPTER IV

"Familiar Letters" and Fiction

A man's letters . . . are only the mirror of his breast.
—Samuel Johnson (to Mrs. Thrale)

The seventeenth and eighteenth centuries saw the flowering of the "familiar letter" into a literary genre of great importance and popularity. The period was not unique in this respect; the semipublic, formal epistles of Cicero, Pliny, the Church fathers, and Renaissance humanists like Erasmus, Politian, Guevara, and Ascham are obvious examples to the contrary. But in seventeenth-century England the familiar letter in the vernacular began to appeal to a large and enthusiastic public, as distinguished from a choice audience of scholars, and to develop the quality of negligent charm which culminated in the famous correspondence of such men as Pope, Walpole, Gray, and Cowper. People apparently became genuinely hungry to read other people's letters, almost anyone's letters; and booksellers were quite ready to satisfy their appetite, as is evidenced by advertisements like the following, from the astute and unscrupulous Edmund Curll:

> Post-Office Intelligence: or, Universal Gallantry. Being a collection of love-letters, written by persons in all stations, from most parts of the kingdom. Faithfully published from their originals, returned, into the General-Post office in Lombard Street, the persons to whom they were di-

rected, being either dead, or removed from their usual place of abode.[1]

We need only remember what a cliché "a letter to a friend" had become by this time, as a vehicle for putting almost anything into print, to realize how completely the image of the familiar letter dominated the literary modes of the age.

Social, economic, and cultural factors favored the growth of letter-writing as a part of common life in the seventeenth and early eighteenth centuries. The English postal service constantly, if spasmodically, increased in efficiency, cheapness, and availability—with the appointment of a postmaster general by Cromwell, the establishment of the London penny post in 1680, the use of stamps. It became easy to correspond on matters of no particular importance and to send and receive letters quickly and often. Thus, the personal letter was no longer restricted to business matters or emergency messages and might become a vehicle for something approximating conversation. At the same time the level of general literacy in England was high, very high indeed in comparison with much of the Continent; the frequency with which young women, children, and even servants wrote letters was remarked on by travelers.[2] On a higher level of society, most grammar schools required the students (usually in the fourth form) to compose epistles in Latin and English as an easily taught, learned, and controlled form of elementary composition. In many schools the students wrote two epistles each week, one in answer to the other, basing them closely upon models in classical rhetorics. This practice could lead to anything from a polite accomplishment to professional writing, depending on the extent to which the writer had an eye toward publication. The semipublic "display letters" of the Restoration wits fared as did the "sugred sonnets" of a century before. Among those whose published letters enjoyed considerable success were Joseph Hall, John Donne, Wotton, James Howell, Robert Loveday, Suckling, and the Restoration courtier dramatists.

At the same time, letter-manuals adapted to the tastes of all social levels found a ready market; but these are not our concern. No very clear line, however, was drawn between collections of letters intended as instructive models and miscellanies of letters designed for entertainment, and these last bridged the gap between Emily Post and epistolary fiction. Here, too, Continental influence played a part, for the letters of French wits—Guez de Balzac, Voiture, Fontenelle, Le Pays, and Scarron—were widely popular, and numbered even Dryden among their translators.[3]

In an age when the essay, the article, and the short story had not taken form, the advantages of the letter as a medium for any short and nondescript piece of prose began to be appreciated. The very amorphousness of the *familiar* letter made it ideal for the writer who chose to produce a variety of diverting tidbits for popular entertainment and did not have the inclination or the leisure for sustained work—who was, to put it baldly, a hack. The importance of the letter in Grub Street, and the variety of forms it might take, are well illustrated in the life and works of the popular Tom Brown. From 1697 to his death in 1704 Brown published letters in some form each year, and a very large proportion of his total work consists of letters, original or translated.[4]

Even a manual of correspondence might contain the elements of fiction. The model letters were often in pairs, the second answering a question or solving a problem presented in the first. The predicaments of the writers would have to be mentioned, and the letters' approximation of fiction would depend on how much detail the author wished to include on the situation and personal feelings of the correspondents. As time passed these elements increased, as model letters broke away from the conventions of the classical formularies, but the break had to be almost complete before true fiction could emerge. It was a change in an author's intention that got through the impasse; for although Nicholas Breton's *A Poste with a Packet of Madde Letters* (1602) superficially resembles a letter-manual, it is clear that he had no didactic purpose. Breton wished to assemble a series of disconnected sketches in the manner of his "characters" and *Fantasticks,* and a variety of letters arranged as in a manual offered a convenient medium. *A Poste* contains no instructions whatever for inditing letters; and although it begins with the device of intercepted correspondence that was to become indispensable to miscellanies of letters, a glance at the introductory statement shows that this can hardly have been meant to be taken seriously.

> You shall understand, that I know not when, there came a Poste, I know not whence, was going I know not whither, and carried I know not what: But in his way, I know not how, it was his hap with lack of heed, to let fall a Packet of idle Papers, the superscription whereof being only to him that finds it, being my fortune to light on it, seeing no greater style in the direction, fell to opening the enclosure, in which I found divers Letters written, to whom, or from whom I could not learne.[5]

Breton made three significant innovations. He wrote crisp, witty, idiomatic English; he emphasized personal situations and telling details in his pairs of letters; and he popularized several stock predicaments for his imaginary correspondents. The style of Breton had only French preciosity as a rival in seventeenth-century letter collections. Other writers who sought to improve their own sales by disparagement simulated dismay:

> I see thou art already bleare-eyed with reading Monsieur Balzac, and the Packet of letters...this stuffs thy memory with stoln French, that with English not worth the stealing; the one commands thee to violate the Laws of all Ancient Rhetorike, the other to observe none,[6]

but such attacks did not counteract the popularity of the brisk Bretonian style. Readers preferred lively and relatively unornamented English prose to the stiff periods of Breton's predecessors.

Such epistles as the following show how far Breton had naturalized the idiom and situations of his correspondents (though here there is certainly an element of satire at their rusticity) and how much he sometimes emphasized the fictional possibilities and the background of the situation:

> The Country-mans Letter to his beloved Sweet-heart.

> Truly Sweet-heart, I am so out of order with my selfe with the extremitie of loue that I beare you, that my heart is euen at my mouth to say Sweet-heart, when I

thinke on you: and if I heare but your name it makes me start, as though I should see you [he tells how he dreams of her and how he "ferreted all night for a rabbet" for her].

...for though the old Crust my Father and the old Cramme my Mother will not come out with their Crownes, I care not, I am all their sonnes, and therefore I shall haue all the Lands: and hauing a good Farme, we shall make shift for mony: and therefore Sweet-heart (for so I well dare call thee,) I pray thee be of good cheere, wash thy face, and put on the Gloues that I gaue thee, for we are full askt next Sunday, and the Sunday after you know what, for I haue your Fathers good will, and you haue my Mothers: if buckle and thong hold, we will load our packs together: I would haue said somewhat else to you, but it was out of my head, and our Schoolemaster was so busie with his boyes, that he would scarce write thus much for me, but farewell, and remember Sunday.

Thine owne from all the world, T. P.

An Answer to her heart of Gold, and best beloved.

Nowne Loue, and kinde soule, I thanke thee for thy sweete Letter a thousand times, I warrant thee it hath bin read and read ouer againe, oftner than I haue fingers and toes: euery night I get vp our Man into my Chamber, and then by my beds side, he sits and reads it to me still, stil til I am almost asleep: but when he reads so often Sweet-heart, and I loue thee: Oh, say I, you doe lie, and he sweares no: and then I said, I thanke you Tom, no loue lost, for I am no changeling [she describes her reactions to the tenderer parts of the foregoing letter]. My Mother hath stolne a whole pecke of flower for a Bride-Cake, and our man hath sworne, he will steale a braue Rose-mary Bush, and I haue spoken for Ale that will make a Cat speake. . . .

Written by our Man at my beds side at Midnight, when the folkes were all a-sleepe.

Your true loving in heart, till death us depart,

E. S.[7]

Similar elementary stories are indicated in other sequences among Breton's letters: in one the girl is calumniated and her lover reproves her supposed unfaithfulness, but after a quarrel they make up and agree upon marriage. In another, consisting of four letters, Rinaldo begins his amorous attack upon Lorina with a high-flown epistle, she retorts pertly, he urges his cause, and she relents and encourages his suit. This sequence represents the maximum of complication and length achieved in Breton's epistolary narratives, but the collection as a whole presents a rich variety of situations and characters, with modifications of style adapted to the various imaginary writers. Many of the letters show the influence of the "character": the seventh letter of Book I, to a virtuous gentlewoman, might well be called a character of such a person.[8] There are letters of advice, love proposals and their answers, railing letters, letters of news, a few letters of business, a letter recommending a servant, a warning against marriage, and so on.

Several kinds of letters and situations in Breton's collection, which became stock types, were used again and again in semifictional letters for over a century. Among these were the facetious letter of news, the railing letter, in which ill-natured and ingenious abuse is heaped on the recipient for no particular reason, the begging letter, the dissuasive from marriage, and the wooing letter. These last are usually from a ridiculous rustic wooer, or from a rich old man who seeks the favors of a beautiful young girl, and are saucily answered. It would be tedious to list their many imitations; but examples are Ned Ward's scurrilous letter "to a Crooked Lady," in *A Pacquet from Will's* (1701), and *The Amorous Pedant* (1719), a variation on the theme of the clumsy wooer repulsed. Both Tom Brown and Ward were fond of the satirical letter of news (which contained such information as that thieves and informers grow fat and that the city is infested with pestilent sectarians) and of the dissuasive from marriage.

Later epistolary manuals included varying amounts of fictional or entertaining material; and as preoccupation with the form of the letter decreased, interest in its content increased proportionately. Richardson's well-known *Familiar Letters* (or *Letters Written to and for Particular Friends on the Most Important Occasions*) demonstrates how, with full intent to compose a practical and useful manual, a writer might be led without being very conscious of it to produce a work with strong fictional elements. Richardson included no instructions on the mechanics of letter-writing in his volume, and, as his well-known autobiographical letter to Stinstra indicates, he was preoccupied with showing his readers "how they should think & act . . . as well as indite." [9] The stress on conduct, combined with the need of vivid examples for moral instruction and Richardson's own story-telling bent, led inevitably toward fiction. Both character and plot are well defined in most of Richardson's 173 letters; several narratives are carried out into sequences of some length; [10] and at a number of points *Familiar Letters* foreshadows elements of Richardson's novels.[11]

While the followers of Breton adapted the letter-manual to purposes of entertainment, other writers were using it for satire, at once ridiculing epistolary conventions and whatever sorts of persons they might choose to be correspondents. *The Quakers Art of Courtship: The Yea-and-Nay Academy of Complements* (1689) furnishes an interesting example of such epistolary fiction. It combines vehement satire on the Quakers as canting hypocrites and enthusiasts with ridicule of the polite conventions of *The Academy of Complements* (1640) and its followers. It purports to furnish Quakers with suitable modes of address, dialogues, poems, and letters, all of which are made to reveal hypocrisy, lust, covetousness, and the like, and which keep up a constant barrage of ridicule against the forms of speech affected by the Quakers. Three chapters are devoted to collections of letters, with descriptive headings such as:

> Certain other Epistles and Greetings, giving a further Discovery of the *Knack* Yea-and-Nay-People are arrived to as to the thing called *Complement*.[12]

One letter furiously denounces a "Priest of Baal," another discreetly offers a bribe for the good treatment of Friends in prison. The following extracts are typical:

> Having been accustomed to the Use of a Yoke-Fellow, thee mayst have some yearnings after Creature-Refreshment. . . . I doubt not but she may prove a Help-meet for thee upon both Accounts, being possessed not only of Youth enough to *set* an *Elder agog*, but having besides a

considerable Stock of what the *World calls Fortune*, besides what she expects from *Pennsylvania.* . . .

Thy Friend as to the Light,

D. F.

From the South-side of
More-fields *this 19th*
Day of the aforesaid
Fifth Month.

A letter from a Friend to an Attorney in *London*,
to Arrest one that owed him Monies.

. . . Therefore I would have thee to employ a *carnal
Officer* called a Serjeant to seize upon his *outward Taber-
nacle*, and lay him in custody until such time as the
Monies be paid down.[13]

Whatever one may think of the satirist's taste and his motives,
the result is clever in its scurrility, and demonstrates the
adaptability of the letter for lively and amusing satire. A similar sort of multiple satire is found in Jo. Savage's lively translation from the Italian Moscheni, *Brutes Turn'd Criticks*
(1695). Its thirty pairs of letters treat of lawyers, courtiers,
historians, legacy hunters, and similar types. The satire is in
fact quadruple. One of its aspects lies in the choice of beasts:
thus the cat and the ass are lawyers, the ant a servant, the
badger a historian, and the "camelion" a courtier. Second, the
beasts rail at various prevalent vices; third, they hypocritically
defend their own failings; and lastly, the letters ridicule the
emptiness of such conventional epistolary addresses as a letter
consoling a son on the death of a wealthy father. The Cat
writes to the Ass,

The Bearer of this is my Client. . . . He has been in Law
a great while; and his Suit has been unmercifully follow'd
by me ever since: But at length finding that his Case required the Assistance of some more Learned and Able
Advocate, I thought I could not do him better Service,
than to send him to you; by whom the Merits of his
Cause being better understood, might be the more judi-

ciously handled. I have bubbled him as long as ever I could,

and the Ass replies,

Be pleas'd therefore to know that in byassing a Judge, I boast a singular Talent.

The Ant recommends himself to the Toad as a salesman.

Sir,
I am so far convinc'd of your Friendship, that I dare recommend my self to your service, for having lately understood you have open'd a rich and splendid Shop, where of necessity you must have occasion for a great many Hands, I was Ambitious amongst the rest to beg you would make use of mine, humbly presuming my self so far qualify'd for a Journeyman, as it may be granted that one who has made it his business his whole Life, is able to bring a weak Argument to a good end.[14]

Many of the letters are more like essays or "characters" than epistles, and often the "answers" are not actually replies; the letters are connected in tone and narrative in only eighteen of the thirty pairs. The fictional element is limited, inhering principally in the situations suggested, and the translator makes little attempt to vary the style or make it appropriate to the varying "social positions" of the beasts.

Robert Beaumont's *Loves Missives to Virtue* (1660) comes closer to fiction in the sense that most of its letters are organized about a slender narrative thread. They suggest the story of an unsuccessful wooing. Beaumont had evidently speculated on the theory of epistolary fiction, as his address to the reader shows (though the letters which follow indicate that his ability in practice was considerably inferior to his theoretical grasp of the matter):

All the other Letters besides are none of Mine. They are (properly) Others Experiences; this only is Mine, that tells you so. The Several Discourses of other Persons, proceeding from their as various Events, brought Matter: I only Form'd this Matter into Letters. Letters are the Engines of Love; and these were only prepared for an Assault, but never us'd . . . every Epistolist hath this privilege above others, that he may personate any *Humor*, and yet not *patronize* it. I may write of the *Indifferency* of one *Lover* and the *Inconstancy* [of] another, and yet be neither *Subject* nor *Predicate*. While other *Authors* are bound to wait upon the *Event* to give its *Relation*, I may anticipate any by a *Supposition*, and so provide *afore-hand* either for the *goodness* or *badness* of the *Event*, by an *Answer* suitable to *Both*.[15]

The collection begins with a series of short letters to an imaginary lady. Although they are clogged with conceits and witty turns of phrase, they contain frequent and tantalizingly vague references to the events of the courtship. The writer begs to become the lady's servant and sends her a New Year's gift. Later, we learn that she is of superior station. He mentions "your Anger" and regrets that "Distance of Place, [and] Discontent of Mind (occasioned chiefly by the Reports of others) have widened this our Difference." He also writes of "your Answer to my former Letter" (which apparently was an angry reply) and again of "the fruitlesse Successe of former Letters." He asks the help of another woman in his suit and apparently succeeds as time passes, for he writes of "having the Honour to waite upon you in the delicate Moneth of May" and of "having the Privilege above Others." [16] He writes to a man that he has been jilted and again (perhaps to the same man) on the frailty of woman. He then offers himself to yet another woman, with blunt levity, but we hear nothing further of the matter. The letters become increasingly miscellaneous, though one contains significantly misogynistic advice on wooing. The remainder include conventional letters of compliment and of thanks and a long narrative satire on enthusiasts.

If Beaumont intended to write a narrative in letters, he failed lamentably, for his principal object as he wrote seems to have been to adorn his letters with jeweled phrases and ingenious conceits that are suggested by the shadowy situations indicated in the letters, but only remotely related to them. Probably, however, the collection represents the assembling of Beaumont's random essays in the epistolary form and perhaps some actual correspondence, written over a considerable period of time. Such jottings would naturally include high-flown love letters as well as those of compliment; their author probably felt that whatever semblance of narrative they contained or could be given in revision would do their chances of success no harm. The alternative explanation is that Beaumont's notion of the requirements of fiction was distressingly vague.

Although the *CCXI Sociable Letters* (1664) of the eccentric Margaret Cavendish, duchess of Newcastle, have often been mentioned as a step in the direction of the epistolary novel, they are a very short step indeed. It is true that she chose to imitate the correspondence of a pair of ladies and that the letters are written in colloquial English and deal with the ups and downs of English country life in a manner that is thoroughly familiar and domesticated; the Duchess prided herself on having deliberately avoided writing in a "Complementing, and Romancical way":

> I fear [critics] will say the letters are not written in a Mode-style . . . with High Words, and Mystical Expressions, as most of our Modern Letter-writers use to do. . . . I do not intend to Present you here with long Complements in Short Letters, but with Short Descriptions in Long Letters; the truth is, they are rather Scenes than Letters, for I have Endeavoured under the Cover of Letters to Express the Humors of Mankind, and the Actions of Man's Life by the Correspondence of two Ladies . . . so that these Letters are an Imitation of a Personal Visitation and Conversation.[17]

The Duchess' brief "Scenes" included family squabbles and domestic intrigues, such as a foolish household brawl over a chine of beef and the love affair of a neighbor with his maidservant, together with digressions on her own travels, her childlessness, her philosophical speculations, and her views on literature. But the situations that give rise to the letters are invariably dismissed in a few lines, to be followed by speculations on life and manners in the most general terms possible. The typical passage that follows is a fair sample of the rapidity with which she passed from narration to reflection:

> Madam,
>
>   I am sorry that Sir C. A. is Kill'd, and as Sorry that V. A. hath Kill'd him, for by Report they were both Worthy and Right Honourable Persons, which causes me

to wonder how such two Persons could Fall out, for surely they were such men as would be Unwilling to Give an Offence as to Take an Affront, and if the Offence was Unwillingly given, as by Chance, they being men of Honour and Merit, would not be Grieved, at least, not Angry at or for it: but many times a Third man will make a Quarrel betwixt Two others, and leave them to Fight it out. You may say, that sometimes Quarrels cannot be avoided. . . .[18]

Nor is any situation continued or developed beyond the letter in which it is first mentioned. It is clear that the flighty duchess seized upon the letter merely as one of a series of media for conveying her riot of speculations on all subjects under the sun; indeed, she herself explained her rather artless views on adopting the form:

> . . . first, that I have put forth Twenty Playes already, which number I thought to be Sufficient, next, I saw that Variety of Forms did Please the Readers best, and that lastly they would be more taken with the Brevity of Letters, than the Formality of Scenes.[19]

The innovations of the noble lady in fiction consist chiefly in the easy language she used and in the fact that she composed a bookful of imaginary letters; she belongs more properly with Howell and Loveday among the early practitioners of the informal personal essay.

The Familiar Epistles of Coll: Henry Marten (1622) is a collection made in a different manner and for a different purpose. Colonel Marten was one of the regicide judges, and the bulk of the collection appears to consist of letters which he wrote to his mistress, Mary Ward, while awaiting trial in prison immediately after the Restoration. These came by some means into the hands of Edmund Gayton, a miscellaneous hack writer and an ardent royalist, who used them to defame Marten's character. The collection begins with a letter which Marten apparently wrote for publication in defense of his conduct and which Gayton filled with angry interpolations. The letters to Mary Ward follow. These bear much evidence of authenticity: they are full of slang and intimate endearments and contain a multitude of references to the personal affairs of the two. Their lack of organization and extreme informality make it almost impossible to believe that they are fabrications. Most of them are brief; Marten often refers to supplies of food which he arranged to be sent to Mary, who was apparently without other support, and to his three children (affectionately called "the brats"), who seem to have been smuggled in to visit their father on occasion. He continually writes of his hopes and fears regarding the coming trial, and of his longing to see Mary and the children. The letters as a whole, though they appear to be arranged in a roughly chronological sequence, do not present much of a connected narrative, but they do give a pleasing and very realistic picture of Marten's personality in brief glimpses:

> My sweet soul,
> Whether I have any thing to send thee or no, I must be scribbling to thee. Perhaps I am as well pleased in the doing of it, as thou in the receiving. First, I give thee an account of myself . . .[20]

Marten's letters are followed by a series of twelve foolish "heroicall epistles" supposed to be written by Mary's page "Dick Pettingall" to his mistress, but actually the productions of Gayton.[21] These are clever but weak and incoherent burlesques of the high-flown epistle of love, full of extravagant phrases and far-fetched similes, as might be supposed to come from a lovesick adolescent. Two mildly rebuking letters to Dick from Mary follow, and the difference between their tone and that of the foregoing ones suggests that they may be authentic. Then comes a very vague letter to "Lady B." concerning Marten's amatory conduct, and an open letter from Gayton to Marten. This last is a violent denunciation, which proclaims the doctrine of Divine Right, attacks Marten's morals, and retails a number of scurrilous anecdotes concerning him. Although the work is only partly fiction, the uninformed contemporary reader would have found some difficulty in telling it from similar "true histories" which were fabrications. It evidently made good reading and was republished a number of years later after Marten's death in 1680 —added spice being given to the title by the declaration that the letters had been "found in his Misses Cabinet."

Anecdotal letters of French *épistoliers* such as Fontenelle and Voiture were eagerly read in England, both in the original and in translation, and were eagerly imitated, either for amusement and the display of one's talent, or, by writers like Tom Brown, for profit. The ancients as well as the Italian humanists furnished grist for Brown's mill, and narrative letters of Aristaenetus and Aeneas Sylvius figured in his miscellanies.

Another popular epistolary type, which was established in England largely through Brown's efforts, was the "letter from the dead to the living." The inspiration for these came from a collection by an anonymous Huguenot refugee, who used the device for violent attacks on the king and prelates of France. Brown's imitative letters either presented a famous late contemporary's account of Hell (it was usually found to be remarkably like London) or the satirical comments of a noted inhabitant of the shades on a living person of parallel character. Antiochus was made to write to Louis XIV, Hannibal to Prince Eugene, Charon to Jack Ketch, Henry Purcell to Dr. John Blow, and the late Mrs. Behn to "the famous Virgin Actress" (Mrs. Bracegirdle).[22]

The public was equally ready to buy collections of letters which purported to be by contemporary English wits. The letters of Dryden, Congreve, Wycherley, Dennis, Rochester, Flatman, Etherege, Farquhar, and others of lesser note were served up again and again in miscellanies.[23] These usually bore the name of the most famous contributor on the title page, but his letters were often few and were followed by a mass of letters of wit, news, anecdote, love, and badinage by professionals and amateurs, sometimes single, sometimes arranged in sequences. Many epistolasters (to coin a term) of both sexes were eager to shine in print, and the table of contents in almost any letter-miscellany printed at the turn of the century lists groups of letters which are either anonymous or signed with initials. Such letters were desirable literary property if they were even faintly witty or could be arranged to tell of an amour, and booksellers were eager to obtain them, as is indicated by the following hopeful advertisement from John Dunton, concerning the second volume of *The Post-Boy Rob'd of His Mail*:

> This is also to give Notice that the Publisher of this *First Volume* has receiv'd from a *Young Lady* all the letters

sent her during a *long Courtship,* which shall be inserted in the *Second Volume* aforementioned, with the Ladies *Ingenious Answers* to all his LETTERS. Further this is to Advertise, that if any other Gentlemen or Ladies have any LETTERS, sent 'em whether from their *Lovers* or ingenious Friends, a Publication of which (with Remarks thereon) will either satisfie them or gratifie the Publick, if they please to Direct 'em for Mr. CHAPPEL, to be left at *Smith's* Coffee-house in Stocks-market, they shall be Printed, together with those Letters design'd for *The said Second Volume:* And those Letters sent in according to this *Advertisement,* shall be mark'd with an Asterism, to distinguish 'em from those taken from the Post.[24]

Either Dunton's request was complied with, or the author-editor Gildon chose for the purposes of realism to pretend that it had been, for in the second volume we find the following passages:

> Here I must inform you, That for some Reasons best known to our selves, and the Parties concern'd, and which may be easily guess'd at, we have thought fit to give our Lovers Names more Romantic than their own.

> Sir,
>   Your Promise to insert what Letters should be transmitted to you in the next Volume of *The Post-Boy Rob'd of his Mail,* prevail'd with me to impart these following *Letters* to you, Since the Persons they relate to being long sice marry'd, it can be no prejudice to them, to have this secret Amour published.[25]

The letters in question concern the amour of Lysander and Belvidera and the troubled loves of Lindamor and Clarinda; they are realistic sequences with a fair amount of narrative and conflict.[26] Both appear either to have been written as letter-narratives or to represent actual correspondence furbished up for publication. Such practices were fairly common at the time, a notable example being the letters of Farquhar. He apparently revised his correspondence with the actresses Mrs. Carroll (later Mrs. Centlivre) and Mrs. Oldfield and contributed it to a miscellany which was being assembled by Tom Brown and others to rescue the financially straitened publisher Samuel Briscoe. After their first appearance, these epistles of "Astrea," "Celadon," and "Chloe" adorned a whole series of miscellanies with which Briscoe was connected. The success of the venture probably inspired Farquhar to produce his *Love and Business* (1702), a miscellany which combined letters and poetry.[27]

These semifictional letters were far from the stiff and unreal epistles which had been written for earlier collections and manuals under the domination of the classical formulary. While they owed something in tone and manner to the elegant epistolary conventions of the French, their form was extremely loose and their content was realistic, colloquially expressed, and thoroughly British. A similar flexibility prevailed in informal letters written for whatever purpose by educated persons around 1700. It is clear that their writers (who naturally would not need letter-manuals) wrote more or less as people write informal letters today; they jotted down whatever came into their minds, content to ramble pleasantly, and caring only for the elegance or wit of the individual phrase, not for the form of the whole letter. Indeed, epistolary negligence was coming to be prized more and more, and he who composed a formal epistle ran the risk of being suspected of insincerity:

> If that Sentences were less artfully twin'd, they wou'd be the more persuasive of the Reality of your Passion. Believe me, one Passionate Expression is infinitely more pleasing to a Woman, than all the witty Things you can say.[28]

The *Portuguese Letters* had by now made their influence felt, and they were considered the epitome of artlessness and true passion in one's letters. That such a passage as the following, from the celebrated letters of Otway to Mrs. Barry, could be fervently admired is eloquent testimony to the decline of the formal epistle in entertainment value.

> To purchase that Pardon, what would I not endure? You shall see me prostrate before you, and use me like a Slave, while I kiss the dear Feet that trample upon me. But if my Crime be too great for Forgiveness, as indeed it is very great, deny me not one dear parting Look; let me see you once before I must never see you more.

Christ! I want Patience to support that accursed Thought; I have nothing in the World that is dear to me but you. You have made everything else indifferent: and can I resolve never to see you more? In spight of myself I must always see you. Your Form is fix'd by Fate in my Mind, and is never to be remov'd. I see those lovely piercing Eyes continually, I see each moment those ravishing Lips, which I have gaz'd on still with Desire, and still have touch'd with Transport; and at which I have so often flown with the Fury of most violent Love. Jesus! From whence and whither am I fallen? [29]

A narrative sequence might be popular, however, without being passionate. Heroes sometimes courted the fair with tongue in cheek, and heroines as practical as Pamela existed in the epistolary miscellanies of 1692–1719 in no less abundance than maidens who palpitated with passion and neither ate nor slept:

[From a gallant to a lady]

I did not see enough of you, to be in Love, and therefore I shall not be such a Fop, as to pretend I am: But I heard enough to like you, in spite of all the Imperfections a Masque can cover.

[the gallant's second letter]

You are surpriz'd that a Man of sense shou'd take a Womans word for her being pretty; It may be you have reason, Madam; but then you have the same reason to be surpriz'd, if I shou'd take your word for your being Vertuous. . . . To decide these two points, I know no method so effectual, as to do me the honour of a Rendezvous; then 'twill be the fault of my eyes, if I don't see the one, and the fault of my Constitution, if I don't try the other; tho' I promise you upon my fidelity, that that tryal shall be made with all the decency in the World.

[the lady's reply]

If I was out in your Constitution before, I'm sure you have in your Last discover'd so much of it, that I dare not now venture an Interview, least with your perfect Health, you shou'd prove that you had perfect Strength too.

[Clarinda to Lindamor]

Mr. Lindamor,

 I am amazed at your Letter of the 7*th* present, and at your breach of Promise therein; you say you must submit, and immediately afterwards you would intice me to run away from my Parents, on supposition of a civil welcome from yours; but I would have you know, I never will consent to such a thing . . . neither would I marry any Man without a rational Prospect of a Comfortable Subsistence, for Money is good to keep Love warm. . . . And I pray, Sir, in what a blessed pickle should I be, if your Father disinherit you; and you soon after die, and leave me, and it may be some small Children, to the Mercy of the Parish! In earnest, I am loth to trust to Charity in an Age wherein it's so cold: Think not therefore to wheedle me into a compliance with your unwarrantable Request.[30]

The forces which promoted such farragoes of letters real and imaginary resulted in more ambitious works which are easier to classify as fiction. Four of these are of particular interest: Mrs. Aphra Behn's *Life and Memoirs*, Mrs. Mary Manley's *Letters* and *The Lady's Pacquet of Letters*, and Charles Gildon's *The Post-Man Robb'd of His Mail*. Mrs. Manley's *Letters* of 1696 were written to an unknown correspondent as she journeyed away from the employment of the duchess of Cleveland in 1694, probably touched up only slightly except for the inclusion of three short "novels," and published either by herself or a friend to prepare the public for her forthcoming drama, *The Lost Lover*.[31] In 1707 a collection of forty-one letters from her hand appeared in two separate parts with the mysterious title *The Lady's Pacquet of Letters*. Three of these letters are first-person scandal-chronicles concerning the "secret histories" of famous contemporaries; two sequences are elementary attempts at the epistolary love story; but the rest of the letters are Mrs. Manley's own correspondence with the feminist wit Sarah Fyge Egerton, the duke of Devonshire, her widowed sister Cornelia, and Richard Steele, with whom she was long acquainted. Some of them date back to the neighborhood of 1700. It is probable that Mrs. Manley was in financial straits in 1707 and sold her collected correspondence to Benjamin Bragg the bookseller, together with the fictional sketches, which might easily be given an epistolary form.[32] Her own letters were doubtless polished and expanded; and being arranged in chronological order they would yield (particularly the letters to and from Steele) some semblance of narrative progression. Thus, she and Steele corresponded about their financial difficulties and his ruinous dabblings in alchemy, which she was apparently trying to persuade him to give up.[33] The contents of *The Lady's Pacquet* and the circumstances that brought it to the public remind one of the "nonbooks" of our own day and give an excellent picture of the literary situation in the 1700's: the poverty of authors and of their methods of composition, the taste of the public, and the lack of rigid differentiation—or consciousness of the difference—between fact and fiction.

Some such complicated process of composition may have produced the *Life and Memoirs* of Mrs. Behn, "Written by one of the Fair Sex," which first appeared in her *Histories and Novels* of 1696. This collection was put together by Gildon, and it has been thought that he wrote or at least edited the *Life and Memoirs*. Its contents are extremely miscellaneous: it contains passages of narrative, purporting to be by the member of the fair sex, interspersed with numerous letters. These include a novella in letter form, which relates an adventure of Astrea (Mrs. Behn) in Flanders, a letter telling of the ridiculous suit made to her there by "Van Bruin" and "Vander Albert" and including her correspondence with them, a ridiculous letter of compliment from a London coxcomb to Astrea in a novella containing his "portrait" and the history of his matrimonial adventures, and a series of eight "Love Letters to a Gentleman. By Mrs. A. Behn. Printed from the Original Letters." The style is decidedly uneven, and appears to be on four distinct levels. The "fair sex" passages contain much bad grammar and seem to have been written in considerable haste. The letters from Van Bruin and the fop are excellent burlesques of the worn-out metaphorical style of the complimentary letter. The novellas are written in a light, brisk style, with great clarity, and in a rather feminine manner. The "Letters to a Gentleman" are realistically confused and cryptic; they lack wit, lightness, or polish, and bear much evidence of authenticity. They are either astonishingly clever fabrications or, as is generally thought, Mrs. Behn's actual letters to her friend John Hoyle. From this evidence of style it seems probable that Mrs. Behn must be credited with the authorship of nearly all of the *Life and Memoirs*. Gildon (an acquaintance of hers) probably brought together all of her unfinished writings that he could find, including her correspondence, the novellas, the burlesque epistles, and perhaps even scraps of a tentative autobiography, and hastily dovetailed them together as best he could. (The novellas could easily have been converted into letters for purposes of authentication by adding superscription and signature and inserting a few short passages.) [34]

Gildon may have used the same method, casting an epistolary coloring over an extremely miscellaneous collection of odd fragments to give it the appearance of unity, in his *Post-Man Robb'd of His Mail* (1719).[35] Many of the "letters" in this volume are actually essays. Some are obviously modeled closely on the successful essays of the *Spectator*; some are letters from type characters to one another, commenting on vices and follies; two series of long letters are addressed to a noble lord and are essays on projects, including a proposal for founding a royal academy of arts and sciences. Other letters are variations on the stock themes established by the Bretonian letter collection. Gildon writes letters to himself commending his own works and patronizingly criticizing "little *Sawny* the Poet" (Pope). His book also includes a psychological novel in letters, *The Lover's Sighs*. He evidently had in mind the success of his earlier collection of letters, which he mentions in his preface;[36] it doubtless seemed to him that a second miscellany with a similar title might share the success of the first and afford a convenient means of selling to a bookseller, as one large work, all the scraps he had on hand, with a minimum of trouble in revision.

Personal correspondence, display letters, manuals of letter writing, and fiction in single letters or short sequences do not add up to a unified genre. But the fact that all these kinds, separately or mixed, passed as "familiar letters" and were widely read, is important for an understanding of the early development of letter fiction. Readers in the age of Swift were eager to read letters which at least purported to be those of some real person or persons, but they were not greatly concerned with the contents of the letters, so long as they were fashionable and entertaining. Casting a story in epistolary form authenticated it and satisfied the reigning demand for true histories; and the letter—flexible, short, and easy to compose—could be an essay in elementary fiction that was neither financially risky nor taxing to the writer's talents. The fictional letter would naturally be more solidly entertaining than a mere display of wit and charm based on general propositions rather than anecdotes. And even those who did not buy and read novels so called were exposed to a certain amount of diluted fiction in the highly popular miscellanies of letters.[37]

The familiar letter, however, when turned to the purposes of fiction, forbade development, length, or complexity. Variety of characters, situations, and incidents would assuredly be found in a collection, and indeed from page to page, but the impressions made upon the reader were constantly dissipated in the absence of a unifying theme or plot. The miscellany could not progress as fiction without losing its form. Later writers often pretended to have discovered "pacquets" of letters, but these were integrated around a central plot or theme; they were written from beginning to end as fiction, and any "miscellaneous" appearance their contents might have was planned beforehand and was the result of art rather than nature.

CHAPTER V

The Writers and Readers
of Letter Fiction[1]

Writing ... is become a very considerable Branch of the English Commerce. The Booksellers are the Master Manufacturers.
>   —Daniel Defoe, in *Applebee's Journal*

The author, when unpatronized by the great, has naturally recourse to the bookseller. There cannot perhaps be imagined a combination more prejudicial to taste than this. It is the interest of the one to allow as little for writing, and of the other to write as much as possible.
>   —Oliver Goldsmith, *An Inquiry into the Present State of Polite Learning in Europe*

We have been considering the environment in which, after the Restoration, a literary technique grew into a literary form. But a description of artistic influences only does not tell the whole story. There were social factors of equal importance—the forces of economics and of public taste. If a literary historian is dealing with an established form during a period when it was unquestioningly accepted by its audience, as with the novel in our own day or the epic in a heroic age, he can afford to ignore extraliterary circumstances if he chooses. But a kind of writing that is scarcely recognized as a definite genre, that is "popular" in nature, surviving by pleasing its readers rather than by imposing itself on them, and that fluctuates in content and quality with the pressure of sales needs another sort of treatment. It must be seen through the eyes of those most closely connected with it—authors, booksellers, and buyers. "Subliterature" requires a "consumers' history." It is less intimately concerned with art than with inventories.

How large a public did early letter fiction reach? Of what classes of people was that public composed? Who wrote letter fiction, and under what conditions? How much did authors receive and readers pay for it? How popular was it? Did it include "best sellers"? Were its particular qualities appreciated? The answers will not be found in novels; we must look to their appendages—booksellers' advertisements, prefaces and dedications, subscription lists, remarks in letters and journals—and to the personal side of economic history, the incomes and expenditures of private persons. But specific facts regarding the economic life of the average Englishman in the time of Queen Anne are not abundant; and statements on fiction in the books and periodicals of the day are dangerous evidence. To speak of novels during the early eighteenth century was either to condemn them out of hand as paltry and wicked or to puff them shamelessly under the guise of criticism. With these cautions in mind, however, we may gather enough information for our purposes.

To begin with, it must be borne in mind that at least until the later eighteenth century the English reading public was in effect confined to London. London set the tone for those who sent from Bath, Bristol, and York for books and papers; the circulating library was yet a rarity, and even if much information were available on the number and tastes of provincial readers, they were unimportant compared with those in the metropolis. Literacy did not guarantee the availability of novels or the desire to read them, and the prejudice against any reading other than Scripture, divinity, history, the classics, and works of practical instruction was still strong enough to be significant. Moreover, novels cost money. The price of a novel compared to a day's wage was higher than it is now, especially in our days of paperback publication.

Attempts to calculate the size of the London reading public in the early eighteenth century have had to be based upon records of the circulation of newspapers and magazines. These figures vary from a circulation of ten thousand for the *Gentleman's Magazine* in 1739 to Addison's estimate in 1711 of sixty thousand readers (or more properly, hearers) for the *Spectator*; a probably very reliable estimate of the total circulation of newspapers in 1704 was 43,800.[2] Between the number of people who bought copies of a monthly magazine intended for men of education and the number who *may* have read an essay-periodical tailored to the taste of both sexes and most levels of society lies an extremely wide gap. So many variables and causes of doubt enter our calculation that on this point we must be content with a vague estimate indeed and assume that the potential readers of fiction (including epistolary fiction) in Addison's England may be numbered conservatively at twenty to thirty thousand.[3] Various considerations, such as that book prices remained roughly stationary, that minimal literacy increased, and that periodicals grew in popularity and variety, have led to the conclusion that the reading public enlarged steadily during the first half of the century. (In any case the population of England increased by almost two million during that period.)

Newspapers cost a penny or twopence; the books in which letter fiction was to be found were priced from sixpence to six shillings—one shilling to two shillings and sixpence being the commonest prices.[4] At the same time wages for a skilled laborer might go no higher than two shillings and sixpence a day. The price of a day's wages, one might think, would put novels out of the reach of the literate working man and his wife. But before ruling them out as readers, another matter must be considered. Early in the eighteenth century certain publishers began the practice of printing popular novels and other fiction in installments as a regular feature of their periodical papers; at least one paper consisted exclusively of fictional reprints.[5] Such books, among many others appearing inexpensively in installments, apparently did penetrate to the lower orders of society (much after the manner of the encyclopedias bought today in parts at supermarkets). In this connection the following comments are of considerable interest, though both are doubtless exaggerated by aristocratic bias. The first is from Sir Roger L'Estrange, who complained of the selling of translations so dog cheap that...every nasty groom and roguey lackey is grown so familiar with Homer, Virgil, and Ovid, as if 'twere Robert the Devil, the Seven Champions, or a piece of George Wither.[6]

The second is from a letter in the *Gentleman's Magazine*, which speaks of

this strange Madness of publishing books by piece-meal, at 6 or 12 Pennyworth a week. . . . What an Age of Wit and Learning is this! In which so many Persons in the lowest Stations of Life, are more intent upon cultivating their Minds, than upon feeding and cloathing their Bodies. You shall see a Fellow spend Six-pence upon a Number of *Rapin*, or Three-pence upon a bit of *St. Matthew's Gospel*, when perhaps his Wife and Children want a Bit of Bread, and himself a pair of Breeches.[7]

The works mentioned are productions of lasting worth, which might well have been bought for their "snob value," as people used to buy Wells's *Outline of History*. Novels, however, were also available for a few pence per part, and it would be strange if the "lower orders" had not craved escapist reading, polite amusement, and gallantry as well as culture. Among the works cheaply issued in parts or in periodicals were several of the most popular pieces of epistolary fiction, including Mrs. Behn's *Love-Letters Between a Nobleman and His Sister*, Madame d'Aulnoy's *Ingenious and Diverting Letters*, the letters of Abelard and Heloise, Mrs. Haywood's *Fatal Secret*, and Mrs. Mary Hearne's *Honour the Victory and Love the Prize*.[8] Publication in parts may sometimes have been a way of testing the market, but this certainly was not the case with these novels. With the exception of *The Fatal Secret* they had all proved spectacularly successful for their time, and the publisher could have had few doubts of the salability of the latest novel by the popular Mrs. Haywood. It seems more likely that these works came out in parts in an attempt to exploit their success further by making them available to a new segment of the public in the "lower income brackets."

In addition to reading cheap novels in parts, people with only a few pence to spend could become familiar with letter fiction through many shorter pieces published in one or more issues of a periodical.[9] Through these indirect channels letter fiction must have had considerable circulation among the lower social and economic classes of the literate. There is also evidence that novels originally intended for the polite world found their way below stairs in the course of time. A writer in the *Universal Spectator* for July 4, 1730, spoke with praise of "some compositions in Prose, such as *Telemachus*, which are very instructive and entertaining," but went on to say:

> It requires some Degree of good Sense to relish them; and therefore People of middling Capacities hardly give them the reading, though every *Footman* and *Chambermaid* are fond of the lewd Inventions of *H*[aywoo]*d*, or *M*[anle]*y*.

It was not a sudden phenomenon that caused Lady Mary Wortley Montagu (who admitted a sneaking fondness for Richardson's novels) to write scornfully years later, in 1750, that *Pamela* was "all the fashion at Paris and Versailles, and is still the joy of the chambermaids of all nations." [10] In fact, such people as servants would most naturally come by novels like Mrs. Haywood's when they were discarded by the gentry, rather than by purchase, for her books were too expensive to be bought outright by those who worked for a living. On the other hand, many women of the upper classes figure in Mrs. Haywood's dedications, and Lady Betty Germain owned a copy of her *Love-Letters on All Occasions.*[11]

Another answer to the question of who purchased works of letter fiction is given by the subscription list. In the early decades of the eighteenth century the practice of publishing by subscription was rarely extended to fiction. Subscription might be resorted to for an expensive volume, a first book by an unknown author, or a work for which the bookseller was unwilling to assume the entire financial risk. Several early epistolary novels contain printed lists of the subscribers which furnish interesting information, but the lists must be used with caution for several reasons. Some of the names included are probably fraudulent; for example, in *Some Memoirs of the Amours and Intrigues of a Certain Irish Dean* (1730 ed.) we find under "G" in the list of subscribers "Capt. Lemuel Gulliver of Redriff." The presence of a subscriber's name on the

list does not necessarily indicate that he read the book when it
appeared, but rather that he paid the solicitor of subscriptions.
A male subscriber might purchase a book as a suitable present
for a lady rather than for his own reading, as Pope bought
French romances for Miss Blount. With these sources of error
indicated, the information from the subscription lists is still
useful. The subscription list for Mrs. Haywood's *Letters
from a Lady of Quality to a Chevalier* (1721) contained 309
names, including 123 women and some persons of rank.[12]
Some Memoirs of the Amours and Intrigues lists 20 women
and 48 men, including a baronet, several army officers, and
"Right Honourables" of both sexes. The 169 subscribers for
Mrs. Davys' *The Reform'd Coquet* (1724) at three shillings,
though mostly Cambridge students, numbered among them
three duchesses, and Pope, Gay, and Martha Blount. *Melinthus* (1728) had 90 copies subscribed by 60 women and 26
men, 29 among the 86 bearing titles. The "Proposals for Printing by Subscription a Novel. Entitled, The Happy-Unfortunate; or, The Female Page. In Three Parts. By Louisa," cir-
culated by Mrs. Elizabeth Boyd, contained a list of 328 persons who had subscribed for 353 copies; it consisted of 188
men and 140 women. Ninety-two of the subscribers belonged
to the nobility.[13] *Secret Memoirs of the Late Mr. Duncan
Campbell* (1732) had 86 copies subscribed by 20 women and
64 men, including 30 persons of rank, among them the duke
of Argyle and the duchess of Ormonde.

Such figures as these entitle us to suppose that the public
for which many epistolary novels were written certainly did
not consist of basket women and seamstresses, but rather of
persons of wealth, education, and sometimes rank. Although
one would naturally expect men to scorn such novels of sentiment and passion (as Swift, Pope, Shaftesbury, and others
certainly did) [14] the surprising number of men named in the
subscription lists (outnumbering women in five of the six
lists mentioned above) leads to the assumption that some of
them at least were interested in reading the novels for which
they had paid such respectable prices. The library of so practical a man as Defoe contained several luscious novels, among
which was Mrs. Hearne's *The Female Deserters*.[15] Dudley
Ryder, a serious young law student and a Dissenter, nevertheless read *Lindamira* (at the behest of his female relatives) and

enjoyed it.[16] Pope was probably familiar with Gildon's *Post-Boy Rob'd of His Mail*, although this work can hardly be called sentimental.[17] The *Spectator* pointed out that brisk young men-about-town also read such novels, either to ingratiate themselves with the "fair-sex" or for frothy amusement of an amatory nature, as Fielding's Mr. Maclachlan read Mrs. Behn. Both Richard Savage and one James Sterling wrote extravagant poems in praise of Mrs. Haywood's performances, and, though it is hard to explain their enthusiasm, the poems make it clear that they were well acquainted not only with her works but with those of Mrs. Manley and Mrs. Behn.[18]

It was clearly for women, however, that many of these early examples of letter fiction were intended. References to such books are found in the diaries and letters of women of the upper classes, as well as in satirical comments on the tastes of feminine readers. The *Tatler* regretted that

> the generality of our Young Women, taking all their Notions of Life from gay Writings, or Letters of Love, consider themselves as Goddesses, Nymphs, and Shepherdesses,[19]

and the *Spectator* described the county family in which, while the father and sons spend the day wandering about the estate,

> the Daughters read Volumes of Love-Letters and Romances to their Mother. . . . the Boys think their Mother no better than she should be.[20]

Love letters in one form or another were a staple in the literary diet of women and were eagerly sought after in the fashionable world. Thus, we find a Mrs. Knight (later Lady Luxborough) writing from Hampshire in 1736 to the estimable countess of Hertford:

> Don't expect I should obey your commands about the letters, for when I mentioned the having drawn the story of Antiochus in a fan (which story I was obliged to inform the company of), I was answered, "What! a married woman employ herself in drawing love stories?" Upon which I immediately changed the discourse to a pudding. Judge, then, if I dare translate love-letters.[21]

The countess herself made a few modest attempts at epistolary fiction; these, together with the book in which they appeared, were a topic of considerable interest among fashionable ladies at their visits.[22] Lady Mary Wortley Montagu was
certainly familiar with the works of Madame d'Aulnoy and
Madame du Noyer as well as with those of Mrs. Manley, and
judging from her avowed fondness for novels she doubtless
read many of the others as well.[23]

Clearly, women must have formed an important, if not
predominant, part of the public for these novels. Mrs. Haywood seems to have profited most from dedications to
women; they were twice as frequent in her novels as were
dedications to men. As early as 1691 the enterprising bookseller John Dunton had recognized the importance of the feminine reading public by devoting monthly numbers of his
Athenian Mercury to matters of special interest to women.
His *Ladies Mercury* first appeared in 1692, and the two periodicals contained occasional letter fiction of an elementary nature in the form of long confessional letters concerning love
affairs. Dunton's project led eventually to the production of a
curious volume of letters called *The Challenge Sent by a
Young Lady to Sir Thomas: or, The Female Warr* (1697),
which had about the same fictional content as the *Spectator*.
But Dunton was only one of many who discerned the profitable connection between women and sentimental-epistolary
fiction; it would be difficult to list the multitude of parenthetical addresses to the feminine reader in such novels. Indeed,
novels of sentiment (including epistolary fiction) had been
particularly directed to ladies from Elizabethan times onward.

Some portions of the reading public, however, may be
tentatively removed from the picture. The devout of all
ranks, and the merchant and shopkeeper classes, would have
disdained most works of letter fiction as belonging in the category of books which were trivial, wicked, or at best unprofit-
able. They might read *Robinson Crusoe, God's Revenge
Against Murther*, and *The Pilgrim's Progress*, together with
works of practical piety (these were the books scornfully
lumped together by Gildon as the property of every old
woman who could afford them), but few novels, with their
amorous intrigues and their atmosphere of debased sentimental Platonism, could have met their requirements. The pious

Mrs. Rowe's fictional but didactic *Letters from the Dead to the Living,* or her *Letters Moral and Entertaining* were exceptions to the general rule;[24] but not until the time of Richardson did most readers of the neo-Puritan "middle class" find novels of which they could approve. The more frivolous among their wives or daughters might secretly indulge in romantic fiction, perhaps concealing novels behind *Holy Living* and *Holy Dying* in their "closets"; but such reading was certainly in disfavor, and one of the clichés of the age was the protest against the corrupting effects of lewd novels upon the minds of impressionable young girls. But the fact that novels or volumes of love letters were so roundly denounced is a significant clue to their popularity.

From all this rather miscellaneous evidence it is not inaccurate to conclude that letter fiction reached an audience of Londoners constituted somewhat as follows.[25] It probably excluded the poor, the learned, or the intellectual, the religious, and the commercial "lower middle class." (There is no question that other members of the *economic* "lower middle class," such as the very numerous group of upper servants, were readers of popular fiction.) It included many members of the nobility and gentry, the bourgeois rich, the young, and the fashionable; and although the tastes of women may have dominated its choices in fiction, it also included many men.

Even if such evidence is discounted, the publication figures for epistolary fiction point to a sizable number of readers. Editions of about two thousand copies seem to have been the rule, at least in the early eighteenth century; and if this is true we may estimate that something like one million volumes containing epistolary fiction were offered to the public between 1660 and 1740.[26] If this figure is too large it is because it cannot take into account the number of "editions" which were merely issues or former editions disguised with new title pages; and there is no way of telling what proportion of the books offered was actually sold. However, of the 203 works loosely defined as letter fiction which we are considering, many proved to be decidedly popular. Ninety-three seem to have appeared only once; but forty-two appeared twice, twenty-one three times, eleven four times, twenty-nine five to ten times, and six more than ten times in the period covered by the listing.

As one might expect, works of the greatest literary merit and highest technical development were not the most popular. The six books with more than ten editions, which we might call "best sellers," were the *Turkish Spy*, Madame d'Aulnoy's *Ingenious and Diverting Letters*, Mrs. Behn's *Love-Letters Between a Nobleman and His Sister*, *God's Revenge Against Murther*, the *Portuguese Letters*, and Mrs. Behn's *Histories and Novels*. These greatly differing works owed their popularity to factors both intrinsic and extrinsic, as do best sellers today; and among these factors the epistolary technique was really important only for the *Portuguese Letters* and the *Love-Letters Between a Nobleman and His Sister*. All six doubtless owed a major part of their success to the fact that they dealt with travel, "secret history," passion, or intrigue. Many works of letter fiction from this period which a critic of today would consider the most important—*Lindamira, Loves Posie, The Perfidious P—*, Mrs. Trotter's *Olinda*, and Gildon's *The Lover's Sighs*, to name a few—appeared only once or a few times. Mrs. Hearne's *Female Deserters* and *Lover's Week*, and Mrs. Behn's *Love-Letters*, probably owed more of their success to their lascivious matter than to the technical innovations which they made. The public was as capricious as it has always been; the epistolary form had not yet gained the power it had later in the century to promote a novel's favorable reception.

This failure to foster the budding epistolary novel was not entirely the public's but rather that of the powerful booksellers, who certainly were not concerned with improving the taste or morals of readers. What the more unscrupulous bookseller was like can be seen from the biographies of such men as John Dunton or the notorious Edmund Curll, which are filled with examples of fraudulent advertising, deception, pirating, the printing of obscenities, and similar practices. Moreover, it was such booksellers as Curll who were chiefly associated with the publication of fiction and therefore of letter fiction. They were motivated purely by an interest in what sold, and their methods, therefore, reveal something about the vogue of fiction.[27] A book worth pirating, for example, must have been popular; sensationalism in advertising or in titles reveals what was thought most likely to catch the public's fancy. The extent to which booksellers pushed letter fiction by means of various catchpenny devices demonstrates that it was becoming an important part of their literary property. Thus, Mrs. Eliza Haywood, when her works had "caught on" about 1724—with her activity perhaps spurred by the enterprising bookseller Chetwood—poured out novel after novel with incredible speed for a few years, after which her production dwindled markedly. It is possible that the wily booksellers, anticipating a change in public taste, no longer found it profitable to encourage her romances of passion.[28]

Booksellers of the early eighteenth century had a stranglehold on their authors, particularly authors of fiction. While authors of religious books, scientific or medical treatises, and other serious works could gain a fairly good living by their pens, the case was far different with fiction writers, who were only a little less despised than hack translators. It is noteworthy that Mrs. Behn, Mrs. Manley, and Mrs. Haywood alike turned seriously to fiction only after writing for the stage, with its far greater financial rewards, was denied to them. (Mrs. Manley and Mrs. Haywood had both failed as dramatists, and political satire against the Whigs in her plays seems to have brought Mrs. Behn into serious trouble.) [29] An author might get from fifty to one hundred pounds for a play, plus the profits from "third nights," and a poet might get as much as ten guineas for a poem of some length (such as Johnson's *London*), but an author of fiction could expect no such fee. The royalty system was not established, and the copy was usually bought outright for a lump sum.

There is almost no direct evidence about what authors received for the copy of a novel before 1740, but it must ordinarily have been from one to ten guineas, probably nearer one than ten in most cases. Mrs. Mary Davys said that in 1700 she had received three guineas for *The Lady's Tale*. Curll gave Ann Brome, the widow of Charles Brome the bookseller, a guinea for the rights to the popular *Gentleman Apothecary*, a bawdy epistolary tale which sold at a shilling. In 1726 he made John Clarke two payments of a guinea each "in part of the coppy money of two [similar] novels, viz. 1. The Virgin Seducer. 2. The Batchelor Keeper." [30] Payments would, of course, vary with the social standing and reputation of the author, but most of those who wrote letter fiction before 1740 did not have much of either for bargaining purposes. It is

stated (possibly understated) that around 1770 fashionable
novels for ladies which retailed at six shillings gained their authors ten to twenty pounds; [31] if we scale down the payments to authors in the earlier period proportionately to the
difference in the prevailing prices for novels, we may conclude that they received two to six pounds for a novel of some
length. Even in a period when a year's expenses for one person's frugal living, as calculated by Dr. Johnson, amounted to
thirty pounds, such sums could hardly have kept the authors
of short novels very happy; although they no doubt often exaggerated their distresses and complained merely because they
could not live as the gentry did, novelists were certainly in a
worse state than authors in general. (Tutchin, for instance,
was paid half a guinea a week for writing the *Observator*.) [32]
They doubtless tended to be extravagant rather than prudent,
but we have considerable evidence to show that Tom Brown,
Gildon, Mrs. Behn, Mrs. Manley, and Mrs. Haywood, were
often in the most serious financial difficulties. When the
Tories fell, Mrs. Manley complained of having "a starving
scene" before her unless she could have further politically
subsidized work.[33] Certainly, Mrs. Haywood, the "Arbitress
of Passion," at the height of her popularity from 1724 to 1726
would not have produced an average of one novel a month
during this period if she could have supported herself in pros-
perity with less vigorous exertions.

Writers in such a financial situation were not in a position to work in a leisurely manner, developing background or
character, even if their abilities permitted them to do so. It is
remarkable that they wrote as well as they did. There was no
incentive for them to write long or complex pieces of fiction;
the need for ready money at short notice was too great, and
the requirements of sensationalism could be fulfilled with a
minimum of time and effort.

The prevalence of women among the authors of these
novels also had its effect. With considerably less educational
equipment than most male writers, they were even more at
the mercy of booksellers. As Mrs. Manley's biographer points
out, "nothing less than notable dishonor and the necessity of
earning her bread was likely at this early period to induce a
woman of respectable family to take to Grub Street." [34]
Writing was something for a woman of wit to turn to when

all other means of livelihood short of manual labor—including concubinage—had failed. Women wrote to please, and therefore wrote brief amatory tales. Mrs. Haywood remarked wistfully in one of her dedications:

> But as I am a Woman, and consequently depriv'd of those Advantages of Education which the other Sex enjoy, I cannot so far flatter my Desires, as to imagine it in my Power to soar to any Subject higher than that which Nature is not negligent to teach us.
>
> Love is a Topick which I believe few are ignorant of; there requires no Aids of Learning, no general Conversation, no Application; a shady Grove and purling Stream are all Things that's necessary to give us an Idea of the tender Passion. This is a theme, therefore, which, while I make choice to write of, frees me from the Imputation of vain or self-sufficient:—None can tax me with having too great an Opinion of my own Genius, when I aim at nothing but what the meanest may perform.
>
> I have nothing to value myself on, but a tolerable Share of Discernment.[35]

She, Mrs. Manley, and Mrs. Behn (all, fortunately, of uncommon ability) had been forced to pick up what education they could in a haphazard manner through reading and conversation. Among the known female authors of epistolary fiction in the period, only Mrs. Elizabeth Rowe and the child prodigy Catherine Trotter seem to have had anything approximating formal education beyond the most elementary level.[36] With such a handicap, and writing in haste, they sometimes displayed a remarkable amount of learning and technical proficiency. The looseness of the artistic requirements of fiction at the time made it a natural field for the efforts of female authors, who were apt to be either very poor indeed or better off than their male counterparts (that is, with means of subsistence other than writing) so that they were either compelled or could afford to accept the wretched prices offered by booksellers. How many of the early letter novels were the efforts of amateurs who were delighted to see their writings in print with little or no payment is unknown, but three of the best—*Lindamira, Olinda,* and *Familiar Letters Betwixt a Gentleman and a Lady*—were probably written in a leisurely manner by women who were in comfortable circumstances or who at least were not industrious hacks like Mrs. Behn, Mrs. Manley, and Mrs. Haywood.[37]

Compelled by necessity, these three women turned to fiction only after writing for the stage, and the technique they had learned for the drama carried over into their fiction. Such a connection with drama in form and style may have influenced the popularity of early epistolary fiction, for it is known that plays were perhaps the most popular reading for the very persons who formed the public for letter fiction. Mary Astell's *Serious Proposal to the Ladies* (1694) equated plays with romances as comprising the typical and worthless reading of women. *The English Lady's Catechism* (1703) contained the following lines:

> "Pray, Madam, what Books do you read?"
> "I read lewd Plays and winning Romances."

A more famous devourer of plays was Addison's Clarinda (*Spectator*, No. 323), who recorded her day-by-day perusal of *Aurengzebe* in her diary. Without insisting too much on the similarity to the reader between a printed play and a letter novel, we may note that the heroic and sentimental dramas most in vogue with female playgoers and readers consisted largely of ranting speeches, declarations of love, and the like, couched in an artificial vein of sentimental Platonism, based on the love-and-honor conflict, and with action often subordinated to feeling. Precisely the same ingredients may be found in many an epistolary tale of the time, except that the speeches are called letters. Certainly, the artistic distance between such plays and such novels is much less vast than that between a sentimental drama and a novel like Defoe's. The manner of narration, with the emphasis on emotion, melodramatic but sketchy plots, and declamatory "passions" rather than upon objective description, would also have been easier and more obvious for fledgling female novelists fresh from the stage. The booksellers were not backward in stressing the sentimental and passionate aspects of some of their wares above the plot or other elements, and since they were interested above all in gauging and satisfying the current tastes of the public, it would be surprising indeed if the parallel between plays and certain types of novels had not occurred to them.

The public, likewise conditioned to the modes of the heroic romance, was well prepared to expect and find letters among the paraphernalia of the popular novel.

Letter fiction survived in its sporadic way and became popular during the period of its haphazard development only because it could command a sufficiently large group of readers and continue to please them. Unlike verse satire, for example, or occasional poetry or conduct books, it had neither accumulated prestige nor the practical needs of readers to rely on. It offered entertainment only, and of a particular kind which was increasingly in demand; this alone counted with the booksellers on whom its production depended. At the same time its appeal was not universal, and its artistic quality was kept low by the economic conditions which bound those who wrote it. Richardson and his works remedied these deficiencies, but the economic conditions that militated against the appearance of an earlier Richardson, continuing through the years before and after 1740, help to explain the amazing acclaim which greeted *Pamela* and *Clarissa* when they appeared. One might say that the public had been waiting in ignorance for just such a pair of novels.

CHAPTER VI

Letter Fiction and
"the Taste of the Age"

> ...there being no possible pleasure in reading a Story
> which we know to be false...[yet] *Romances* have always
> been allow'd the most apt to make Impressions upon the
> Mind...
>
> —Daniel Defoe, *A New Family Instructor*

Anyone searching through formal English literary criticism
for discourses on fiction that can compare with the many significant essays on poetry, epic, and drama may be justified in
saying that no one bothered to think critically about prose
fiction before Fielding. Even so important and copious a critic
as Dryden gave prose fiction the merest glance, and his major
contemporaries seem to have ignored it completely in their
critical works.[1] But prose fiction was not among the literary
"kinds," and such matters as the Rules left critics no leisure for
literary forms unknown to the Ancients.

   Modern scholarship has assembled scattered brief comments on "histories" and "romances" which are in general
agreement about the values and aims of fiction. These may be
called a critical corpus of a sort, but in sum they add up to
very little. We find without astonishment that the Augustans,
when they discussed fiction at all, felt that it should instruct,
move, edify, and amuse the reader, and depict the life he saw

around him.[2] So should any nonabstract art; such canons are as conventional as they are vague. They also belong, clearly, to that primitive stage of criticism from which English discussion of poetry and the drama had largely disengaged itself—the defensive. They are designed to clear fiction from the imputation of sinfulness and frivolity.

The same prudent defensiveness can be found in the preface or dedication to almost any early novel: the reader will find the work that follows both innocent and veracious. Any Grubstreet author who took the trouble to write a preface to his novel or any bookseller who wanted to recommend his wares was sure to begin somewhat as follows:

> [The abuse of novels] requires a few words . . . for the removing of such Prejudices as that Abuse has occasion'd against all Performances of this Kind.
>
> Had not the original Design of these Imitations of History been to instil the Noblest Sentiments after the most Agreeable Manner, which is always the surest; and were not the grand Moral of them, the Rewarding of Honour and Virtue, and the Punishing of Dishonour and Vice [Bishop Huet would not have written his essay on romances] . . . . the utmost Care has been taken, that no Novel shou'd have a place, which cou'd possibly offend the Gravity of the Aged, or the Modesty of the Young.[3]
>
> N. B. In these Letters, the subject Matter throughout is new and amusing; the Sentiments are refined and pure, and the Expression apt and Elegant; in short, the utmost Decency is every where preserved: So that no Book can be fitter for the Perusal of young People at our *Boarding-Schools* . . . to guard them against the polluted Writings of the Age; to form their Minds aright, and give them a just and amiable Idea of Morality and Virtue.[4]

The purpose of such comments is so obvious that they may be disregarded as criticism—as may the constant protestations that novels are not novels, but "true histories." While some authors and many readers may have felt that they owed a duty to truth, most of these remarks were born of the knowledge that the public wanted stories which were true, or seemed to be. The injunction of I Timothy (4:7)—"But refuse profane and old wives' fables, and exercise thyself rather unto godliness"—and the attitude which "seyde that Omer made lyes" were still taken too literally by too many people to be ignored. (But the insistence upon veracity had more effect on fictional technique than that upon virtue, since it promoted a search for mechanical devices to make a story *seem* true, rather than a reliance on the mere announcement that it was.)

A few specific comments on epistolary fiction from this period have been recorded, but they are vague and hardly differ from those on fiction in general.[5] We might think at first that no one before Richardson himself had paid attention to the particular qualities and virtues of a story in letters, but something closer to criticism is to be found. It does not occur in formal essays, however, for those who wrote letter fiction operated not to exemplify critical canons or professed intentions but to satisfy the desires of the public. Accordingly, their novels contain many hints to the reader, thrown off with a casual air to avoid the forbidding appearance of literary theorizing, but showing that writers were sensitive to what the reader wanted to find and were ready to demonstrate that it was available in plenty. In letter novels these hints are very specific and lead to conclusions which cannot be gathered from any outside source. They merit no more dignified name than advertising paragraphs or "blurbs," but it is from these alone that one can gain a notion of how much individuality letter fiction had in the eyes of authors and readers during the early years of its development.

Briefly, it appears that authors, booksellers, and the public associated two particular characteristics with a story in letters: authenticity and the depiction of passion, sentiment, or feeling. Letter fiction shared the first of these with all other kinds of fiction except the fairy tale, the allegory, and the romance, but the latter was almost peculiar to it at the time.[6]

I

The use of letters afforded a writer many advantages in meeting the almost universal requirement of authenticity. Everyone is familiar with Richardson's elaborate and reluctantly discarded pretense of being merely the editor of letters which had fallen into his hands. In this he was merely repeating a device practiced by most of those who wrote letter fiction in the previous seventy years—a device of whose earlier use he can scarcely have been ignorant.[7] Letters might be found by the author in a deserted house, confided to him by a friend, made public to correct misinformation, or revealed after having been kept in secrecy.[8] All these situations piqued the reader, stimulated his interest in what followed, and made him believe that the letters he was reading were genuine. The letters of actual persons were being eagerly read by a large public (the history of Pope's letters and their publication shows the intense interest that such collections aroused), and volumes of letters partly authentic and partly fictional met with equal success. The reader of the time, unlike his modern counterpart, would not have had his suspicions excited by finding the letters signed with enigmatic initials or with manufactured romantic names like Strephon or Parthenia; such names were commonly used in gallant correspondence and would merely have led him to speculate on what famous contemporaries might be concealed behind the high-flown appellations.[9] The initials he would immediately have attempted to identify with various gentlemanly wits of the day. The "common reader," living in an age of (modified) belief, did not find his credulity overstrained by a series of letters which told a story and which purported to be authentic, especially when elaborate devices to stimulate his suspension of disbelief were provided. He could hardly tell it from a collection of authentic letters unless he happened to move in circles where the facts were known.

The author might be content with a short prefatory statement of veracity, or he might elaborate it into a technique of presentation extending through the entire work. In the preface to *The Illegal Lovers* (1728) we find the mere statement:

> Some letters (since the sad Catastrophe of his Fate) falling into my Hands, I thought I could not more oblige the Publick than by communicating them; and also some Particulars of his History, which I was informed of by those about him, and are yet known to but few.[10]

On the other hand, Defoe, master of "lying like truth," once went to extraordinary lengths in using letters as a device of authentication. He wove them into the whole fabric of his semifictional *The Storm* (1704), an account of a great tempest which devastated England in November 1703. It begins with a portentous sermon on misrepresentation:

> Where a Story is vouch'd to [the writer] with sufficient Authority, he ought to give the World the special Testimonial of its proper Voucher, or else he is not just to the Story: and where it comes without such sufficient Authority, he ought to say so; otherwise, he is not just to himself. In the first Case, he injures the History, by leaving it doubtful where it might be confirmed past all manner of question; in the last he injures his own Reputation, by taking upon himself the Risque, in case it proves a Mistake, of having the World charge him with a Forgery....

> I confess here is room for Abundance of Romance, because the Subject may be safer extended than in any other case, no Story being capable to be crowded with such Circumstances, but Infinite Power, which is all along concern'd with us in every Relation, is supposed capable of making true.

> Yet we shall no where so Trespass upon Fact, as to oblige Infinite Power to the shewing more Miracles than it intended....

> I thought to make some Apology for the Meanness of Stile, and the Method, which may be a little unusual, of Printing Letters from the Country in their own Stile.

> For the last I only leave this Short Reason with the Reader, the Desire I had to keep close to the Truth, and hand [*sic*] my Relation with the true Authorities from whence I receiv'd it, together with some Justice to the Gentlemen concern'd, who, especially in Cases of Deliverances, are willing to record the Testimonial of the Mercies they received, and to set their Hands to the humble Acknowledgment. The Plainness and Honesty of the Story will plead for the Meanness of the Stile in many of the Letters, and the Reader cannot want Eyes to see what sort of People some of them come from.

> Others speak for themselves, and being writ by Men of Letters, as well as Men of Principles, I have not Arrogance enough to attempt a Correction either of the

Sence or Stile; and if I had gone about it, should have injur'd both Author and Reader.

These come dressed in their own Words because I ought not, and those because I could not mend 'em. I am perswaded, they are all dress'd in the desirable, though unfashionable Garb of Truth, and I doubt not but Posterity will read them with Pleasure.[11]

Defoe writes a chapter on the causes of winds, culled from various scientific writings, and then describes the effects of the tempest on the city of London, probably from his own observation. Wishing to include accounts of the damage in other parts of England, he summons letters to his aid:

As the Author of this was an Eye-witness and Sharer of the Particulars in the former Chapter; so, to furnish the Reader with Accounts as authentick, and which he has as much cause to depend upon, as if he had seen them, he has the several Particulars following from like Eye-witnesses, and that in such a manner, as I think their Testimony is not to be question'd, most of the Gentlemen being of Piety and Reputation. ... Besides, as most of our Relators have not only given us their Names, and sign'd the Accounts they have sent, but have also given us leave to hand their Names down to Posterity with the Record of the Relation they give, we would hope no Man will be so uncharitable to believe that men would be forward to set their Names to a voluntary Untruth, and have themselves recorded to Posterity for having, without Motion, Hope, Reward, or any other reason, impos'd a Falsity upon the World, and dishonour'd our Relation with the useless Banter of an Untruth. ... And first, I shall present such Accounts as are entire, and related by Men of letters, principally by the Clergy, which shall be given you in their own Words. ... From *Oxfordshire* we have an Account very authentick, and yet unaccountably strange. ...[12]

The letters from the clergy are followed by others from country folk, for whom Defoe apologizes as follows:

The following Letters, tho' in a homely stile, are written by very honest plain and observing Persons, to whom entire Credit may be given.[13]

He is careful to modify his style to suit his "honest plain persons":

> At *Evercreech*, three Miles from *Brewton*, there were a
> poor Woman beg'd for Lodging in the Barn of one
> *Edmond Peny* that same Night that the Storm was, she
> was wet the Day before in Travelling, so she hung up her
> Cloaths in the Barn, and lay in the Straw; but when the
> Storm came it blew down the Roof of the Barn where
> she lay, and she narrowly escaped with her Life, being
> much bruised, and got out almost naked through the
> Roof where it was broken most, and went to the dwell-
> ing House of the said *Edmond Peny*, and they did arise,
> and did help her to something to cover her, till they could
> get out her Cloaths; that place of *Evercreech* received a
> great deal of hurt in their Houses, which is too large to
> put here. . . .
>
> Hu. Ash.[14]

The effect of this cloud of epistolary witnesses is clinched by
a letter from "Mr. Anthony van Lauwenhoek, F. R. S.," who
used his microscope on the sea water blown against his win-
dows by the gale. Many of the letters in *The Storm* are, in all
probability, authentic. Defoe mentions that an advertisement
asking for such accounts of "deliverances" was published,
though he neglects to say when or in what periodical.[15] But
the very vehemence of his protestations that all is true, and
the amount of space he devotes to them, lead the reader to be
suspicious, especially since it is Defoe who is speaking. A great
many of the letters in this, Defoe's first work of reportage, are
probably of his own invention, though perhaps based on written or oral accounts.

Such an extensive use of the letter, authentic or fabricated,
by the first acknowledged English expert in literary verisimilitude, can only indicate that he considered it a sovereign device for his purposes. Letters, of course, had long been conventionally regarded as especially intimate revelations of a
person's true nature; witness the early collection of letters by
Thomas Forde, significantly titled *Foenestra in Pectore*
(1660). A prefatory poem to the popular *Epistolae Ho-
Elianae* of James Howell declared:

> Speech is the index, letters ideas are
> Of the informing soul; they can declare,
> And show the inward man.

Such ideas were connected with the classical placement of the letter in the "familiar" branch of rhetoric; since they were so commonplace, they probably directed the thoughts of authors rather forcibly to certain advantages of the epistolary method. Gildon's *Post-Boy Rob'd of His Mail* furnishes further examples of the elaborate devices of verisimilitude thought appropriate and necessary in an epistolary collection. The "Bookseller's Advertisement to the Reader," perhaps written by the publisher John Dunton, is an unusually long-winded document in which the book is painstakingly defended against all suspicion of being fictitious:

> I thought proper to advertise these few things.
> *First,* that the Post has too often here in *England* . . . been rob'd. . . . There have Accidents of this nature happ'ned in other Countries; as in Italy, as the Letters of *Palavicino* demonstrate; so that there can be no doubt of the Truth of the Matter of Fact, or at least of a Probability of that Truth.
> *Next,* It may be wondered that in all these *Mails* pretended to be robb'd, there should in such a *time of Action* be no Letters of News, or any Account of the late *Intreagues.* But I desire these Gentlemen to have Patience till they see the *Second Volume.* . . .
> *Fourthly,* In the next Volume will be an Explanation of the *Letter* in *Figures* that is in this, one of the Company having found a *Key* for it, but too late to have it inserted, the whole being printed off.
> *Fifthly* [on libel], . . . may there not be hundreds of the same Christian and Sir-name in *England?*
> *Sixthly* [explanation of the lack of business letters], . . . if it were either safe or convenient, they could send such *Doubters* to many of the Persons that receiv'd the Letters.
> *Seventhly* [on obscenity], . . . upon this *Condition only* was the Copy delivered to me, that I should leave

out none of those *Letters that the Company thought fit to publish*.[16]

The Epistle Dedicatory justifies the genuineness of the letters on the basis of their style:

> As for the Book . . . I shall only say, 'twill discover the difference betwixt *these Letters*, prompted by the several *immediate Occurrences*, that occasioned the writing of them, and those which some *Epistle-Writers* have publish'd for Examples for the World to Copy after: *Nature*, and *Easiness* appear in the first; and Study and *aukward Pains* in the latter. 'Tis not to be expected there should be the same Wit, and Language in e'ery Letter, since the Occasions, and Writers are different: and they are generally more remarkable for their Import, than Words, and Phrase.[17]

The reader is also given a long and highly circumstantial account of how Church, Chappel, Temple, Grave, River, Brook, Fountain, and others robbed the post-boy, what adventures they met with, and how they retired to a secluded country seat to sort over and comment on their loot. If all this authentication were not enough, the whole first volume is cast in the form of a letter to a friend, at the end of which the writer apologizes for not being able to include all the letters taken from the post (and incidentally stimulates the reader's interest in the sequel). Dunton's ingenuity did not stop here. He inserted an advance review in his *Compleat Library* for June, 1692, praising the authenticity of the performance, and wrote himself a flurry of questions in the *Athenian Mercury*, assuring himself in the answers that the letters were unquestionably genuine. He later inserted an advertisement in the *Athenian Mercury* asking readers to send their own letters to "Mr. Chappel," and thus secured copy for the forthcoming volume while insuring that at least some readers would believe all its contents to be the letters of real persons.[18]

Authors and booksellers showed astonishing fertility in contriving situations to account for the existence of letter stories. Mrs. Manley's *Lady's Pacquet of Letters* was explained in its preface by a single enigmatic paragraph, plausible and matter-of-fact, which spurred the reader's curiosity to know more.

The Letters at the latter End, are part of a Parcel that was taken, as the Title says, from an English Lady in her passage to Holland: the Officer, of whom I purchac'd 'em, told me, that they were show'd him by a Privateer Captain, who desir'd him to let him know what they were. The Exchange happening immediately after, the *French-Man* not remembring to ask for 'em, they remain'd with him. I justly thought 'em so easie, so natural and entertaining, that knowing none to be offended by them, I quickly resolv'd them for the Press.[19]

O-Brazile (1675), a wild tale of an enchanted invisible island off the coast of Ireland, was authenticated in a manner worthy of Defoe. The story consists of a letter of eleven quarto pages, dated from Londonderry, March 14, 1674, and signed "William Hamilton." It is addressed to his "honoured cousin" in London. The letter mentions Captain John Nisbet, who still lives and who once saw the island, and relates that a patent for its possession if it should become visible was taken out in the time of Charles I. The island, it seems, has just become permanently visible, having been liberated from a Druid spell together with its inhabitants when a party of Christian mariners lighted a fire on its shores. The letter concludes with a number of affidavits and a postscript in which the "honoured cousin" is reminded to tell "Cousin *Lesly*" of the occurrence if he is still in London, since it was his father who had taken out the patent on the island. The letters of Philander and Sylvia in Mrs. Behn's *Love-Letters Between a Nobleman and His Sister* (1683–87) were asserted to have been "found in their cabinets, at their House at St. Denis, where they liv'd together, for the Space of a Year." [20] Readers were carefully assured on the title page of the second part of Mrs. Haywood's *A Spy on the Conjurer* (1724), an account of the "Dumb Philosopher" and fortune-teller Duncan Campbell, that it was "a COLLECTION of letters found in Mr. Campbell's Closet." In addition to such precautions many writers took care to see that the letters in their collections were properly and recently dated and signed with realistic names or at least initials.

The author (or translators) of the *Turkish Spy* made sure that that enormous and rambling collection of letters was adequately authenticated. The address to the reader begins disarmingly:

> I here offer you a Book written by a Turk...I do not doubt but you would know when 'twas written; and perhaps, whether the Author be living; and whether you must expect a *Romance*, or a real History.[21]

There follows the story of finding a mass of manuscripts left by a mysterious lodger who, after arriving in 1664 and staying eighteen years, suddenly disappeared. The "editor" learns Arabic and begins to translate the manuscript. As an aid to realism the third volume contains a letter with no beginning, since "the Arabick paper had been torn asunder, and one Part was missing." [22] But in addition to these devices the frequent comments on the Spy's personality and manner of writing take the matter of authentication across the dividing line between a mere mechanical trick and a technique for the creation of character. Thus the preface points out:

> 'Tis no Wonder, if, in the Course of five and forty Years, which he pass'd away at *Paris*, both his Genius, and Conversation, may seem to vary at some critical Seasons, through the natural Force of Time...it would be unequal, to expect the same Method of Writing from him, either as to Sense or Style, Matter or Form, when he was But Thirty or Forty Years Old, as, when he was Threescore.[23]

These remarks were put in to forestall criticism of any inconsistencies of style, but they also prod the reader to look for evidence of the maturing mind and changing opinions of the Turk.

Letters also helped the authors of secret histories and scandal-chronicles to establish at once the mysteriousness, background, and genuineness of their revelations. *The Secret History of White-Hall* (1697), made up in the manner of Madame d'Aulnoy from a variety of written and oral sources, seeks in its preface to disarm "such scruples as may be suggested in general, concerning the Authentickness of the ensuing *Letters*." We are given a circumstantial account of the author (a dispatch clerk), told of the dangers of his position and the necessity of suppressing his name, presented with the bill of fare from "the Dark, and almost inscrutable Recesses of the French Cabinet-minutes," and informed that some of the letters "were written in Cyphers, which I retain by me, as I do the rest of the Original Papers, for my own and the Worlds satisfaction." [24] One passage significantly indicates the author's appreciation of the usefulness of the epistolary method to his technique:

> And 'tis hoped no body will quarrel, that this *Piece*, which is Entituled by the Name of a *Secret History*, &c. should be written in an Epistolary way, when it be considered that such a *Form* was indispensably necessary under the Circumstances of the *Author*, and his *Noble Correspondent*, and that there is a very engaging part naturally couched under such a method of bringing *State-Arcana's* to light, by way of *Letters*, which, in the very Notion of them carry something of Secrecy; Though after all, the *Reader* cannot but observe an Air of History to run, in a manner, through the whole composition. [25]

The letters which follow are carefully dated; they extend from January 8, 1676, to February 27, 1689, and tell of various intrigues of the French, including attempts to subvert Charles II's Protestantism and the appointment of Louise de Kéroualle as spy and *agent provocateur*. The dryness of the contents in general, and their failure to "reveal" much of interest, emphasize the importance of the spectacular preface in promoting sales.

The value of letters to the compilers of "secret histories" no doubt suggested them as a useful vehicle for the scandal-chronicle, although their employment in the famous *Histoire amoureuse des Gaules* had already gained them a place in its technique. If one could convince the reader that he had before him the actual letters of the living persons who were being unmasked, so much the better; here were their very words and inmost thoughts with no author as go-between. Booksellers were careful to stress the intimacy of revelations presented in letters as adding to the value of a work. Thus, *The Fair Concubine* (1732) concerning Miss Vane, the mistress of Prince Frederick, announced on its title page that it contained faithful copies of several of her letters, particularly one to P. Alexis on her first finding herself pregnant; and another to the Q[ueen] concerning her condition.

Curll's miscellany *Atterburyana* (1727) adorned its title page with

> Court secrets: or the ladies chronicle, historical and gallant, from the year 1671 to 1690. Extracted from the letters of Madame de Sévigné, which have been suppressed at Paris.

When the *Letters from a Lady at Paris to a Lady at Avignon* finally appeared in English in 1716, the translator gloated in his preface over the excellences of epistolary scandal:

> The Materials scattered up and down in these Letters furnished Sir *Richard Steele* with two *Guardians* upon the Life and Conduct of [Mme Maintenon]. But...the Stories are much more natural and agreeable in the manner [in] which this Lady has related them, than in his Papers.[26]

If something sensational occurred to a person of note, booksellers quickly seized the occasion to present the public with letters purporting to be his. The letters of Colonel Henry Marten the regicide judge (partly real and partly fabricated) followed hard upon his imprisonment. When Hortense Mancini, duchess of Mazarin, came to England and its king in 1676, she was promptly followed by her *Mémoires*, written by St.-Réal; before the year was out they appeared in English as the familiar "letter to a friend" recounting her history. Forde, Lord Grey, eloped with his sister-in-law, Lady Henrietta Berkeley, in 1682 and was involved in the Rye House Plot in the following year. The public was quickly treated to a broadside "letter" from the injured wife to a friend, and in 1683 Mrs. Behn's *Love-Letters Between a Nobleman and His Sister* appeared. Although the characters were called Philander and Sylvia and were said to be French, the disguise was doubtless thin enough to be penetrated by most readers, since we have evidence that the book was recognized as a scandal-novel. As Grey continued to provide material, subsequent parts detailed "Philander's" intrigues and his unsavory involvement in Monmouth's rebellion.[27]

The style of letters was also a useful means for compelling the reader's belief. "Editors" early learned to refrain from attempting to retouch the artless graces of the "author's" style. "A Faithful Account of how a Young Lady was Lately Seduced and Imposed Upon, by an Abbot at Lisbon"

> was sent in a letter from a Lady at Lisbon to her Correspondent at London: and we give it to our Readers in the natural and beautiful Style, in which it was writ by the ingenious Author.[28]

Tom Brown made a similar statement (probably truthful) in the preface to *Lindamira*.[29] Madame du Noyer's letters were proclaimed to be full of natural beauties not to be found in a more connected narrative;[30] and Marivaux's *Vie de Marianne* in translation was said to carry the stamp of its authenticity everywhere upon it.

> As this History may probably be suspected of having been contrived purposely to amuse the Publick, it may not be improper to acquaint the Reader, that I had it from a Friend who actually found it in the Manner immediately mentioned.... The Truth is, that, was this History a meer Fiction ... Marianne's Reflections would be neither so long nor so frequent. It would contain more Facts and less Morality; In short the Author would have indulged the universal Inclination of the present Age, which, in Books of this Kind, does not relish Abundance of Arguments and Reflections. When they read Adventures, it is only for the Sake of the Adventures themselves. But Marianne, when she wrote, did not in the least regard this. She pleased herself in setting down indifferently the whole Compass of her Reflections on every Incident of her Life.[31]

The concept of the ideal letter as a natural and unstudied outpouring of the heart, so pronounced in the later eighteenth century, had gained headway much earlier, at least among certain classes of readers. Letters had long been praised for revealing the soul's motions, but this quality had been thought of as a result of their being frank and private, not as the fruit of artlessness and spontaneity.

To list in detail all the ingenious devices by which letters authenticated fiction would require a volume; but the examples given sufficiently demonstrate that letters played an important part in satisfying the public demand for "true" stories. Letter fiction enjoyed its peculiar advantages in this respect, but other devices, notably the trick of saying "I was there" or "I heard it from a grave old manservant who had been with the family for years," which Aphra Behn and Defoe used so often, and the piling up of specific detail such as Defoe's famous "scoured-silk dress," were equally effective and were very widely used. It is not surprising that we find no direct comments on the epistolary technique's usefulness for verisimilitude. The "editor" of a collection of letters cannot plume himself publicly on his cleverness if he wishes to preserve the deception. Authors could afford to be more explicit on another strong point of epistolary narrative: its power to depict the processes of the mind—emotions, changes of feeling, traits of character, complexities of motivation. In prefaces and asides to the reader scattered through the texts of novels, they made it abundantly clear that letters were admirably adapted to exhibit the human heart.

II

Considering the highly practical interests of Defoe's characters, for instance, and the down-to-earth tone in his novels or the stories of intrigue popular in his era, we may be surprised that other authors should have pointed out the sentimental elements of fiction during the same period or given them so much importance. Perhaps the most interesting and detailed piece of early theorizing on the qualities of the new "novel" is the preface to Mrs. Manley's *Secret History of Queen Zarah* (1705), a scandalous attack on the duchess of Marlborough. Mrs. Manley violated her own precepts flagrantly in the book (she wrote it hastily for the purposes of the Tories), and the essay does not specifically refer to the epistolary technique. It nonetheless indicates that she had given considerable thought to narrative methods, and in it she discusses rather carefully the very qualities which had been and were being stressed in letter fiction. Although this document may be an echoing of commonplaces (it is true that similar statements had been made by Mlle de Scudéry and others), its insistence on the detailed depiction of specific emotional processes in a character is striking at this early date, more particularly since Mrs. Manley definitely applied her comments to the novel rather than to the romance, which she regarded as outmoded. From the modern point of view it can hardly be called a good critical essay, but in contrast to the absurdly vague remarks of Mrs. Manley's contemporaries its attention to detail is remarkable. She begins by condemning the romances (which she says are now replaced by short novels, "much more agreeable to the Brisk and Impetuous Humour of the *English*") for their sprawling construction, their lack of realistic modern setting, and their enormous casts of characters. She also condemns the digressive episodes of the French "historical novel," and emphasizes the necessity for compression and rapid movement in a novel. Next she decries the impossible virtues of the hero of romance and the vagueness with which he is described and gives her own recommendations for characterization:

> The Characters are better managed in the Historical Novels, which are writ now-a-days; they are not fill'd with great Adventures, and extraordinary Accidents, for the most simple Action may engage the Reader by the Circumstances that attend it; it [he?] enters into all the Motions and Disquiets of the Actor, when they have well express'd to him the Character. If he be Jealous, the Look of a Person he loves, a Mouse, a turn of the Head, or the least complaisance to a Rival, throws him into the greatest Agitations, which the Readers perceive by a Counterblow.... Most Authors are contented to describe Men in general, they represent them Covetous, Courageous, and Ambitious, without entering into the Particulars ... they don't perceive nice Definitions ... the Genius of the Author marvellously appears when he Nicely discovers those Differences, and exposes to the Reader's Sight those almost unperceivable Jealousies which escape the sight of most authors, because they have not an exact Notion of the Turnings and Motions of Humane Understanding; and they know nothing but the gross Passions, from whence they make but general Descriptions.... the Turn of the Mind, Motion of the Heart, Affection and Interests, alter the very Nature of the Passions, which are

different in all men. . . . 'tis not by Extravagant Expressions, nor repeated Praises, that the Reader's esteem is acquired to the Character of the Heroe's, their actions ought to plead for them.[32]

Furthermore, Mrs. Manley observes, several personages may have the same characteristic, but in differing degrees, and these should be carefully differentiated; the author should appear impartial rather than show his hand in the conduct of his tale or make moral reflections. She praises simplicity in fictional conversation, together with realistic brevity in the characters' speeches.[33] She anticipates our own day in her emphasis on the reader's being allowed to draw his own conclusions from the speeches and actions of the characters.

This essay presents a highly idealistic program for the author of Mrs. Manley's age; she might have been writing of the novel long after her time. Unhappily, neither she nor her contemporaries often succeeded in carrying out her recommendations in practice. Yet many authors, in their prefaces and parenthetical remarks, paralleled her emphasis on the minute depiction of emotional states and minor changes of feeling, praising the emotions to be revealed in their books at the expense of any mention of the events. The *Portuguese Letters* assured the reader in L'Estrange's brief foreword:

> You will find in [the letters] the Lively Image of an Extravagant and an Unfortunate Passion; and that a *Woman may be Flesh and Blood in a Cloyster, as well as in a Palace.*[34]

Among the wares in his *Post-Boy Rob'd*, Gildon found it expedient to offer "Petty Jealousies, little Love-Quarrels and Excuses," and "the *several Passions* that Influence all the Life and Actions of Mankind, *the softnesses and the wrecks of Lovers*, the Intreagues and Extravagancies of Lust." [35] Even letters whose interest would seem primarily historical came in for their share of comment: the reader was notified that the last letter of Anne Boleyn to Henry VIII

> is by far the most to be admired; for as the Occasion of it required the utmost Effort of the Mind, so nothing could be Penned in a more exalted Strain.[36]

The Double Captive (1718), a miscellany of letters and poems said to be written by a political prisoner to a girl he had loved from afar, contained

> only the Genuine, and artless Ramblings, of a poor, unhappy, miserable, and double Chain'd Man . . . the jealous Notions of an amorous Mind, and the variety of Whims they put into my Head.[37]

But it was collections of narrative love letters, supposedly authentic, that drew forth the most lengthy and detailed encomiums on the passions they revealed, these being carefully described for the benefit of the buyer. The first letter of Heloise to Abelard (translated earlier than 1694, perhaps by L'Estrange) was prefaced by a note which contained the following comment:

> That Letter (says he who has collected the Works of Abelard) is very proper to shew how far a Woman is capable to carry the Sentiments of the Heart, when she joyns a violent Passion to a good Education.[38]

The complete collection, in John Hughes's translation of 1713, was opened by an elaborate preface which gave a historical account of the lovers and pointed out the beauties of their letters:

> It is very surprising that the Letters of *Abelard* and *Heloise* have not sooner appear'd in *English*, since it is generally allow'd by all who have seen them in other Languages, that they are written with the greatest Passion of any in this kind which are extant. And it is certain that the *Letters from a Nun to a Cavalier*, which have so long been known and admired among us, are in all Respects inferior to them. Whatever those were, these are known to be genuine Pieces occasioned by an Amour which had very extraordinary Consequences, and made a great Noise at the time when it happen'd being between two of the most distinguished Persons of that Age.
>
> These Letters therefore being truly written by the Persons themselves, whose Names they bear, and who were both remarkable for their Genius and Learning, as

well as by a most extravagant Passion for each other, are every where full of Sentiments of the Heart, which are not to be imitated in a feign'd Story, and Touches of Nature, much more moving than any which cou'd flow from the Pen of a Writer of Novels, or enter into the Imagination of any one who had not felt the like Emotions and Distresses. . . . Monsieur Bayle says, he had been inform'd [the French translation] was done by a Woman; and perhaps he thought no one besides cou'd have enter'd so thoroughly into the Passion and Tenderness of such Writings, for which that Sex seems to have a more natural Disposition than the other. This may be judg'd by the Letters themselves, among which those of *Heloise* are the most Tender and Moving, and the Master seems in this Particular to have been exceeded by the Scholar. . . . The Letters between him and his beloved *Heloise* were not written 'till long after their Marriage and Separation, and when each of them was dedicated to the Life of Religion. Accordingly we find in them surprizing Mixtures of Devotion and Tenderness, of Penitence and remaining Frailty, and a lively Picture of Human Nature in its Contrarieties of Passion and Reason, its Infirmities and its Sufferings.[39]

Each letter was equipped with a prefatory argument which dwelt more upon the turns and twists of passion it expressed than on what it had to say:

Letter III. If [Abelard] seems by some Passages in it to have begun to feel the Motions of Divine Grace, they appear as yet to be only by Starts, and without any Uniformity.

Letter IV. The Passion of *Heloise* breaks out with more Violence than ever . . . an unhappy Woman abandon'd to all the Transports of Love and Despair.

Letter V. [Heloise] yet discovers some Emotions which make it doubtful, whether Devotion had entirely triumphed over her Passion.[40]

Writers who wanted to demonstrate that their works combined the two great merits of letter fiction felt or professed to feel that mere authors of "feigned histories" could not duplicate the genuine accents of passion. Gildon wrote in the preface to his *Post-Man Robb'd* (1719):

> I can't but recommend too the passionate Love-Letters of the fair Stremunia, I think the most valuable we have seen in Print of that kind. I suppose they are genuine; and indeed they bring their own Credentials, for no Body that was not fully possest of that Passion, cou'd write so feelingly of its Torments and Pangs.[41]

Mrs. Eliza Haywood, like her predecessor Mrs. Manley, had evidently thought long and fruitfully on the problems and benefits of certain narrative techniques, for she prefixed to the second edition of the *Letters from a Lady of Quality to a Chevalier* (1724) a "Discourse concerning Writings of this Nature, by way of Essay," in which she dwelt for twenty-nine pages on the virtues of love letters. The "discourse" is of extremely loose texture to be dignified by the name of essay, but it indicates copiously its author's belief concerning love letters (or at least what she wished her readers to believe):

> If we make never so many Resolutions to contain ourselves in the bounds of the most strict Reservedness, we cannot be sure but some unguarded Moment may arrive, in which *Passion* may triumph over *Reason:* Paper cannot blush, and our Thoughts, in spite of us, will often take a greater liberty in expressing themselves that way, than the natural Bashfulness of Virtue will permit 'em to do any other.... I have somewhere read,
>
>   The *Pen* can furrow a fond Female's Heart,
>   And Pierce it more than *Cupid's* talk'd-of Dart:
>   Letters, a kind of Magick Virtue have,
>   And, like strong Philters, human Souls enslave! ...
>
> There is certainly an Influence in an artful, tender, and passionate Way of Writing, which more sensibly affects the Soul, than all the Tongue can utter.... Tho we know each Line is an Arrow aimed at our Virtue or our Peace; our Curiosity, or our Inclination, seldom fails engaging us to peruse them: from that we fall to examining the happy Turn of Thought,—the Elegance of the Expression,—the easy Flow of Stile,—discover unnumbred Beauties in every Sentence ... thence we reflect on his

Behaviour while he was writing—think in what manner he look'd—how he sigh'd—what he wish'd—imagine we dive into his very Soul—find out Meanings there, to which, perhaps, he is a Stranger. . . .

The Lady, whose Letters I have taken the liberty to translate, tho she has been cautious enough in expressing any thing (even in those the most tender among them) which can give the Reader an Assurance she had forfeited her Virtue; yet there is not one, but what sufficiently proves how impossible it is to maintain such a Correspondence, without an Anxiety and continual Perturbation of Mind, which I think a Woman must have bid farewel to her Understanding, before she could resolve to endure.

In the very first she plainly discovers the Agitation of her Spirits, confesses she knows herself in the wrong, and that every Expression her Tenderness forces from her, is a Stab to her Peace; she dreads the Effects of her Lover's too powerful Attractions, doubts her own Strength of resisting such united Charms as she finds in him, and trembles at the Apprehensions, that by some unlucky Accident the Secret should be known. Every thing alarms her . . . so this unfortunate Lady, divided between Excess of *Love*, and Nicety of *Honour*, could neither resolve to give a loose to the *one*, nor entirely obey the Precepts of the other, but suffered herself to be tossed alternately by both. . . . the Disquiets she suffered in that time of Probation, were, I think, if no worse ensued, too dear a Price for the Pleasure.[42]

Mrs. Haywood stresses the power of letters to reveal the emotions passing through the mind of their writer and to produce reverberations in the bosoms of their recipients. We have already seen that letters too artfully and elegantly expressed were beginning to be suspected of having no passion behind them; passion, it was felt, promoted the very qualities of touching incoherence for which the Portuguese Nun was so celebrated. The Lady of Quality became suspicious when she received a letter too well penned:

The Letter you writ to me this morning, seems to have more of Gallantry than Sincerity—the Style appears more studied, and the Sentiments are expressed in a man-

ner, which carry a greater share of Art than Nature.—
What is your Design?

But when the next letter was properly artless and tender:

> —I trembled, with an apprehension, that I might have
> forgot something in it: and yet there was not one engag-
> ing Syllable that I had not read over a thousand and a
> thousand times, before I could resolve to put it out of my
> power to read it any more.[43]

Pre-Richardsonian epistolary fiction, full of not very discreet hints to the reader that the style of letters will tell him
much about the character of their writers, is no less crowded
with elaborate descriptions of the stunning effects of letters
on "a fond Female's [or male's] Heart." The following are
typical:

> What were her Pains when all those Fears were con-
> firmed from that never-failing Mark of a declining
> Lover, the Coldness and Alteration of the Style of Letters,
> the first Symptom of a dying Flame! *Oh where*, said she,
> *where, oh perjured Charmer, is all that Ardency that
> used to warm the Reader?*

> He fansied she had put great Constraint upon her natural
> high Spirit to write in this calm Manner to him, and
> through all he found dissembled Rage, which yet was
> visible in that one breaking out in the Middle of the Let-
> ter: He found she was not able to contain at the Word,
> Common Mistress.

> You may easily see by this Letter she was not in a Hu-
> mour of either writing Love or much Flattery.[44]

> The Prince was sensibly affected with this Letter, which
> gave him great Uneasiness, and [was] now convinced of
> Vanella's sincerity.[45]

> I needed no other Proof than the Style and the Shortness
> of this *Billet*, to inform me, that I was, indeed, as
> wretched as I could be.[46]

> If I could once see a Letter of hers like those I would
> adore her, nay I would turn raving Mad for her sake.[47]

And in *The Tell-Tale* (1711, pp. 39–41) a lover is depicted anxiously trying and discarding phrase after phrase so that he may fan his mistress' flames to the requisite degree without seeming too fulsome.

Addison and Steele, on a somewhat higher level of criticism, were very much aware of the pathetic possibilities of letters. They wrote appreciations of the last letter of Anne Boleyn and of a letter written by a sergeant after a battle, being profoundly impressed by both. Addison found greater merit in "natural eloquence" than in artificiality:

> Grief has a natural eloquence belonging to it, and breaks out in more moving sentiments than can be supplied by the finest imagination. Nature on this occasion dictates a thousand passionate things which cannot be supplied by art.[48]

Steele defended the sergeant's letter against criticism by rules, insisting that a revelation of the writer's feelings transcended wit or elegance:

> This is, said I, truly a letter, and an honest representation of that cheerful heart which accompanies the poor soldier in his warfare ... the picture of the bravest sort of men, that is to say, a man of great courage and small hopes.[49]

Formal questions of epistolary style were not confined to manuals of rhetoric or complete letter writers. The latter agreed in general that the soul of the familiar epistolary style lay in the appearance of informal discourse or familiar speech, shorn of conceits and graces. The critic John Dennis, on the other hand, was willing to allow more latitude. While he stated in the preface to a collection of his letters in a miscellany

> that the Style of a Letter was neither to come quite up to that of Conversation, nor yet to keep at too great a distance from it,

he also conceded

> that if the sublime were easie and unconstrained, it may be as consistent with the Epistolary Style, as it was with the Didactique.[50]

Steele devoted a *Tatler* to the question of what style was suitable to letters of gallantry; his verdict indicates a reaction against the languishments of the love letter, real or imitated.[51]

But the authors of sentimental or passionate letter fiction were not writing to please Richard Steele. Their frequent comments on the beauties of the natural style must not be construed to refer to the simple, blunt manner that Steele praised in the soldier's letter, but rather to an artificially disheveled style of incoherent exclamation derived from the sensationally popular letters of the Portuguese Nun and the heroic drama. A style of epistolary writing which to us seems the very reverse of natural evidently looked convincingly artless to its readers in comparison with the stilted, conventionally ornamented style of the formal letter.

Some of the comments recorded here not only point out the emotional storms revealed in letters or experienced by their writers and recipients, but also suggest that the reader should take part in them, that indeed he cannot help being moved by their intensity. The idea of the reader's participation gained rapid acceptance with the passage of time and is very evident in the comments of Richardson and his contemporaries upon his novels.[52] A striking earlier example of just this insistence on the reader's participation is Samuel Humphreys' preface to his translation from Crébillon *fils, Letters from the Marchioness de M*** to the Count de R**** (1735). Together with Crébillon's own account of the letters, this essay might be said to sum up most of the comments made during the previous two generations on letter fiction to direct the reader's taste into profitable channels. To catch the reader's eye, Humphreys' title page is adorned with a quotation from a critical journal.

> If any LOVE-LETTERS may be rank'd with the celebrated ones of *Abelard* and *Eloisa;* those of a Religious *Portuguese* Lady, and those of the *Chevalier de Her—;* They are These of the Marchioness *de M—* to the Count *de R—*. They have the *Fire*, the *Turn*, the *Spirit* and easy *Air* of *Those* we have mention'd: They furnish us besides with this useful Lesson, That Guilty Love must expect to meet with unhappy Consequences.
>
> Journ. Liter. 1734 [53]

His extravagant preface, declaring that sentiment and propriety reign in the ensuing letters, reminds the reader of the uncontrollable sympathy with the heroine which he will experience:

> [The letters] paint, in the warmest Colours, the Progress of an unfortunate Passion, from its seducing Birth, to its fatal Period; and represent an amiable Mind variously agitated by the Impressions of Tenderness, and the Dictates of Duty.... She distrusted the natural Softness of her Soul, and neglected no Endeavours to extinguish a Flame from whose Prevalence she had Reason to be apprehensive of such unhappy Events. Her Breast was, perhaps, a scene of the sharpest Conflict that was ever sustain'd by Love and Innocence; and if the latter had not the Glory of being victorious, it was because the other had the Fatality to be invincible.... we shall consider, with Astonishment, that uncomplaining Softness of Soul ... and will find it difficult to suppress our Impatience to behold her awaken'd into Resentment.... But when we at last trace her in the Pangs of Death, and read the moving Flow of her agonizing Penitence ... we intermix our Tears with hers; we intreat Heaven to be propitious to her.... I am almost persuaded that some of these Impressions, at least, will be experienced by the generality of those who read the Letters I have attempted to translate.[54]

The author's opening letter makes sure that everything possible is done to convince the reader that the letters of the "Marchioness" are authentic:

> An Extract of a *Letter* from Madam de *** to M. de ***.
>
> I have lately made a very agreeable Discovery; for I found, among the Papers that belonged to the Count of *R****, a collection of Letters written by the Marchioness of *M****.... Perhaps they may not present you with that Accuracy of Style, in which our Writers place so considerable a Part of their Merit; but the little Negligences of a Woman of Wit have that amiable Air, which might be difficult, even for your fine Genius to imitate. ... I have only transmitted those to you, which I imag-

ined worthy to be read; and though I have selected no more than seventy out of five hundred which are in my Possession, you are not to conclude that the rest are inferior to these. . . . I found my self a little disgusted at the excessive Warmth that glows in some of these Letters. . . . I have likewise rejected several others out of Regard to the strict Rules of Decency; but at the same time, I have endeavoured to disconcert, as little as possible, the Order in which they were written; and yet, after all my Caution, you will sometimes find the Connection interrupted.

The same Expressions are frequently repeated in them; the same Situation of Circumstances is as often presented, and the same Object perpetually rises to the Reader's View. Little Dissatisfactions, Reconciliations, Flights of Caprice, warm Resentments and flowing Tears, Joys, Jealousies and Apprehensions, Fears, impatient Wishes and Despair, are liberally diffused; and tho' these Emotions are varied in the Description, yet Love is the only Cause from whence they derive their Existence and receive their Extinction; Love still appears in this Diversity of Shapes, and the Uniformity of the Subject must infallibly be disagreeable, notwithstanding the Variety of the Sentiments.[55]

Although Crébillon thought fit to apologize for a series of letters in which almost nothing took place and whose matter consisted of endless slight variations on the same theme, he evidently felt that the public would like it, and the English translator seems to have shared his enthusiasm. Their confidence was justified; the English version reached its second edition within two years. The increasing popularity of similar novels in the decades before 1740 seems to indicate that the public was by no means so startled by Richardson's method as has sometimes been supposed.

III

To point out an obscure phenomenon of letters is some service to literary history, but to demonstrate that it was significant or influential (if this can be done) is more useful. It is interesting that early letter stories were thought easy to believe true because of their form and that fictional letters were accorded a high place in intimately depicting the movements of the heart. If they had been uncommon, nothing more could be said. But popular novels seldom contain statements that will not be read with patience, and these tales rivaled Defoe's in popularity. The preferences which they indicate need to be taken into account in assessing the state of literary taste in general in "neoclassical" England.

Swift's and Pope's war on Grub Street should be enough to indicate the double current of taste in their day, and when considering poetry or the drama, religion, or popular philosophy we are ready to concede that such a division of taste existed. The forces of unreason and anti-"common sense" were equally strong in the fiction that people read, but because so much of it was inferior and is forgotten we are prone to take the best for the whole and assume that Defoe was the only fiction writer between Bunyan and Richardson. Mrs. Haywood's public thought otherwise, and made its tastes felt before Defoe's time. Thus, a standard modern work on the history of popular taste in fiction asserts that in the earlier eighteenth century the "middle-class" reader had no desire to hear about high life, totally lacked interest in feeling or sentiment, liked brisk, business-like narration, and was devoted to facts about material possessions, and that these qualities were typical of the popular writing before Richardson's time.[56] The early epistolary novel flatly contradicts every one of these statements. Its two prime characteristics, carefully considered, show how and why.

It might seem that the demand for stories which appeared to be true, so well satisfied by the devices of letter fiction, is evidence of a highly realistic, common-sense, down-to-earth taste. But "real," "true," "authentic," "verisimilitude," are all notoriously vague terms. They do not in themselves differentiate between the possible and the probable, the plausible or likely and the conceivable. "True" stories could lead in many directions, and after the "Augustan" reader had salved his moral or aesthetic conscience (whichever it was) with the preliminary premise that he was reading a true history, he (or she) settled down contentedly to tales of the wildest improbability. It was not only Mrs. Behn and Mrs. Haywood who gave them to him. A modern reader, if he compares Defoe's treatment of time and childbearing in *Moll Flanders*, or Fielding's of coincidence and concealment in *Tom Jones*, or the tricks of fate in *Robinson Crusoe* and Prévost's *Cleveland* with the events in such a novel as *Madame Bovary*, will see that "realism" need not pervade all the departments of fiction to be realism. It is true that from scene to scene the atmosphere of early epistolary fiction is far less decorous than in Defoe and the emotions far more theatrical and fiery, presented with far less realistic control. As for down-to-earth, homely realism, it was exceptional in early letter fiction. The locale was likely to be France, Italy, Spain, or an English haunt of fashion such as Bath, with an occasional excursion to Barbary or Bengal. Protagonists, usually female, seldom finally married below an earl or experimented with courtship below a knight. In these novels the details of physical setting, which critics have so often celebrated in Defoe, were usually confined to naming a chair, a sofa, a flowery bank, or a chamber richly adorned, though gold pieces (never counted) were flung about with abandon. Plots were sketchy and ill-constructed, and clearly no reader was expected to pay much attention to them. Incident, however, reached its most fantastic extravagances in this fiction. A devotee of letter fiction between 1680 and 1740 could have read of ghosts and apparitions, elopements (one of a nun from a convent in a diving bell), the imprisonments, escapes, abductions, and seductions of distraught maidens, duels, murders, robberies, rapes, concubinage (in both directions), fornication, adultery, incest (at least twice outside of *Moll Flanders*), and pederasty (once).[57]

The critic must condemn such stuff, but the historian of taste is obliged to take note that it existed and that its popularity among a significantly large public meant a craving to hear of extravagant goings-on in an unreal world of high life among fascinating rakes and impossibly beautiful heroines, whose antics could be credited because anything might happen in foreign parts. On one level we may call this vulgar sensationalism, but if it had been of higher artistry we should be constrained to think of it as preromanticism. The European *comparatiste* Paul van Tieghem divides the manifestations of the preromantic movement into "internal" and "external." He identifies the external with the remote in time, space, and culture: medievalism, balladry, primitivism, *chinoiserie*, the Ossianic cult, and so on, and the internal with the exploration of the irrational, with sensibility, sentiment, passion, and the individual mind.[58] Although the authors of pre-Richardsonian epistolary fiction confined themselves to the recent past and neglected China, they cultivated external romanticism in their crude way, and their readers evidently responded with enthusiastic purchases long before the exoticisms of Walpole, Beckford, Laclos, and Restif de la Bretonne.

Internal romanticism was not being neglected. The sentimental novel of the mid-eighteenth century has long been recognized as a breeding ground for revolt against classicism and cultivation of sensibility; we need only to amplify this idea by emphasizing that at least a few novels of pure sensibility were widely read in England before the death of Charles II and that such novels increased in number and influence during the next half century. In the letters of the Portuguese Nun action, plot, and events count for nothing; the Nun's sensibility is all. The same goes for the Nun's many descendants, whose creators grew increasingly articulate in their comments concerning passions on paper. The early reader of letter fiction was expected to luxuriate in its fantastic emotional crises just as much, though perhaps not so tenderly, as the later readers who "sobbed in a most scandalous manner" over Richardson's works.[59] It might be argued that while readers *could* have reacted in this fashion to sentimental letters there is no evidence to show that they did. But passages that point out in detail the emotional waverings of a letter-writing heroine and direct the reader to participate in them can hardly be interpreted as benevolent attempts on the authors' part to refine public taste. Their motives were less disinterested; their prefaces performed the same function as the cover of today's paperback novel. They had perceived that certain tastes existed where we have hitherto failed to find them.

The Nun, in *Seven Portuguese Letters*, writes to her lover:

> If you hand a Lady over the Kennel, I am for all that day like a Distracted Creature, raving under the highest extremities of despair.[60]

Mrs. Haywood writes:

> I have heard some Ladies (in the Infancy of Love) dispute very warmly in [passion's] behalf, declare that they

look'd on a state of *Indifference,* to be no better than a
state of *Stupidity;* and that they would not part with
their Passion, with all the little Fears, Hopes, Wishes,
Languishments which attend it, for the World.[61]

They and the author of the original *Portuguese Letters* were
only a step from proclaiming that it was fashionable to weep
or from attaching an index of tears shed. The excesses of deli-
cacy, sensibility, and refinement into which popular-novel
heroes and heroines ran in the latter part of the eighteenth
century have long been ridiculed as the silly results of carrying
a fresh and valuable literary emphasis too far. We might say
instead that modes of writing which had had a long "under-
ground" existence in inferior fiction were gradually moving
up into novels of greater merit.

The part played by women in fostering early letter fiction deserves consideration. We should remember the serious-
ness with which a largely feminine public took the French
romance and the heroic-sentimental drama, the feminine milieu in which the novels of Richardson germinated, the high
proportion of women among the authors of fiction in the
years preceding his work, and the many women who followed in his footsteps.[62] Perhaps it is oversimplifying to say
that women preferred emotions and sentiment in their fiction
while men preferred action, but this notion is widely accepted.[63] To see the trashy but popular melodramatic letter
novel as a bridge between seventeenth-century romances and
dramas and the sentimental epistolary novel of a hundred
years later is not far from the truth. We might hypothesize a
sort of reverberatory effect: an atmosphere of rationality and
common sense bred an inevitable reaction to itself from its
earliest days, and a craving for sentiment in the Restoration
produced novels which generated a stronger inclination for
such fiction. This, in turn, produced more and better sentimental novels in letters, until the tendency exhausted itself
shortly after 1800.

The importance of Mrs. Haywood's readers ought not
to be overstressed. Defoe and his public, however, have so
long and so completely engrossed attention that a corrective is
due. We cannot ignore languishing ladies in our admiration
of Moll Flanders if we wish to look objectively at English

fiction just prior to *Pamela*. Bizarre events and settings and an emphasis on feeling for feeling's sake, which have every right to be called essentially and even exaggeratedly romantic, pervaded the potboilers of the "Age of Reason" and shaped public taste earlier than we have recognized a romantic groundswell as arising in the novel.[64] For this reason if for no other, the letter fiction of the early eighteenth century has an importance in the history of English literature which its small artistic merit might deny it.

CHAPTER VII

"Icing on the Cake"

❧

The whole interspersed with curious letters of love and gallantry.

—*The Secret History of ... Beauties*

We have explored the literary tradition in which letter fiction grew up before Richardson, the stimulating effects which French novels and the familiar letter had on it, the economic facts that conditioned it, and those particular qualities which made it important to its authors and readers. It now remains to examine early letter fiction in isolation in order to determine how well the epistolary method succeeded in dealing with artistic problems of narration.

We have seen that fictional letters were commonly associated with the display and analysis of a character's emotions and thoughts, a quality rarely present in the conventional narrative of the time. If the two kinds of writing could be combined, the letters would furnish the tale with an emotional dimension quite distinct from the bare recital of events. Readers could be given a chain of happenings to pique their interest, and at the same time the portrayals of emotion could act upon their feelings. But if the emotional elements were not fully integrated with the fabric of the tale being told, they would function as a sort of delightful overlay, unnecessary to the relation of what happened, but desirable—a sort of icing on the cake. Such "icing" appeared more consistently in early

fiction in England than we recognize; and its relation, or lack
of it, to the "cake" it ornamented furnishes an interesting
chapter in the history of fictional technique.

English epistolary fiction from 1660 to 1740 may be
roughly divided on the basis of structure into two categories
—stories in which letters are the sole narrative medium and objective prose narration in which interpolated letters take up
varying amounts of space, sometimes as much as half of the
work. The purely epistolary type, which received its first
great impetus from the letters of the Portuguese Nun and its
second from the novels of Richardson, flourished with vigor
until well into the nineteenth century. The semiepistolary
form, though popular as early as the time of Elizabeth and
increasing in favor until Richardson's day, began to fall into
disuse with the overwhelming success of purely epistolary
fiction. If the inserted letters in sixteenth-century fiction may
in some cases be dismissed as merely a kind of rhetorical orna-
mentation, such letters acquired a very real importance to narrative in the next hundred and fifty years. The stories which
they adorned may be thought of as curious hybrids between
the objective narrative and the novel in letters. They were mutations which flourished for a time but gradually died out
when a new variety more adaptable to survival (in this case,
possessing a more artistically satisfying and flexible technique)
appeared on the scene.

These mutations were remarkably similar in form to
some of the most popular examples of Tudor fiction, which
indeed was far from forgotten. Perhaps for this very reason
Lucres and Eurialus found favor nearly three hundred years
after its original composition in Italy with no changes beyond
the modernization of its diction and tone, while *Euphues*
went through several eighteenth-century editions in a condensed version; [1] and we have seen that novels like Mrs.
Behn's and Mrs. Haywood's were essentially developments,
without really basic modifications, of earlier novellas and the
"histories" from romances. The French novels of the age of
Louis XIV, so popular and so widely imitated, were the results
of a parallel though somewhat more rapid development. But
the new importance and new uses which inserted letters gained
in English and French novels after 1660 cannot be attributed
solely to the influence of forces of tradition.

Letters had a notable place in the mechanics of the intrigue-plots typical of these novels.[2] Heroines who are kept in virtual or actual imprisonment by harsh parents and rascally abductors, or who dare not speak their love,[3] must have some means of communicating with lovers or possible deliverers if the plot is to go on, and letters were the only answer. (Indeed, though they are surrounded with an abundance of realistic bourgeois scenery and properties, Pamela and Clarissa are as much in durance vile as any Emanuella of Mrs. Haywood's. Their creator had to imprison them in order to maintain the maximum dramatic tension possible in a letter narrative, and to avoid the difficulties he later failed to surmount in the handling of *Grandison*).[4] Forged letters (the most popular of all epistolary tricks at the time) may be used to implant unjust suspicions in the minds of lovers or to create false security, as in *Clarissa;* the discovery of the forgery may resolve the plot. Correspondence lost, dropped out of someone's pocket, or glanced at on a table while its recipient is out of the room may provide a character with new information, and give the plot a new direction; letters may be withheld, delaying action, or opportunely produced to reveal the identity, blamelessness, or villainy of a character and thus effect a resolution. Such uses of the letter are purely mechanical, and in all these common letter-situations the exact contents of the letter need not be reproduced for the purposes of plotting. Objective description of the gist of it is enough, though the effect for the reader is enhanced if he receives the revelation in the sender's own words.

Letters brought about these basic situations not only in the Renaissance tales and the French romances, but all through the early development of letter fiction. In matters of intrigue they were exploited with great ingenuity, if not with taste. In Mrs. Haywood's *The Agreeable Caledonian* (1728), the heroine Clementina, who is generally believed to be the mistress of a cardinal, receives a reproachful letter from a more humble admirer. It is intercepted by her father, who is enraged to discover that her affections are not devoted solely to the cardinal, with whom he is trying to arrange a match for her, the cardinal having promised to renounce holy orders. Clementina writes to beg her plebeian lover to rescue her, and he replies, offering to duel with the cardinal if the latter will doff the cloth. Her father publishes the reply to clear himself and his daughter from aspersion and packs her off to a convent. In the cloister a letter carelessly dropped by the fair Miramene informs Clementina that Miramene is pining for a certain Baron Glencairn. He and Miramene frequently exchange letters, but she is not permitted to speak to him. Clementina proposes a stratagem with a double purpose: she will send a letter of her father's to the baron so that he may counterfeit the writing and compose a letter of introduction to the abbess, presenting himself as a relative of Clementina's. Thus, he may see both the girls at the convent wicket, since no inmate may talk there alone. Clementina, by deceiving the abbess, promptly arranges to have poor Miramene deprived of all privileges and presents herself at the wicket as the transmitter of letters. She plays the part of go-between so well that one of Glencairn's fervid epistles is presently addressed to her; and before long the baron, disguised as a friar conveying a relic to Rome, smuggles her out of the convent in that relic, a miraculous diving bell. The first part of this short novel contains no less than seven long letters, while others are mentioned, and most of the plot revolves around the employment of letters. In the second part Clementina's maid plays upon her the same epistolary trick she had played on Miramene.

Again, Marmillio (the earl of Scarborough) in Mrs. Haywood's *Court of Caramania* is temporarily in disgrace and forbidden to have private conversation with his sovereign. He reinstates himself by means of discreet epistolary blackmail presented before all the court in

> a little Billet, which it was easy for him to deliver to him, though in the presence of all the World, because it was usual for all Petitions and Addresses to pass through his hands.[5]

The hero of *The Gentleman Apothecary* (1670), having by chance imprudently performed a service of shocking intimacy for his mistress, is bidden never to see her again and must effect a reconciliation by a series of letters.[6] Mrs. Behn's Sylvia, the heroine of *Love-Letters Between a Nobleman and His Sister*, in an imprisonment strikingly similar to Clarissa's at Harlowe-place, is forced to smuggle letters to her Philander by her maid. Later, when the maid is discharged by her parents, she lowers letters on strings to a friendly gardener. In the second part of the novel Sylvia uses elaborate stratagems to obtain a sight of a letter written by Philander to one of his friends, in order to be assured of his perfidy.[7] In Mrs. Davys' *The Reform'd Coquet* (1724) a mysterious love letter, concealed in a glove and thrown into a summer house, starts a whole train of events. The novel contains no less than thirteen letters, but all are essential to the plot. They include warnings of danger from an unknown friend, letters making assignations, a letter of introduction, and several letters connected with the basic deception around which the plot revolves: the coquette Amoranda's formal guardian, Formator, turns out to be a worthy lover in disguise, somewhat of the Sir Charles Grandison variety. A letter presents him as her guardian; another reveals his true identity. Many other novels might be cited in which letters are vital to the plot-mechanism and hence have very good reasons for being included in the story.[8]

Practicing writers of fiction are familiar with the way in which characters seem to acquire a life of their own as a novel is being written and struggle for an importance or a direction which the author had not originally intended to give them. Some process such as this may have taken place with the inserted letters in the early novels of France and England. Letters were often given in full when this was unnecessary for the purposes of the plot; they began to occur without much relevance to the plot, or even to be unconnected with it. At times they were not only useless, but blocked the progress of the story and diverted the reader's attention from its main purpose.[9]

It is useful at this point to reflect on the form generally taken by Western fiction from the Greek romances to the eighteenth century. With the exception of the Renaissance Italian and Spanish novels, which were notable for their objectivity, economy, and concentration, fiction lacked focus; it was rambling and disorganized. The narrative, as a matter of course, was constantly broken up and impeded by ornaments —descriptions, soliloquies, poems, letters, and harangues. Such fiction may be described as a patchwork, or more accurately as a series of more or less unrelated segments, some of which were functional, some merely decorative. The author might pause at any moment in the narrative to reflect upon events in his own person, exhibit his virtuosity in description, or lecture the reader. The texture of early fiction was seldom so smooth and uniform as the modern reader of novels commonly expects it to be, as when, for example, the whole story is seen through the eyes of a single character.[10] Writers in general had devised no effective way of making fluid transitions between objective or purely functional narrative—the bare relation of what happened and who said what, to get on with the plot—and the "set pieces" whose purpose was to amplify and give depth to the picture. Readers tolerated narratives rather arbitrarily filled with long complaints, descriptions of scenery, discourses, and letters, as in the French romances. Such mélanges had to be, because neither the author nor the reader could be contented with the adventures of wooden puppets; their minds and motivations must eventually be explored.

To solve this problem the reader of today would suggest long and frequent scenes in which the characters exchange ideas and opinions, expressing their feelings by means of dialogue imitating actual conversation or by action. But this expedient, obvious as it seems to us, was not obvious to French and English writers before the middle of the eighteenth century. Anyone who glances through the novels of this period will be struck by the near absence of what we now call normal dialogue. Harangues, passions, tirades, and lengthy unrealistic speeches are found in abundance; conversational exchange scarcely exists.[11] Instead, one finds a surprising amount of indirect discourse. When the author has what would now be called a heaven-sent opportunity for a "big scene," he (more often she) hurries through it quickly, clumsily, and with evident embarrassment. The following scene from Mrs. Haywood's first novel, *Love in Excess,* (1719) is typical:

> [The Chevalier d'Elmont, newly married to Alovisa, has just discovered that she has been tampering with his letters to her former rival Amena, with the result that Amena has taken the veil in despair.]
> *Alovisa* . . . ran in to know the Certainty. . . . You have done well, Madam, (said *D'Elmont,* looking on her with

Eyes sparkling with Indignation) you have done well, by your impertinent Curiosity and Imprudence, to rouze me from my Dream of Happiness, and remind me that I am that wretched Thing a Husband! 'Tis well indeed, (answer'd *Alovisa*, who saw now that there was no need of farther Dissimulation) that any thing can make you remember, both what you are, and what I am. You, (resum'd he, hastily interrupting her) have taken an effectual Method to prove your self a Wife!—a very Wife!—insolent—jealous—and censorious!—But, Madam (continued he, frowning), since you are pleas'd to assert your Privilege, be assur'd, I too shall take my turn, and will exert the—Husband! In saying this, he flung out of the Room, in spite of her Endeavours to hinder him, and going hastily through a Gallery which had a large Window that look'd into the Garden, he perceiv'd Melliora lying on a green Bank, in a melancholy, but a charming Posture ... he in a Moment lost all the Rage of Temper he had been in, and his whole Soul was taken up with Softness.[12]

With artistically useful dialogue and realistic, significant action in this embryonic state, authors continued to rely on the older expedients of fiction, the "set pieces," for their explorations into emotion, thought, or motivation. As time passed some of these devices were discarded, and the novel presented less variety of texture. Verse lost the favor it had once possessed, and after the Restoration few novels contained any verse beyond an occasional song. The quips and nips, "frumps," and orations of euphuism were likewise discarded; but the "portrait" (condensed), the soliloquy, and the letter were retained. Coming into the vacuum created by the absence of other devices, they increased in frequency and value to the novelist. The soliloquy might sometimes be given as a speech, but more frequently it was rendered indirectly, introduced by such a sentence as "But with what words shall I represent the wild distraction of *Placentia's* Soul when she receiv'd his Letter!" [13] In letters, however, subjective narration found its most effective fulfillment. They became an almost inevitable device in novels in which the authors felt it necessary to deal with the feelings of the characters. Letters even took the place of dialogue when dialogue was not only possible but logical. The novel of writers like Mrs. Haywood, unless it were purely epistolary, was the euphuistic novel modernized, with its subjective elements furnished chiefly by numerous interpolated letters.

English novels of this period in which the characters' feelings and motivations are analyzed more or less in the modern manner, by the author's description of what went on in their minds, are so rare and striking that historians of fiction have noticed and praised them as important forerunners of the modern novel. Such are Mrs. Behn's *The Nun: or The Fair Vow-Breaker*, parts of Mrs. Manley's *New Atalantis*, and Mrs. Haywood's *Life of Madam de Villesache* and *The Fatal Secret*.[14] More frequent are novels in which the same end is more crudely accomplished by inserted letters. Mrs. Haywood's short story "The Witty Reclaimer" in *Love in Its Variety* (1727) is an example. Don Fabritio loves Christiana, ruins her, and marries the wealthy Villaretta. Love and remorse soon make him repent, and Christiana retires from the world, having exacted from him a vow that he will marry her if it is ever in his power to do so. Fabritio and Villaretta quarrel; she yields to the importunities of Don Diego del Piramont and grants him an assignation. A mysterious letter advises Don Fabritio that he is about to be cuckolded, and he discovers Villaretta and Don Diego together. Don Diego is revealed as Christiana in disguise. After divorcing the unchaste Villaretta Don Fabritio marries the "witty reclaimer" and all is well. Told thus baldly, the plot is an ingenious intrigue in the manner of the Italian novelle; [15] but Mrs. Haywood makes the story somewhat more plausible by inserting an exchange of five letters between "Don Diego" and Villaretta in which the gradual undermining of the wife's chastity is shown as her letters alter in tone from cold disdain to eager acceptance. The letters are not really necessary to the progress of the plot. They are inserted because the author and her readers liked love letters and because they help to make Villaretta something more than a puppet.

A similar use of the letter for characterization occurs in the story "The Wife's Resentment," in Mrs. Manley's *The Power of Love* (1720). Mrs. Manley added two letters to the story of Didaco and Violante, from Bandello by way of the version of Painter or Boaistuau. Perhaps the letters were ex-

pected as ornaments, but also they gave individuality and
realism to the invincible chastity of "Violenta" (Mrs. Manley's spelling). In all the earlier versions we are told merely
that Violante, the virtuous and educated daughter of a goldsmith, rejected the attempts of the profligate young lord
Didaco to seduce her. Mrs. Manley makes her rebuke him
roundly:

> I have a Mind truly intrepid in the Cause of Vertue,
> which neither the Preservation of your precious Life, nor
> that of my Mother, Brothers, or of my own, can ever in-
> duce me to forsake; I would see the whole World in a Con-
> flagration, and my self in the middle of it, before I could
> be brought to do any thing contrary to the Rules of
> Modesty. Wonder not, that a Maid so meanly born and
> educated, should have such exalted Ideas of Vertue: I
> have study'd her well, all her Ways are lovely, Peace and
> Honour attend her Votaries in this Life, a fragrant Report
> when they are dead, and a Crown of Glory hereafter!
> How despicable are those Advantages which you offer me
> in exchange? Consider of it, and farewell.[16]

(Violenta's anticipation of Pamela is not confined to the ex-
altation of humble virtue over lordly vice; we later learn that
she is holding out for marriage.) The story contains two
other letters from Violenta, their contents being given in full
in indirect discourse, and two complaints by her. Except for
these ornaments the story is told with considerable economy
and is even drier than in Painter, since the style lacks his Elizabethan richness of diction. There is almost no dialogue.

If we consider merely the progress of the plots, both of
these brief tales are hampered by the epistles. The story is at a
standstill while the letters deal with matters which Boccaccio
or Bandello would have dismissed in half a paragraph. But
clearly Mrs. Manley and Mrs. Haywood were at least dimly
conscious of the technical contributions the letters made and
were willing to let the action suffer for the sake of characterization. Blocking the narrative was nothing new; ornament
had been far more seriously oppressive in the proto-"psychological" novels of Lyly, Pettie, and their followers.

Another interesting example of how authors regarded interpolated letters is furnished by Préchac's *L'Illustre pari-*

sienne, translated by Mrs. Haywood as *The Disguis'd Prince* (1728). The plot, rather like that of the modern *The Student Prince*, begins as follows. A German prince, wishing to send his son to be educated in Paris, cannot do so openly because of a state of war which makes it probable that the son would be arrested as a hostage. He therefore sends him disguised as Samuel, the son of Solicofane, his banker. For the sake of improving his French, Samuel is the "pen pal" of Blanche, the daughter of a Paris banker named Bonnin. Although it is stated that the real Samuel and Blanche corresponded frequently, the author remarks:

> I hope my Reader will excuse me for not inserting the Letters, because those of *Solicofane* were far from any thing of that Delicacy which alone can render Writings of that Kind pleasing, and those of *Blanche* cold, and design'd only to oblige Answers that might excite laughter in herself and Father.[17]

But when the false Samuel arrives in Paris and Blanche is smitten with his charms, the situation is different. Although they have ample opportunity to converse at meals and in the evening, they write letters, which are given in full. "Samuel" writes to Blanche, giving the ridiculous reason that his strait-laced tutor might forbid them to talk intimately. Blanche writes to him over the name of Sophia, her German maid, and forces from him the admission of his real love. Presently, "Samuel" is forced to flee to England, and the correspondence continues; the first part of the novel, containing fifty-eight pages, has no less than eight letters. *The Disguis'd Prince* indicates how the combined forces of letters for plotting and letters for the treatment of character might result in a story which a modern writer might manage excellently without using letters for either purpose.

Again and again the reader of these novels detects instances in which the writer seems to shy away from opportunities for dialogue, preferring letters even when their use is absurd. The full-fledged epistolary novel seems to be struggling to take shape. Such is the case in *Some Memoirs of the Amours and Intrigues of a Certain Irish Dean* (1728), a scandalous tale about Swift and the Blount sisters (and perhaps Stella and Vanessa), anonymous, but almost certainly by

Mrs. Haywood.[18] The book bears every evidence of having
been written in the utmost haste or rushed into print before it
was finished; it is an undigested mixture of scandal-chronicle
and romantic tale of passion. The two plots (if plots they
can be called), one dealing with Swift's "amours" and the
other with those of the Blounts, are alternated without explanation or transition and are quite unconnected. The ninety-six
pages of the book contain twenty-four numbered letters, each
running from half a page to several pages in length. The contrast between the epistles and the narrative passages is striking: the latter are careless, hasty and flat, full of inconsistencies and abrupt transitions, seeming almost improvised;
the letters are long, evidently written *con amore*, and exploit
emotions and reactions to the utmost. Polidore (Swift) courts
Satira and Sapho, who writes poetry. Although he has every
opportunity to speak to them, the conversations are not reproduced; the letters are. Polidore finds it necessary to leave
town for a while, but all we are told is that

> some Days past in mutual Endearments, in which time,
> when they had not Opportunity of conversing alone,
> they employ'd it in writing to each other. The day before
> they were to part, *Polidore* wrote the following Epistle
> to put into her hands as he took his leave.[19]

The epistle, given in full, does what might have been done
better for the story by a farewell scene between the two.
Polidore and Sapho have a quarrel, which ought to have been
put in dialogue, but which is given in thirteen pages of short
letters with brief paragraphs to link them.[20] Although Polidore is often away from his mistresses so that he must write to
them, his absences are unexplained. In a similar situation the
heroine of Mrs. Haywood's *Cleomelia* finds it necessary to
implore her betrothed, Heartlove, to feign that he wishes to
renounce her, in order that she may carry on an intrigue with
the handsome rake Gasper. Although they constantly see one
another, the whole scheme is carried out by means of high-
flown letters, and all we learn from the narrative is that

> The Pleasure with which *Cleomelia* receiv'd this Grant
> of this Request was very much damp'd by the Grief she
> knew it caus'd in him who oblig'd her; but as it is natural

to prefer ones own Satisfaction to that of any other Persons, excepting the Man one loves, it easily wore off.[21]

Letters were often the focal points of shorter narratives. A famous example is Steele's *Tatler*, No. 82, which tells the story of the bridegroom who accidentally shot his bride on their wedding day. Steele tells the story with the utmost economy, placing the principal burden of the narrative on the two letters which climax and end it, one written to the bride's father after the wedding, the second after the accident. A similar short story built around epistolary matter, "The Heroick Cavalier," is in Mrs. Jane Barker's *A Patch-Work Screen for the Ladies* (1723). The story, which is simplicity itself, is narrated as sparely as possible by a gentlewoman to the company in a coach. A girl whose parents disapprove of her lover is immured in a convent, but the resourceful lover smuggles his page, disguised as a novice, into the convent with a letter. Here the gentlewoman-narrator reads the letter and the answer to it aloud to the company; "she had procured a copy." The cavalier persuades the nun to attempt to free herself. She replies:

> Sir,
>   Your letter has so ruffled my whole Interior, that I know not how to write common Sense: Therefore, if my Answer be unintelligible, blame me not, for I am utterly lost in an Abyss of Confusion: The Thought of breaking my holy Resolutions on one Hand, and the Sufferings which the keeping them, makes us both undergo, on the other, distracts me. My dear Chevalier! change your Reproaches into Pity: I will endeavour to repair my Faults: Faults! did I say? Ah me! it is a Crime, to call this my Religious Enterprize a Fault! My Thoughts, Words, Writings, on this Occasion, are Faults! The very Corresponding with the young Lady you placed here, is a Fault! Yet a Fault so sweet, so delicious, that I cannot refrain, because she recounts a thousand tender Things of you; repeats your Sighs and Grief in such soft and melting Words and Accents, as would soften the most obdurate Heart.
>   Then, what Effect, think you, must it have on mine, which is prepared to be set on Fire by the least Spark

struck from your dear Sufferances, which she most indus-
triously blows into a Flame, not to be suppress'd by any
devout Sighs, Tears, or other Religious Mortifications; by
which I suffer a perpetual martyrdom, and see no Way of
Delivery, but by adhering to your Advice sent by her,
and come to your Arms: those dear glorious Arms! those
Arms, that have honoured your Family, Friends, and
Native Country! Those Arms, that have crown'd the
Hero with Lawrels, and the Lover with Myrtles. Those
Arms, that have greatly help'd to subdue the Enemies of
France, and built Trophies in the Hearts of the Fair. O!
can I refuse my Hero? Can I refuse my Lover? Can I
refuse my dear Chevalier? Indeed, I cannot! No, no, I
cannot! I will not! The Temptation is too great to be
resisted by frail Mortality.

Wherefore, my beloved Chevalier, I will comply
with those Measures you and your young *Hugonot* have
taken.[22]

At length she resolves to defy her parents and proclaim her
love at the public ceremony of taking the veil; she is released
by the bishop to join her lover. So rapid and colorless is the
nonepistolary narration that the letters by comparison take up
far more space and attention in the conduct of the story than
they deserve. On the other hand, the story revolves around
the nun's change of mind as pictured in her letter; her character is given a touch of depth and credibility when we are
allowed to see her mind in the process of struggling and forming its resolution.

The importance of letters in these divided narratives is
vividly apparent when we compare the amount of space they
get with that given to expository passages, and still more so
when we compare the two kinds of prose to see how much
attention is given to passing events. Perhaps "degree of intensity" is a suitable term to describe this. Comparison shows
that a Haywoodian novel may present the most important
events, or even plot reversals, in a hurried paragraph or so
without color or interest, while in its letters fleeting emotional
states or the most trivial events are dwelt upon, amplified, and
intensified with the utmost resources of the author. *Some
Memoirs of the Amours and Intrigues of a Certain Irish Dean*
is an extreme example. Polidore raves to Sapho:

My beautiful Angel, its impossible for me to express the immense Grief I suffer'd last Night; for, Oh, I miss'd my Pocket-Book, wherein, besides Notes and Letters, there was the dear Symptoms of Love I receiv'd from you: I fretted, raved, and stormed, but in vain, to lose those dear Pledges of thy Faith; and that those unparrallel'd Effluvias of thy divinely inspir'd Muse, was present Death to me; but to my wonderful and transporting Joy, found it about an Hour ago: Thus, from the lowest Abysses of Sorrow and Distraction, am I again elevated to my former State, and now I can feast all my ravish'd Senses on the sight of thy lovely handy Works.

Eternally Yours.[23]

But on the following page an important change takes place; it is dealt with in the following summary manner.

This [another letter] came very opportunely to relieve *Polidore* from the distracting Thoughts and Perplexity of Mind he was in at the Thoughts of her having bestow'd, what he believed only himself had a Right to, on some more happy Man.

Besides, *Satira* began to grow extremely troublesome, and he was half distracted, not knowing what he could do; at length he was in short forc'd to grow vastly cool, and give her to understand he could not think of marrying her, because his Mother had a great dislike to her, and as affairs stood he could not upon any Terms think of disobliging her.

This was like a Thunderbolt in the Ears of *Satira*, and the Love she bore to him turn'd to the extreamest Hate.[24]

Earlier in the story a long and passionate letter [25] is followed without the slightest attempt at transition by this abrupt passage:

About this time a young Relation of [Sapho's], to divert herself and others, came there upon a visit, with an Intent to pass away the Summer. She was very witty, entirely agreeable, full of Amusement, and Coquet enough,[26]

and the story goes off in a new direction. The passage from *Cleomelia* quoted earlier is a further example of how casually matters might be dismissed when they were not to be treated in epistolary form. While such inversions of the values assigned to important and unimportant matters doubtless owe their existence largely to the clumsiness of hack writers, they also foreshadow later developments in the novel. If the feelings of a moment or the loss of some love letters can be made to assume greater importance than the cooling of a lover's ardor or the beginning of a subplot, the novel has blundered to a point not very far from the conscious experimentation with time and psychology which marks the novels of Proust or Faulkner—or, to approach these tales more closely in time, Sterne's *Tristram Shandy*.

Examples like these (and they could be multiplied many times) indicate that the letters with which novels were often advertised as being "intermix'd" frequently played a more important part in giving the story whatever depth, atmosphere, and characterization it had than did the narrative they adorned. Earlier, the ornaments in the Elizabethan novel had created what in effect was psychological fiction, though the writers were thinking rather of developing their subject rhetorically than of psychology. A story thus ornamented and amplified with psychological elements was said to be "discoursed." [27] In the same way Richardson's *Pamela*—called in its time a "dilated novel"—was discoursed by making the plot advance slowly, while each step of its progression was reflected in the consciousness of the heroine-narrator and voluminously commented on by her instead of being sparely and hastily recounted by the author. One way of looking at the half-epistolary novels written before Richardson's day is to consider that they represented a development of the Elizabethan technique of discoursing, still somewhat bound by artificial conventions but refined by being narrowed down to the one device of discourse which the unskilled author could most easily make realistic and moving.

In the hands of the more extravagant writers letters came closer to the form and appearance of speech, or of actual mental processes, than did the stilted speeches put into the mouths of their characters. Letters were used typically in moments of crisis to intensify the moment rather than to advance the action, and the author called in every mechanical and rhetorical device in his repertory to show the agitated thoughts and emotional disarray of the transported writer. The rant of the stage, apostrophe, exclamation, and dashes in profusion, indicated disorder and violence. Earlier examples of such letters written in moments of crisis were not very different from the formal epistles of the previous age, as the following extract from *God's Revenge Against . . . Adultery* indicates:

> To my Deliverer, Captain Conrade.
> The service you have done me does challenge a far greater acknowledgment than lies in my power to give you, and I hope will excuse me if I say something to you kind and extravagant. I have no other way to requite your civilities but to tell you what power they have over a soul so sensible as mine is, and it is your own fault that you have not more acceptable proofs of my love and affection to you. Since you are going to the wars, perhaps I may never be put to the blush by seeing you again; but pray remember as you have set my body free, you have made my heart your captive, whilst I am
> Anne of Werdenberg.[28]

After 1678, however, the *Portuguese Letters* furnished new models for passionate expression. Together with the diction of the heroic drama they furnished out the letter of passion in its heyday. What such a letter could be in its extreme form is shown by one from Melantha to Bellario (Eustace Budgell) in Mrs. Haywood's *Memoirs of a Certain Island*.

> To the most Ungrateful of Mankind, the Perjur'd, but still Dear BELLARIO.
> It is then true that I am lost, betray'd, abandon'd; your Silence, and your Absence confess your Inconstancy, and show me what a wretched Fool I have been, to trust a Man who I knew had been false to others.—Oh! I could curse myself, and tear out my own fond credulous Heart.—It is not in your power to be just, or good: Ingratitude is ingrafted in your very Nature, 'tis a part of your Being, and you cannot shake it off without parting at the same time with Life.—Blind and stupid that I was, to imagine there could be a Reformation in him whose whole Soul is made up of Hypocrisy, and Deceit, and

whose every action, since he could write Man, has show'd the Villain.—Oh! I am mad!—pardon the harsh Expressions of my jealous Frenzy—I mean not as I say—I love you still, nor scarce repent the Ruin I have yielded to—all Men are false—all Men are Hypocrites in Love, and you but as the rest, only more lovely, more endearing far—and if you have the Vices incident to your Sex, you have, to excuse the Woman they undo, Perfections which not one besides yourself can boast—Never were any Eyes so form'd to charm, as yours.—Never had any Tongue persuasive force like yours.—The Gods of Love and Wit, conspire to aid you.—Thou more than Angel!—thou God of my Desires! Thou something more than Words can Speak!—Oh! I grow wild again, Remembrance of those extatick Joys your Kindness has bestow'd, is as dangerous to Sense, as those Heart-rending Agonies your Falsehood now inflicts. Neither are to be borne, each is enough to overthrow Reflection; how is my divided Soul then rent 'twixt both!—Pity me, ease me, see me once more, and tell me if *Clarina* must engross you all—give me but the Satisfaction of knowing whether I ought to love or hate you—Oh! that I had never known a Cause to doubt which Choice to make—Curse on the vain officious Tongue that rais'd this jealous Fury—Curse on my Readiness to listen to such destructive Tales—But doubly curs'd be my own want of Charms, which had not power to hold you, yet flatter'd me they had.—Torture—Distraction—Hell—what will become of me—I cannot—I will not survive the Knowledge that you are mine no more—Yet this Suspence is worse than all yet ever bore the name of Horror—Let me not linger in it, if you have Humanity—Declare my Doom at once—be kind in Cruelty at least, and let one Death conclude the thousand, thousand Deaths which every Minute of Uncertainty brings with it, to

The Miserable, but
Still Adoring
MELANTHA.

P. S. I have order'd the Messenger to bring an Answer; if he comes without, depend I will murder him, and then myself.[29]

One example of such epistles should be enough, but their prevalence makes it clear that many readers of 1725 differed in their tastes. Other letters displayed some virtuosity and a certain amount of realism, even by modern standards, as they concentrated on the veerings of emotion or the rapid progression of thoughts through a character's mind. When a writer of today attempts to depict such processes, we call it the "stream of consciousness" or (perhaps more correctly) the "interior monologue" technique, but something very much like the "interior monologue" was used by Dostoevski, Flaubert, Dickens, Jane Austen, and Richardson, and in a limited sense by the Elizabethans. Writers of the early eighteenth century did not have Freud and the psychopathology of everyday life to rely upon, but they did have diluted and popularized Lockian theories of associative processes.[30] They certainly restricted the range of matter in their interior monologues, and they presented them more formally than did Joyce, for instance; but their basic method and intention were much the same—to show a mind in action, forming thoughts. With due allowance for the difference in literary conventions and literary merit, the results are strikingly similar. Unless a character is experimenting with automatic writing, his thoughts must be far less disjointed on paper than they are in his mind, and for this reason the letter is a less grateful medium for the interior monologue than is an imitated direct transcription of thought, such as the ruminations of Molly Bloom. The reader absorbed in the story, however, is not likely to think about such matters until he puts down the book, and the devotees of these tales of passion probably did not reflect that they were reading something more like broken speech than any conceivable epistle.

Mrs. Haywood showed herself a votary of mental monologue in her maiden effort, *Love in Excess*, where in Part III, the unfortunate Camilla dashes her thoughts down as fast as they occur. She is torn by longing, angry self-pity, vituperation, desire, and concern for her lover's safety. From time to time she checks herself, describing her own actions, noting the advent of each new feeling. She alternates between complete absorption in her own feelings and more detached contemplation of them:

Ten whole Nights and Days, according to the vulgar Reckoning; but in mine, as many Ages have roll'd their tedious Hours away since I last saw you; in all which time my Eyes have never known one Moment's Cessation from my Tears . . . restless I wander through this hated House —Kiss the clos'd Wicket . . . then, with wild Ravings, think of past Joys, and curse my present Woes—Yet you perhaps are calm, no sympathizing Pangs invade your Soul, and tell you what mine suffers; else you would, you must have found some Means to ease yourself and me— 'tis true I bid you not attempt it—but oh! if you had lov'd like me, you could not have obeyed . . . —But whither am I going? I say I know not what—Oh, mark not what Distraction utters! Shun these detested Walls! 'tis Reason now commands! fly from this House, where injur'd Love's enslav'd, and Death and Treachery reign—I charge thee come not near, nor prove thy Faith in so hazardous a Way—Forgive the little Fears, which ever dwell with Love—I know thou art all Sincerity!—all God-like Truth, and can'st not change—yet, if thou should'st—tormenting Thought . . . a deadly Cold runs through my Veins, Congeals my Blood, and chills my very Soul! [31]

Some Memoirs of the Amours and Intrigues of a Certain Irish Dean is particularly rich in monologues of this kind, especially from Polidore as he wallows in the pangs of love. Readers who were fond of "little Jealousies, Hopes, Fears, Languishments" found what they wanted in its pages. Polidore begins a passionate letter to Sapho, breaks it off and begins again, with

> I have been interrupted by a tedious Visit, and now have looked over all I wrote, must beg ten thousand Pardons, having been too much transported,[32]

but although he begs ten thousand pardons, the reader has not been spared a full transcription of his earlier transports. In other letters he describes minutiae of feeling and action with all the careful attention to detail that characterizes Pamela's artless pen. Polidore's letters in general, though high-flown, are written in a more idiomatic style than most of their species, and succeed in giving a fairly realistic picture of an agitated mind at work, in which free association runs riot:

Epistle the Eleventh, *Polidore* to *Satira*.

I was just now making myself happy, as cruel approaching Absence would let me, with my Goddess's letter. Oh! there is Ten Thousand Darts in every Line; my Angel has shown so many pretty, charming irregular Expressions, that as I read, I see Sighs and Kisses on the cold Paper.—I kissed it a thousand Times, and feel the Rigour of the dear Hand that wrote it; and yet it has kept a struggling Life from ending. Oh! Good Heavens, the Tyranny of parting.—By your Self my Thoughts croud so thick and so fast, that I know not which to sigh to you first: Your cruellest Letters are all Charms, and I sometimes read them to fright me, that the comforts of the rest may put me out of it: I run over every Passage of our Life every Day, every Hour: I have said enough of it,—love you for ever till I dye, constant, true, and— Good Heavens am I not all over you, is the least Thought a Moment from your Presence: God forgive me, my prayers are full of you.—Well, 'tis Madness to expect one Jot of Happiness upon Earth.——But I expected all this, I did so,—and I expected Death too, tho' God knows how little I am provided for either: I dare not say I will dye; No, I will not if Heavens permit, 'tis your Life, and I'll keep it for you.—Ah, Heavenly *Sapho*, and can you do less for me—I am resolved soon to return and lay Happiness at your lovely Feet, the Charms, the Heaven I saw in your Face to Day. Thus, my Charmer, the Sun looks, brightest when it is just setting, and it is the worst malice of Fortune to add all the lustre she can to these Blessings she is just going to take from us.—God! I am falling a talking like a Fool, running into Speculations on my H—n, my Happiness, my eternal Dear. Oh G-d! You know what I would say, what I us'd when I had my Heaven before me: Well, I don't know what I am saying, what will you expect from a transported Madman: Be happy, or else by H—s I'll dye: I must bid you be true, and yet you're Truth it self; I know you are, and all the World are Lyars: My kind preserving Dear, I cannot think of parting with you: my Heart is not prepar'd for so great a

Change; don't desire to stay me long, if you do I shall dye in your A—s: Blockhead that I am, I forget that you cannot read this till we are parted; That cruel Word, invented by some stale, envious, ugly Maid, to spite, to kill Lovers. Well, I am stark mad, and don't remember any thing, but that I am, and ever shall be, *Sapho's,*
                                        Adoring, Dying Slave.

Epistle the Twenty-Third, *Polidore* to *Leonora.*

I'll tell you how I receiv'd your Letters; it was on Sunday last, and I was full of the dear Expectations, crouded with Hopes and Fears, as if the Sentence was to determine my Life; and tho' I expected one from I—l—d [Ireland], which was absolutely necessary for my Business, yet I never thought the least of it while you stood in Competition: Well I waited, at last some Body knock'd at my Door: Pray let me be a little impertinent, I felt every stroke at my Heart; I opened it, and a Servant gave me the dear Characters; and I was so little Master of myself that I chang'd Colour three or four Times, and in Transport gave him all the Money I had about me; he ask'd me what I meant, I told him, 'twas all too little to pay for that letter, and bid him begone; but by and by call'd him again, and bid him take no notice of what I said. By all that's good this is true and I must boast of it. I flung myself down on the Couch, and hug'd the divine Paper, and kiss'd the Superscription for above an Hour and then open'd it, and was less happy than before, for you kill me with your News of being the Toast of that Place....[33]

The technique of having the writer minutely describe his circumstances as he writes, and the arrival and departure of each fleeting emotion, certainly stems from the *Portuguese Letters.* It steadily increased in favor with authors, it is notable in Richardson, and with the flood tide of sensibility it became one of the most frequent and often one of the silliest devices of epistolary fiction. A character might even describe his own death throes, pang by pang.[34]

Several other avenues of psychology were explored in letters. "The Prudent Husband: or, Cuckoldom Wittily Prevented" in Tom D'Urfey's *Stories Moral and Comical* (1706) is a rather bawdy tale of intrigue, adapted from the *Heptameron* of Marguerite of Navarre. In it the foolish matron Leonora falls in love with the learned and eloquent Father Jovus through hearing a series of his Lenten discourses. Her husband surprises her page with a letter addressed to the monk. He procures a habit, visits his wife at night disguised as Father Jovus, and, professing to believe her seized with an unclean spirit, scourges her with cries of "Temptation! Temptation!" until she is thoroughly cured of her infatuation. D'Urfey's original contribution to the tale is the text of

Leonora's Billett to Father *Jovus*.

When my Perans would first have a me be bound To a husben, I dud prea every day and neet that it might be with a Coller, and won of Laning and Devoution for their Sweat honi instrucksions still incaesd my licking which as I found religoose and Sage, bread Butter thoughts and gaue my Sins of Vnderstanding more plasher, than any other dillicat dud in the whole worl, I am vary much ashemd but prea dere Fader forgive a me if I sea my heart is wounded now more than ever with your define apillitys your graue but strong Doctern has lately twice ravisht me and the great measure of your hollinesse has soe farr Inflounct me, that my brain is possett with desire, and without your pitty and privitys in this bees nest I am undonn and urin'd for evar.[35]

This letter is clearly designed to amuse the reader with its obscenity, but it also furnishes examples of what is nowadays called the "Freudian slip" as the sexual, gustatory, and scatological imagery in Leonora's mind unconsciously breaks out by means of puns and misspellings into what, written correctly, would have been an elegant if agitated billet. (The story makes the point that Leonora believed her feelings to be spiritual or platonic.) It might seem absurd to credit D'Urfey with such a degree of psychological sophistication, but a passage he added following the letter indicates that he had at least some glimmerings of what he was doing.

[The husband] (in the midst of his Vexation for his Wife's Ridiculous and Contemptible Passion) could not forbear laughing at her frantick kind of Spelling, which clearly exprest the hurry and confusion of her mind, she formerly using to write otherwise; nor could he help a Smile when he read over the Breakfast of Bread, Butter and Sage that she had sent her adorable Monk; or when she pray'd to be bound in Wedlock with a Coller, instead of a Scholar.[36]

Moreover, D'Urfey was a dramatist, and the comedy of the misspelt or mispointed letter was a device of the theater as old as the malapropism, anticipated in Medwall's *Fulgens and Lucres* and brought to perfection in the hero's wonderful letter to Dame Custance in Act III of *Ralph Roister Doister*. Whatever the source of D'Urfey's clever contrivance, he seems to have been the first to exploit it in fiction. Here it is not the contents of the letter in themselves which contribute to the dismay of the characters and the amusement of the readers, but rather the distortion of the contents in the hands of an ignorant or foolish writer. It is tempting to theorize that Fielding or Smollett might have known of Leonora's letter; at any rate, they did little better with Mrs. Honour's hilarious letter in *Tom Jones* (Bk. XV, ch. x), the unintentionally obscene letter to Miss Tishy in *Jonathan Wild* (Bk. III, ch. vi), or the celebrated letters of Tabitha Bramble and Win Jenkins in *Humphry Clinker*. D'Urfey's "billet" contains true "portmanteau words"; and we may consider it the most remote ancestor in fiction of the wordplay that passed from Smollett to Dickens and Lewis Carroll, and to its culmination in the verbal complexities of *Finnegans Wake*.

To compare these crude, early efforts at the "close-up" depiction of mental processes with present-day techniques makes the defects and the stilted writing of the early examples glaringly apparent. But even in their crudity the passages show that their ill-paid authors had considered the process of thinking as it actually occurs and were trying to imitate its chaotic and disorganized appearance. They were taking the first steps in what we think of as an important part of literary realism—deliberately breaking up organized, formal patterns of discourse to reflect the disordered processes of actual thought and speech.

Authors also experimented with interpolated letters which revealed something of their writers' idiosyncrasies, or with letters in dialect, much as dramatists used dialect in speeches. Mrs. Mary Davys in her autobiographical narrative of provincial life, *The Merry Wanderer*, gives the reader all the necessary information about a boorish squire by reproducing a "Rustick Love-Letter" from him:

> Madam,
>
> Last Thursday I was very sick with eating Goose-Giblets, and our *Nan* says I am in love. Now if I am in love, I am sure it is with you, for I always loved strange Faces dearly; and our *Nan*, who is a very good Woman, bid me tell you so: and now I tell you so, and tomorrow I will tell you so again, when I come to see you: and I have Three Hundred Pounds a-year, and will keep you a good Pad, and you shall never go to Church on foot, and you shall have Furmety as often as you please, and our *Nan* shall make it for you; and so no more at present, but that
>
> I am your loving Sweetheart,
J. B.[37]

Gildon made a closer approximation to speech in *The Post-Boy Rob'd of His Mail* with a letter in Somersetshire dialect:

> These are to let you know, that cham got zafe to *London* Zity, where the Volk walk up and down e'ry Day, thicker than at *Taunton* Vair, every Door is a Zhop . . . Then there's such a din Night and Day, that the noise *John Tabour* the Drummer of the Train'd-Bands made . . . was nothing to't. . . . nay, by all the Vlesh o've my Bones, if *Zimon* the Clerk of our Parish were to give out a Zalm in one of the groet Streets here, with as tearing a voice as he does on a Zunday at Evening Prayer . . . you'd zwear he did but whisper. . . . Chave zeen a groet many other Zights, but upon the whole, cham o'th' mind thou hadst better keep whaure thee art, vor cham zure, thee cout not lye, swear, nor steal, and Godsbodikings, unless thou canst do twon o've 'em, thee mayst e'en blow thy Nails here. Cham thy loving uncle,
>
> OBADIAH WHEATSHEAR.[38]

The Somersetshire boor was already a minor comic figure in the dramatist's repertory of type characters; if Fielding immortalized the type in Squire Western, the most popular

figure in *Tom Jones* for his contemporaries, we may at least
credit the inventive Gildon with being probably the first to
transfer the type from the stage to fiction.

The heroine of Mrs. Haywood's *Fantomina* (1725),
more clever than scrupulous, manages to enjoy the fickle
Beauplaisir by disguising herself successively as a courtesan, a
chambermaid, the wealthy widow Bloomer, and the fair Incognita, who never under *any* circumstances takes off her
mask. At one point in the story Fantomina and the reader see
two letters, differing widely in style and sentiments, written
by Beauplaisir in the same hour to the courtesan and to the
supposedly rich widow. Mrs. Haywood allows the reader to
discover for himself from Beauplaisir's own pen the state of
his mind and the motivations which sway him.[39]

In some of these novels the inserted letters adumbrate so
much of the action that the story is in fact told twice over—
once in the bare narration of the events and once through
what the reader can pick up from the characters' reporting on
them in the correspondence. In the first part of Madame
d'Aulnoy's *Memoirs of the Court of England* the duke of
Buckingham is recounting his amorous exploits to two friends,
when the conversation turns upon a certain countess with
whom he claims to have had an affair:

> You shall be convinced of what I have told you, to be
> true, reply'd the Duke. You know her hand; look here are
> her Letters, for I sent for them on purpose, just as I was
> come away from her Lodgings, to read them to the Earl
> of *St. Albans;* if you have patience enough to hear them
> read, you shall judge for yourself what place she had
> given me in her Heart.[40]

The duke, no precisian about "kiss and tell," produces the
countess's letters and reads them aloud one by one in chronological order. He alternately comments on the occurrences
reflected in each and describes the progress of the affair, reading the relevant letters at appropriate points. The story is a
thin tale of love: the duke feigns an amour to make the
countess jealous, she fears that her husband may have found
one of her "billets" and that he will duel with the duke, the
duke goes to Holland as ambassador, and the countess pursues
him with amorous epistles. She discovers that she has a rival in

the duke's affections and writes an indignant letter terminating the affair. In this "novel" of thirty-nine pages, containing twenty-six letters of varying length, the very slight plot is given in double narrative, either side of which would have been sufficient to convey its essentials. The narration in letters, however, filtered through the countess's passionate feelings, amounts to a series of speeches; the duke's story, although a first-person account, lacks emotional overtones and concentrates on the events rather than on their impact. The duke comments on the various passions expressed in the letters and the amount of tenderness they show with all the fervor of a guide conducting his thousandth group of visitors through a museum.

It is pleasing to record one instance at least in which double narrative was used with a mature understanding of its liabilities and assets, and what is more, with a refreshingly satirical approach to the clichés of passionate correspondence. *Love upon Tick* (1724) tells the story of Urganda (the name is that of a loathsome sorceress in *Don Belianis of Greece*), who is an old maid with her amorous conquests far behind her. For pure amusement she assumes the character of Phillis, a lady of high degree enslaved by Cupid, and for two years dupes the silly coxcomb Philander by purely epistolary means. Philander never sees Phillis; he is made to hope and fear, to go on constant wild-goose chases into the country in order to leave billets or to keep assignations which never materialize. Like Malvolio he wears absurd ribbons as a signal of love, he dreads several duels with Phillis' imaginary male relatives, and he hires equipages to ride about in the park to no purpose. Urganda is frequently put to her shifts to keep him dangling; her knowledge of Philander's foibles is severely tested again and again. The forty-three letters sustain the story, for the intervening passages do little more than comment on one and prepare for the next. The plot is purified into nothing more than Urganda's playing her gudgeon upon the hook, but the reader is continually curious to know by what stratagems the lady will keep the farce going and avoid discovery. Not content with frequent comment on the follies of coxcombs in general, the author makes Philander's foolish letters reveal his selfishness, meanness, wretched style, and empty conceits. Her dedication (to Philander as quintessential fop) makes it clear that he is to be the object of contempt throughout:

> the Author apologizes for rectifying the *Orthography* of your *Billets;* but had much rather charge the Printer with it than incur your Displeasure, for having divested them of a graceful Illiteracy, which may perhaps be their greatest Ornament.[41]

Love upon Tick may be the work of Mrs. Manley. The author is a woman who writes with an unusually masculine, ironic style, and knows it. Urganda is represented as having been the favorite of a very great lady (as Mrs. Manley was of the duchess of Cleveland), though callously discarded; what is more telling, both Urganda and Philander are very familiar with the version of the story of Beau Wilson told by Mrs. Manley in *The Lady's Pacquet of Letters;* [42] Philander hopes to emulate his happy fortune. It is true that Mrs. Manley died in 1724, but the story need not have been written for a pittance on her deathbed, for she was living comfortably as the mistress of Alderman Barber. Though judgments from style and merit are scarcely applicable in the field of primitive, popular fiction, one is tempted in this case to paraphrase the attribution of a later epistolary satire: *aut Manley, aut diabola.*

Double narrative had long been characteristic of fiction in the Renaissance-Ovidian tradition. The Elizabethan *Lucres and Eurialus, Arnalte and Lucenda,* and *The Castell of Loue* depend heavily on interpolated letters for the progress of their action. The main facts of each could be conveyed to the reader by the letters alone if they were equipped with introductory titles. Analysis of the post-Restoration novel shows many examples of the same sort of double narrative: in some of them the inserted letters, with their content somewhat amplified or with use of the "flash-back" device, would have sufficed for the exposition and resolution of the plot without need of the narrative passages between them. If the authors' aim had been no more than telling a story, this doubling of the narrative was indefensibly wasteful and inartistic and would probably have seldom occurred. (As a matter of fact, the six volumes of Croxall's vastly popular *Select Collection of Novels* [1720 and later], consisting of some of the best novels of the day, chosen from Cervantes, Scarron, Brémond, and other Continental writers, contain no such double narratives. The novels are in plain expository prose; the few letters in them are used in plotting.)

The technique of double narrative reached its logical dead end—the literal splitting of the two kinds of writing into two completely separate versions of the same story—in at least two novels: one of the "histories" in *The Present Court of Spain* (1693), and *Love-Letters Between a Certain Late Nobleman and the Famous Mr. Wilson* (1723). In the first, "the enamored Teresa" tells the sad story of her unconsummated love for the marquis of Mansera to her friend Eleonora in fifty-three pages of first-person narrative. This is followed by one hundred and twenty-four pages of letters from her to the marquis (seventy-five of them) which retell the story. If this had been tortuously complicated, such a procedure might have been faintly justified, but the plot is as follows: Teresa and the marquis love one another from afar; she is disquieted by the thought of possible rivals; he attempts to get into her presence, but never quite succeeds, though twice he manages to steal into her house undetected; her parents become increasingly angry, and she is at length made a prisoner in her own house and resolves to steel herself to forget him. The fact that such a literary monster was created not by an unknown hack but by the accomplished and prolific French novelist Mme d'Aulnoy—and that it went through two editions in five years in its English translation—demonstrates plainly the magical sales powers which fictional love letters were thought to have, and the difficulties which the epistolary novel was undergoing in breaking free from its trammels of conventional narrative. Could Mme d'Aulnoy have doubted her readers' ability to piece together a story from letters alone? If she did, her fears were groundless.[43]

The second of these stories at least justifies the technique of the twice-told tale. It begins with twenty letters which are confusing in extreme; we do not know the identities of the two correspondents or precisely what is happening to them. The letters are full of what seem to be personal allusions and a sort of private language; many passages have been cut out. We can only gather that the writers are lovers who are going through various personal and social difficulties. The narrative then solves the mystery. The "editor" reveals that the correspondence is between the famous Beau Wilson, who was killed in a duel without ever revealing the mysterious source of his large income, and a certain late nobleman, who was homosexual and who was keeping him in splendor. The excised passages were too obscene, it seems, to be printed, and the mysterious troubles arose from the difficulties of persuading the world that both Wilson and the nobleman were having affairs with women. A crisis came when Elizabeth Villiers, mistress of William III, marshaled all her resources to find out the truth about Wilson, but she was eventually outwitted. The anonymous author evidently built his story around a technique of mystification, for he constantly prepares the reader for a second part in which a "key" will identify all the persons mentioned. (So far as is known, it was never written.) The letters skilfully characterize the noble patron as arrogant and haughty, Wilson as basely fawning and full of protestations. But a literary puzzle is hard to elevate into an art form, and unless we wish to see Beau Wilson's story as a forerunner of detective fiction we may dismiss it as a curiosity of literature, an unusual variant of the scandal-novel.

Literary curiosities and monsters notwithstanding, there was a good market for subjective narrative, and authors provided it. The majority of them seem to have been unable to conceive of such a new departure in technique as a novel entirely in letters that might combine subjective narration with the treatment of a fairly complex plot. The characteristic modern novel, which shows personality, character, and feeling through dialogue and action, represents a step which they were in general not technically prepared to take. They therefore resorted to an easier method: developing the resources of the familiar old-fashioned tale by combining bare narration with static pieces of subjective display. The most useful set pieces were developed with much ingenuity and elaboration; at the same time writers cultivated a smooth and readable style for the narrative passages. The growing importance of the set pieces (notably in the works of Mrs. Haywood and similar romancers), aided by the public's delight in them, the writers' consciousness of their technical and financial value, and their adaptability to various purposes, threatened to choke off the narrative; its importance diminished in contrast to the rhetorical glitter of the intense letters. Yet in spite of this absurd imbalance of the narrative elements, authors seemed reluctant to fuse them together. The story with inserted letters remained—clumsy, incoherent, and archaic—until Richardson's time, and even thereafter dwindled away only slowly.

The explanation of the form's persistence is fairly obvious. Poorly paid fiction writers were willing to let well enough alone, and if the public bought their wares they were satisfied. They had neither the time nor the inclination to consider artistic effectiveness. To eliminate easily understood expository passages might have risked sales; to imbue narrative with subjective overtones, as authors commonly do at present, would have been too much trouble. It was certainly not an innovation which most authors of popular fiction were artistically equipped to make, but rather a matter for a Fielding or a Sterne.

However clumsy such stories may have been as fiction, they made significant advances in the effectiveness of the fictional letter. Hampered by lack of precedent in developing realistic dialogue or methods of describing what went on in a character's mind, their authors succeeded in making letters serve for a time as useful substitutes. Although the language used was dominated by artificial conventions and stagy rhetoric, the efforts to depict mental processes and tumults showed realistic insight. The authors dimly realized the importance of concentrating on "the moment" and describing its minutiae and experimented feebly with the manipulation of time and with characterization by accretion. They managed to give the letters an organic connection with the fabric of the story, as Richardson was to do later, by making their existence, writing, concealment, and so forth of high importance in the movement of the plot. Many of the most useful techniques of modern fiction appeared in their works, but only sporadically and in primitive form.

Although few novels between the Restoration and Richardson's time were entirely without letters, the novels in which interpolated letters figured importantly were nearly all either translations from the French or, if native English works, appeared after the turn of the century. They may be considered transitional forms immediately preceding the full development of the purely epistolary novel. The growth of this semiepistolary method—the elaboration and extension of an older one—was a sign that a new fictional dimension was coming to be appreciated and desired even before the technique for handling it adequately had been mastered. The early efforts of popular novelists to provide fiction with an emotional overlay in letters, and to integrate this with the fabric of their stories, show that the ground was being prepared for novels of greater depth and richer texture.

CHAPTER VIII

The Epistolary Novel Arrives

❧

The pen is almost as pretty an implement in a woman's fingers, as a needle.
>   —Samuel Richardson (to Lady Bradshaigh)

When the *Portuguese Letters* appeared in English in 1678,
they did more than popularize a style of epistolary expression.
L'Estrange's book introduced the English public to a new departure in fiction—a long, complex story told (or suggested)
in letters alone. Five years later came Part I of *Love-Letters
Between a Nobleman and His Sister*, the first original English
novel entirely in epistolary form. The many similar tales appearing in the next decades ranged from single short letters to
long novels and differed greatly in complexity and literary
merit. Some few of them—ten to twenty—can be called
epistolary novels without straining the definition. Because of
their pioneering steps in fictional technique, they merit comparison with the work of the greater novelists after 1740.

These novels advanced fictional technique in four ways.
Their authors tried to deal with fairly long stories and complex plots with subtlety, and they used many technical devices
typical of mature epistolary fiction, such as Richardson's.
They gave their work a depth largely new to fiction by concentrating on details of character, motivation, and action, by
using multiple points of view, and by maintaining a uniform
tone and texture in their novels, in contrast to the uneven nar-

rative of the partly epistolary tales. They began to forsake impossible aristocratic characters and melodramatic plots of amorous intrigue for accounts of ordinary people who behaved in a believable fashion. Lastly, the style and settings of the stories began to change. The authors wrote plain, idiomatic English, and their stories took place in a milieu of British domestic life, not in operatic lands of passion and violence. This is not to say that all early letter novels made all these changes at once; but a few of them did. Others progressed more hesitantly, but their improvement, particularly in the manipulation of letters, was striking. (*Lindamira*, in a modern edition, is an easily accessible example of the early improvement in epistolary fiction, but this novel was not unique in its day. Some works, in fact, displayed a far greater mastery of the epistolary technique in fiction, and integrated it more thoroughly with their structure.)

These novels originated in imitation of such highly successful translated works as the *Portuguese Letters*, the *Turkish Spy*, and Mme d'Aulnoy's *Ingenious and Diverting Letters*, but some of their most significant characteristics could not have come from Continental models. Popular and influential as the stories from France were, most of them were not of much literary value. They lacked plot and structure. The *Portuguese Letters*, the *Five Love Letters Written by a Cavalier*, and the *Seven Portuguese Letters* were designed after the same pattern—a series of passionate utterances without replies —and contained only a tiny amount of background, supplied in retrospect. We learn from the five original letters that the Nun saw the Cavalier from her balcony, that they fell in love, and that he deserted her when he returned to France. She speaks vaguely of her parents. She says that she has been made portress of the convent, and later that she has given the picture and gifts of her faithless lover to "Dona Brites" to be burned. She writes that the Cavalier's lieutenant is waiting to carry her message and that she has heard from him of her lover's being cast ashore by a storm at "Algarve."[1] She mentions "Emanuel" and "Francisque," but we do not even know who or what they are. This is all the background and setting the story has; what in our time has been called "the sense of place" is absent. While the cryptic references undeniably contribute to the realism of the letters, they do not give the figure of the Nun solidity. The "plot" of the story is nothing more than her vacillations between rage and lamentation, rejection and pleading. The letters tell a story which is all character— we see into the innermost recesses of the Nun's soul, perhaps, but we do not know what she had for dinner. There could scarcely be a better example of Aristotle's dictum that to string together a series of speeches expressive of character is not to make a tragedy.

The seven imitative letters written anonymously after the appearance of the first five are no better. They record the Nun's violent reactions to a series of minor vexations: the Cavalier has expressed the idea that her love might cool, she has seen him talking to another woman, he has been obliged to go away for a few days, and so forth. *The Five Love Letters Written by a Cavalier* make no advance in plotting or background; their author merely took care to pick up all the hints in the original five, since the Cavalier's letters are intended to represent replies. Emanuel and Francisque become "lacqueys," [2] the Cavalier deprecates the Nun's protestations of humility and wonders how his letters can have miscarried, but the new set of letters makes no addition to the minimal setting the Nun's letters had provided. They are no more than mirror-images of the originals.

Other French novels in epistolary form were not much better as to setting. The anonymous *Le Commerce galant*, translated in 1686 as *Loves Posie*, consists of a long letter from Timander to Madame D., in which he inserts his correspondence with young Iris. The two exchange letters more as finger exercises in gallant correspondence than anything else; they "draw Deductions and Corollaries touching Love tenderness," [3] and that is nearly all. Timander's interpolated comments on the letters and on the adventures which befell the pair provide a little background. Iris complains that she is so strictly watched that writing is difficult; at length Timander goes to Paris to forget. These rudimentary hints are not developed in the twenty-seven letters into anything resembling a plot, and the "commerce galant" takes place in a nearly total vacuum. Boursault's and Crébillon's psychological novels, *Treize lettres amoureuses* and *Lettres de la Marquise de M*** au Comte de R****, developed the method of the *Portuguese Letters*, but did not go far beyond it. They treated at great length and in great detail the mental anguish of the *honnête femme* who progresses from unruffled virtue to guilty love and then to repentance, but they were not enriched with background or important events. In the former the Lady of Quality experiences a long series of hopes, fears, and jealousies, tormenting herself all the while with imaginary apprehensions. The crescendo and decrescendo of her feelings are handled with skill and at such great length that the reader cannot help finding them credible, but external action is remarkably infrequent. The lady dissects her feelings on seeing her lover talking to another woman, agrees to meet him in the Tuileries gardens, and fears—needlessly, as it turns out—that her husband suspects her.[4] Presently, her lover has to go to England, and she gradually and painfully reconciles herself to his absence. The reader does not even know whether the affair was consummated. The marchioness de M*** has an unfeeling and neglectful husband, and she yields to her lover after much soul-searching; her husband soon retires to his estates, and she has to accompany him. She repents, falls into a decline, and dies. But the bulk of the narrative is taken up with events of minimal importance, magnified in the marchioness' thoughts: visits postponed, remarks misunderstood, sudden and unfounded apprehensions.

These novels are diametrically opposed to the romances of adventure, in which plot predominated and characters were two dimensional; they represent a reaction against such types of fiction. But the reaction has gone too far. The plot has been so attenuated that it cannot be a framework for the story. The multitude of tiny glimpses of character assembled by the authors lacks the general outlines which would keep it from being a disorganized mass.

The problem is different with two other early and influential pieces of French epistolary fiction, the *Turkish Spy* and Mme d'Aulnoy's *Ingenious and Diverting Letters*. Both contain many well-told and interesting stories, but this does not make them novels. The Turk gives accounts of historical personages, intrigues, customs, and events and describes his own adventures and reactions; a few of his experiences are narrated at some length through a sequence of letters. But no element binds the whole rambling narrative together except the character of the Turk and his very miscellaneous adventures. These are not enough, because although the author (or translators) tried hard to make the Turk serve as a focus for the whole work, he did not develop or sustain his personality sufficiently for that purpose. The eight volumes contain long stretches in which the Turk scarcely appears among the essays and descriptions, and the relation disintegrates as a story. The *Ingenious and Diverting Letters* are a mixture of travel journal, "novels" supposed to be related by acquaintances made on the road, descriptions of places and people, and historical matter. The personality of the "writer" is spread—though thinly—over the entire tale, but the only integrating plot factor is the journey itself. This is not made to be of much importance; the reader does not know why the lady is going to Madrid or what she will do when she gets there. The accidents of the road are not woven together nor importantly connected with the writer's character. They are simply parts of a panorama that drifts by.

These, the most popular models on which English authors could base their early efforts at letter fiction, had much to offer in particularizing character and making discourse lifelike, but they provided no structure which could be imitated if a writer wished his story to hang together. It is to the credit of the English popular writers that they often planted their epistolary vignettes on solid ground and gave their characters something to do besides watch scenery or torment themselves on paper.

Purely epistolary tales varied in length and complexity. The simplest were the single short letters which appeared in miscellanies and periodicals. These might be of several kinds; in one of the favorites, the "my story" letter, the writer recounted the history of his or her life and usually concluded by drawing a moral or asking the "editor" for advice. Steele was particularly fond of this contrivance and used it in his appealing stories of distressed girls who had been inveigled into a life of sin. A particularly good example is his letter from "Octavia" in the *Spectator*, No. 322. The story is told without heroics, in plain and simple language: Octavia married secretly, but prudently secured a certificate of marriage. This was accidentally destroyed by fire through a boorish squire's practical joke; her husband immediately deserted her, and she was left in misery. Single letters might also tell gossipy stories

concerning persons other than the writer or convey brief
sketches of character and situation which could be made vivid
by adapting the style to the writer's station or by putting him
in a typical and amusing predicament, as Gildon did in his two
miscellanies and Mrs. Haywood in her *Spy upon the Conjurer*. One of Gildon's letters, from a bawd to one of her col-
leagues, asks for advice in setting up a new establishment; two
others present a ridiculous epistolary quarrel between a village
schoolmaster and a gardener about the merits of their respec-
tive professions.[5] The schoolmaster's letter is larded with absurd pedantries; the gardener's by contrast is illiterate but
vigorous and (appropriately) earthy. Mrs. Haywood employed the ingenious device of having a group of type characters write letters to Mr. Duncan Campbell, the famous dumb
seer of the 1720's, asking advice in a variety of amusing (and
mostly amatory) perplexities. Two of the letters come from a
servant girl named "Abigal Jump," who is precisely in
Pamela's situation. Abigal, however, has more prudence than
"vartue," and her principal concern is whether her master will
continue to keep her once she has yielded. The style and
sentiments of her letters give an economical and vivid sketch
of her character and way of thinking:

> Now, Sir, it is very hard to be in Place, and not give Con-
> tent neither; and if I were sure, he would keep his Word,
> it should be the first Thing I would do: For you must
> know, Sir, the Talk of the World is nothing; and what
> need I care what any Body says, if I want for nothing.
> I don't see that any People are so much despis'd as the
> Poor; and if I have Money, I warrant you I shall find
> enough to respect me.... All that frights me is, that a
> young Woman of my Acquaintance went away in this
> manner with a Man, a little while ago, and he turn'd her
> off presently and left her as poor as *Job*.[6]

A similar method enlivened and unified Captain Charles
Walker's *Authentick Memoirs ... of the Celebrated Sally
Salisbury* (1723). Fifteen long letters, in response, we are
told, to a newspaper advertisement, from friends, customers,
and victims of the celebrated courtesan, give lively accounts
of her life, her behavior (she seems to have resembled Nell
Gwyn in wit as in other ways), and her rapacity and lewd-

ness. The documentary method not only allows Captain Walker to avoid telling a feigned story, but enhances the variety and interest of the collection. The correspondents both retail anecdotes and relate their own sad experiences, and while all are rueful, their styles and manners are well differentiated, and the letters are filled with vivid little scenes and dialogue.

The miscellany letters of Tom Brown and Ned Ward were of the same kind. They presented lively sketches of characters and situations, usually with considerable coarseness. But the importance of Brown and Ward to the history of letter fiction (and, it is thought, to the development of Addison and Steele) lies in the fact that their narratives were realistic, thoroughly British, and completely contemporary. They satirized beaux and fops, card-playing women, and stupid rural gentry in situations with which every reader was familiar.

With this foundation, the miscellany of short stories in letters was turned another way by Mrs. Elizabeth Singer Rowe.[7] This lady, who combined strict piety with a good education, took advantage of the great popularity of epistolary miscellanies like Brown's to disseminate moral instruction. Her *Friendship in Death* (1728) was a series of "letters from the dead to the living," like his, but they described the pleasures of Paradise and the pains of Hell as felt by persons recently translated, who warned their freethinking friends in this world to prepare for a future life before it was too late. Her *Letters Moral and Entertaining* (1729 and later) was more successful as narrative. Some of its tales ran into sequences several letters long, and in its second and third parts she provided sequels to earlier letters. Reformed rakes told of their conversion, pious maidens fled the houses of atheistic relatives for rural innocence,[8] and George Barnwells rebuked the Millwoods who had seduced them. Not all the stories are so forbidding as these summaries indicate; as Mrs. Rowe continued to write she began to inject a strain of gentle satire into her pious exhortations, even though their tone and purpose kept out any matter of sensational interest. One of her best tales is the "Six Letters from Laura to Aurelia." Laura, though virtuous, is in love with the giddy delights of the town, and she chafes when she has to accompany her brother to his country seat:

> The Smell of Violets gives me the Hystericks; fresh Air murders me; my Constitution is not robust enough to bear it; the cooling Zephyrs will fan me into a Catarrh if I stay here much longer ... Daylight ... has in it something so common and vulgar, that it seems better for Peasants to make Hay in ... than for the Use of People of Distinction.[9]

She is further perturbed by her brother's atheism and by finding his mistress established at the rural retreat. Presently, she becomes more adjusted to country life, aided by the presence of a "handsome Hermit" who plays the flute in a bower and reads Marcus Aurelius. Two plots now progress to their denouements. The brother repents, his reclaimed mistress is sent off to the protection of her good uncle, and the handsome hermit dies and appears to Laura in angelic form on the following night. Laura becomes resigned to a life of innocence and devotes herself to preparations for meeting the handsome hermit in a better world. We may find both the morals and the manners of these tales too ridiculous to be instructive, but Mrs. Rowe's contemporaries thought otherwise. Her letters went through many editions, and we have evidence that they were widely read and discussed; but more than this, some of them were incorporated in Arthur Masson's *A Collection of Prose and Verse*, a grammar-school reader highly esteemed throughout the century, and so contributed to the education of Robert Burns among others.[10]

Some of Mrs. Manley's and Mrs. Haywood's more skilful short narratives appeared in miscellanies of letters. Mrs Manley's *Lady's Pacquet of Letters* (or *Court Intrigues*) [11] contained, in addition to some actual correspondence fictionalized, several long narrative letters and a few tales three or four letters in length. Interpolated letters between the characters diversified the structure of the longer stories. The first letter, a narrative supposed to be written by one lady to another, tells the "true" story of how the famous Beau Wilson rose from pennilessness to four thousand pounds a year. The tale, too long to retell here, is a fascinating one: Wilson, it seems, acted out the legend of Cupid and Psyche in reverse with the countess of Orkney.[12] Letter XXIV is the history of a gentleman who stumbles into the country retreat of a mysterious and beautiful woman. Smitten with her charms, he later returns, but she has vanished, and he never succeeds in discovering her identity. These two tales have been called the peak of Mrs. Manley's fictional achievement, and they are certainly told with a realism, vividness, fluency, and strength that are rare in the fiction of their day.[13] But their epistolary form provides them with nothing more than a slight authenticating framework and a faint coloring from the "narrator's" personality and comments. They are really excellent short stories called letters. Letters XXV–XXXIII are organized into four narratives of more technical complexity but less merit. First, a brother writes two letters to his sister from Versailles and gives a lively account of the latest court scandals. The next five letters are exchanged between the prince of Hesse and the princess of——. They contain more emotional agitation than plot. Letters XXXII and XXXIII are lively, realistic stories of contemporary British life; each includes several other letters. The first tells of a widow and her management of her two gallants. She writes for a loan from Mr. C., he refuses banteringly, and she accuses him of having made her first letter public. The second story is a letter from one woman to another concerning an intrigue with a young man in Bristol. The writer includes letters from other persons, and the reader thus sees the story from several points of view. Except in the extravagant letters to the prince of Hesse, the material in these tales is thoroughly domesticated and believable.

Mrs. Haywood's *Love-Letters on All Occasions* (1730) contains single narrative letters, letters in pairs, three sequences of four letters each, and one of twenty-four. The shorter tales deal with a variety of situations in which lovers may be involved: ladies are deserted, they protest their constancy or resolve to continue coquettes, they reflect bitterly on their ruin.[14] Mrs. Haywood seldom forgot that she was "Arbitress of Passion," and her letters of love are less down-to-earth and more rhetorical than those of Mrs. Manley, although she showed considerable ingenuity in inventing the situations which occasioned them. "Theano and Elismonda," the story which occupies letters XIII-XXXVI, is a miniature epistolary novel, made up of exchanges between the two. As the story opens we learn that Elismonda has granted Theano "the last Favour" and is consequently in a flutter. She fears that he will desert her; later, he fails to keep an appointment and she is thrown into the most violent agitations for the space of several letters. Theano is forced to go away to settle his estate; Elismonda trembles for the outcome, but at length, after several agonizing delays, Theano writes that he is about to arrive in London. The story, like its French prototypes, is built upon a series of trivial occurrences which do not justify its extravagances. Theano writes, "Recollect, Sweet Distruster! how terrible a Storm arrived with that hour in which you intended to visit *Clarinda*," in order to excuse himself for having thrown Elismonda into fits by missing a visit.[15] The narrative has some faint elements of background, since the correspondents mention specific persons and events: the reader knows the names of their friends and that Theano's early return from the country was prevented by "Sir Thomas' illness." But on the whole the story improves only slightly on the method of the *Portuguese Letters*, and the reader is disinclined to be interested in the fate of the lovers.

Equally poor results were obtained by allowing plot to obliterate character. The untitled novel in letters which forms the first section of *The Polite Correspondence* (1730?) involves two pairs of affianced lovers in a bewildering maze of complications and the author in an equally labyrinthine manipulation of fictional letters. Both parents of each girl suddenly take umbrage and labor to frustrate the nuptials; each lover employs the friend of the same sex as confidant(e) and forwarder of letters; every character labors under an important misapprehension which is at length cleared up. An elopement, imprisonment, an intriguing French housekeeper, mistaken identity, and misdirected letters contribute to the plot, the characters exchange letters in every possible combination, and both they and the reader are kept thoroughly mystified until the end as to why the parents oppose true love and a good match. Unfortunately, the cruel parents turn out to have had little more motive than whim, and the author's technical edifice collapses. Worse, there is little characterization beyond the use of "masculine" and "feminine" sentiments and attitudes; it is impossible to assign letters to a particular character by style alone. Though this volume was in Sterne's library, as the sale catalogue reveals, it could have taught him little.

Short epistolary narratives imitating the *Turkish Spy* and the *Ingenious and Diverting Letters* also appeared in England before 1700. The second volume of Gildon's *Post-Boy Rob'd of His Mail* begins with a series of thirteen letters to an English gentleman from "the wandring *Honan,* an Asiatick." Gildon was evidently doing his best to reproduce all aspects of the method of the *Turkish Spy:* he commented bumptiously in the preface that "the manner of the *Asiaticks* not being very common, it may surprize a Vulgar Critick" [16] and proceeded to ornament Honan's remarks with "Oriental" metaphors and exclamations. The story also has the usual introductory discourse about the English gentleman who has been prevailed upon to communicate a packet of letters from his Oriental friend. If Gildon's narrative has the virtues of the *Turkish Spy,* it has its vices as well. Honan begins his narrative with an account of a storm at sea, visits Cadiz, Madrid, and Seville, falls in love with a nun of Seville and elopes with her, escapes to India, lives in retirement with the nun, and finally goes to Siam. This is certainly plot enough for an exciting tale, but Gildon mingles long essays with Honan's personal reflections. The storm at sea occasions speculations on the soul; dreaming of the nun inspires Honan to write of "Zilphs and Salamanders." The death of his correspondent's kinsman in a duel provokes a long essay on dueling. The story goes to pieces when Honan leaves Spain: he writes two extremely long letters describing the religions of Asia and a letter on a revolution in Siam, the latter being a thinly disguised essay on the revolution of 1688. While Gildon's story is necessarily more compact than the *Turkish Spy* because it is shorter, it has no quality other than brevity to give it a greater unity; neither the traveler's adventures nor his personality is sufficiently particularized to offset the diluting effect of the essays on the fiction.

Mrs. Manley's *Letters* of 1696 also profited from brevity, but more from being based on her actual correspondence of the summer of 1694. When she revised the letters and inserted three short novels, she retained her lively style and vivid brief descriptions of persons and sights encountered on the road.

Indeed, the letters' vivid and authentic pictures of the English countryside and provincial life and manners are scarcely to be duplicated in fiction before the *Spectator*.[17] The book is clearly based on Mme d'Aulnoy, but the writer's personality is much more in evidence than in the *Ingenious and Diverting Letters*. Events are reported in the present tense, while they are happening or have just happened, and Mrs. Manley's reactions are much more particularized and pointed than those of her predecessor:

> I have left the Limb of the Sheep to the Mercy of my Companions (whose Stomachs are thus early prepar'd for any Digestion) to tell you, with what unfeign'd Respect I shall be ever
>
> > Your true
> > Faithful Servant,
> > Dela. Manley. . . .
>
> *Beaux* continues his Assiduities: I think no one was ever so plagu'd with dying Eyes; his are continually in that posture, and my Opposites, that I am forc'd to take a good deal of pains to avoid 'em. The two other Fellow-Travellers were never so promoted [as to be in a coach] before, and are much troubl'd their Journey is to last no longer, and wish the four Days four Months. I hope every Jolt will squash their Guts, and give 'em enough on't.[18]

The pertness of Mrs. Manley's language and the homespun details with which she fills the letters give them a thoroughly English atmosphere and setting. The same is true of her "novels," one of which is adapted from a highly romantic tale, but domesticated and brought down to earth in her revision.[19] She describes lively scenes with a fop and the irritating "Mayoress of Tatness" with a truth to life which anyone who has tried to fend off a bore on a train will appreciate, falls in love with a handsome preacher, and reflects on the annoyances of a country life in a manner which convinces the reader that she is really in the country. Although the collection cannot be called a unified novel, it gains integration from the handling of the journey-plot and the overlying personality of the narrator. It may be compared to the "fortunes of the road" sections of later picaresque novels, which are themselves rather rambling and disorganized. It is certainly one of the liveliest pieces of fictional writing before Fielding.[20]

The stories discussed up to this point are undeniably epistolary, since letters bear the burden of the narrative without assistance from other fictional forms, but they are far from being epistolary novels. The epistolary novel is not a rigidly defined genre like the sonnet or even like the short story as it was written in the early part of this century; the definition of "novel" must include *Roderick Random* and *Finnegans Wake*, and to write a novel in letters does not hopelessly restrict its range. Without being arbitrary, however, one may propose some elementary requirements for the form. It should, in the first place, be a long story of some depth and complexity, unified in tone or focus and by one or more structural devices; in short, a work which gives evidence of having been executed according to a definite plan. Elements such as plot, characters, and setting should be presented with enough richness and detail so that if they do not convince the reader they at least impress him. These requirements are certainly a minimum for the "novel" part of the definition.

That the story is in letters should be important, not incidental, for the "epistolary" part. Letters should have a vital and organic connection with the conduct of the narrative— the epistolary technique should permit effects which would otherwise be difficult or impossible to achieve. The writing, receiving, suppression, and discovery of letters, as well as the fact that letters have a receiver and sender, should have more than merely mechanical importance; they should be worked into the texture of the novel. Letters should have the same importance to the epistolary novel that the Jamesian register character, the specialized use of certain tenses, or the stream-of-consciousness technique has in today's novels.

This last requirement removes many good stories in letters from the category of epistolary novels and puts others in dubious standing. The *Ingenious and Diverting Letters*, *Lindamira*, and *Marianne*, for example, are in essence autobiographical narratives which have been cut into sections called letters. However rich the stories may be in incident, character, or personal tone, the epistolary method is not essential to them, but is merely a conventional framework used either because authentication had become a fetish or because the author could not conceive of an intimate personal account except in the form of letters to a friend. Each might have been told as effectively in the manner of Defoe's *Moll Flanders*, since the personality of the "writer" is revealed equally well by either method. Their occasional salutations or "asides" to the imaginary recipient help to maintain the illusion of correspondence, but they are not lengthy or frequent enough to be significant for the total effect. The immediacy of reporting which is such an important contribution of the epistolary method to fictional technique is not a part of such narratives. On the other hand, these three and others like them are of greater literary merit than some stories in which letters are used more skillfully. In the late seventeenth and early eighteenth centuries the convenience of the "letter to a friend" device as a catchall for miscellaneous matter, fictional or not, encouraged writers to use it when it was not necessary. By creating fictional situations where it *was* necessary, some authors strengthened narratives that were defective in other respects. But with all possible allowances made, most of the stories just discussed are too slight, too rambling, too feeble, or too unevenly developed to merit a place among true novels in letters.

Most of the genuine pre-Richardsonian epistolary novels appeared after 1700, but two of great interest were published in the 1680's. The first of these, *Love-Letters Between a Nobleman and His Sister*, is significant for its technical innovations, its length, and its popularity; the second, *Love Letters [of] Polydorus . . . and Messalina*, is a scandal-chronicle in letters, a slighter work with a notable technique. *Love-Letters Between a Nobleman and His Sister* is a pioneering scandal novel—its first part being an epistolary novel of outstanding technical virtuosity with strong romantic and even "Gothic" tendencies; and it is the first lengthy and original piece of English fiction to adopt the method of the *Portuguese Letters*. It is probably the first published fiction of "the English Sappho," Aphra Behn. One of the most popular "best-sellers" of its time, it has received only the briefest mention from literary historians.[21]

The novel is in three parts. The first came out in 1683, the second in 1685, and the third in 1687 with the title *The Amours of Philander and Sylvia*. The novel itself makes the time-lag evident; the three parts are written with different techniques and are not tied together very well, though each is a narrative unit. Part I is entirely epistolary; Part II combines narrative with a high proportion of letters; Part III uses letters more infrequently, reserving them to accentuate emotional crises. The novel tells the story of Forde, Lord Grey of Werk (later earl of Tankerville), who eloped with his wife's sister, Lady Henrietta Berkeley, in 1682 and was involved in the Rye House Plot to murder King Charles in the following year. (Part III is largely concerned with his involvement in Monmouth's abortive rebellion, in which he betrayed his command, afterward turning informer.) Grey becomes "Philander," Lady Henrietta "Sylvia," and Monmouth "Cesario." The first part was published anonymously, and the dedications to the second and third parts were signed with the initials "A. B."; the novel is generally attributed to Mrs. Behn, and all the available evidence points to her authorship. The setting is nominally French, but careless or deliberate references to "Cowley's lute" and to visiting the sights of the Tower destroy any illusion created by the preface, which attempts to mislead the reader (and protect author and bookseller) by speaking of a French book from which the novel was translated.[22]

Part I, in spite of the modern reader's justifiable impatience with the "Portuguese" mode of writing, is artistically the best of the three. It is carefully focused on the elopement-plot. Philander besieges his wife's sister Sylvia with passionate letters; she resists, but finally weakens. After long, agonized indecision on Sylvia's part and vain attempts to enter the house on Philander's, the amour is consummated. The guilty pair are nearly discovered, but Philander escapes in disguise. Sylvia's family have meanwhile become suspicious, particularly her sister Myrtilla, the wife of Philander. Myrtilla warns Sylvia in veiled language, and a match with the loathsome but wealthy Foscario is hastily arranged for her. Sylvia decides to renounce Philander, but on his threat of suicide she yields. Philander duels with Foscario, and Sylvia's father learns the whole story by coming on a letter from Philander. Sylvia is imprisoned in her room and her conniving maid is discharged. Philander arranges for Sylvia's flight to Paris by coach; Foscario attacks him in a woods as he is coming to escort her, and Sylvia in a frenzy of terror escapes to Paris with Philan-

der's valet Brilliard. Philander, who has killed Foscario, is
wounded himself and is arrested and imprisoned in the Bastille.
Meanwhile, the police are searching for Sylvia. On Philander's instructions she marries Brilliard so that her parents will
lose their authority over her. Philander corrupts his guards
and flees to Holland; the last letter contains directions for
Sylvia to join him in flight, disguised as a boy. The plot in
parts II and III becomes so labyrinthine that it cannot be reproduced here. Sylvia and Philander drift apart, with much
raging and lamentation from the unhappy Sylvia; at length,
however, she rivals him in the frequency and complication of
her conquests. The story gradually disintegrates in a multitude
of confusing episodic subplots. Sylvia becomes an elegant female rake, and Philander's adventures fade away in a general
account of Monmouth's intrigues, laden with satire against
the Whig party and the earl of Shaftesbury in particular.

Apart from its continuations, Part I is a truly astonishing
feat of epistolary narrative for its early date. Mrs. Behn seems
to have thoroughly mastered the method of the *Portuguese
Letters*, grasped its drawbacks, and given it life and depth by
seasoning it with the techniques of plotting and of handling
points of view which she had learned as a practicing dramatist.
There is as much plot as the reader can desire, and each new
turn is firmly established by several pages of correspondence.
Character and setting are less impressive. Philander is hot-
headed and passionate, Sylvia is proud and vaguely "noble."
(The characters, particularly Sylvia's, are better developed in
the second and third parts of the novel.) The physical setting
amounts only to a few conventional descriptions of pastoral
scenery. The minor characters contribute something to the
background: the spiteful sister Myrtilla, Sylvia's maid Melinda, the loutish Foscario, and Prince Cesario are each given a
letter in which to characterize themselves, and this they do as
well as the single letters permit.[23] Cesario is a noble Roman,
Melinda is bawdy and opportunistic, Myrtilla is affected,
hypocritical, and catty; as for Foscario, the reader agrees
with Philander's remark: "By the Style he writes, I dread his
Sense less than his Person." [24] But though the background is
superior to the empty scene of the *Portuguese Letters*, its fur-
nishings are rather sparse.

Yet in skillful and complex management of epistolary

material, Mrs. Behn was second to none before Richardson. Like him she made her characters indefatigable letter writers; Sylvia's passionate request, "Fail not to send a hundred times a Day, if possible," [25] is better complied with than we could wish. This prolixity assures thorough comment on the smallest events. From Philander's first letter to the couple's first night of love, 268 pages (in the 1684 edition) are devoted to analytical variations on the theme of virtue gradually sinking beneath inclination, while all the subsequent events up to the flight are related in seventy-six pages of letters. Sylvia's feelings toward Philander gradually alter by the smallest degrees; they are handled by Mrs. Behn with a relentless slow variation that would do credit to Richardson at the height of his powers. Tiresome as Sylvia's emotional display becomes, its endless change-ringing makes a powerful impression on the reader who has the patience to get through the many pages.

The story comes to him from several points of view. Most of Part I is taken up with the correspondence of Philander and Sylvia, but we have a below-stairs view of the intrigue and a lively change of style and tempo in the maid Melinda's letter to Philander. The outside world breaks in with Cesario's letter; the prince rebukes Philander for wasting time in an amour when revolution is brewing. Foscario's boorish letter to Sylvia and the threatening letter from Myrtilla show that others besides the lovers are pressingly involved in the situation. The letters from the "outside" also break up the monotony of the A to B, B to A exchange. Both Sylvia and Philander introduce extraneous affairs into their letters: Philander writes briefly of the political plotting that distracts him from love and of the farmer's cottage where he is hiding, and Sylvia describes the tension in the household after the discovery and her maid's dismissal:

> I will try to corrupt my new Boy, I see Good-nature, Pity, and Generosity in his Looks, he is well born too, and may be honest.... Thus far, *Philander*, I had writ when Supper was brought me, for yet my Parents have not deigned to let me come into their Presence; those that serve me tell me that *Myrtilla* is this Afternoon arrived at *Bellfont*; all is mighty close carried in the Countess's Apartment. I tremble with the thought of what will be the Result of the great Consultation: I have

been tempting of the Boy, but I perceive they have strictly charged him not to obey me; he says, against his Will he shall betray me, for they will have him searched.[26]

Part II, though its technique is not purely epistolary, contains a revealing double exchange of letters. Philander, exiled at "Collen" (Cologne) protests his love to Sylvia while at the same time he corresponds with his friend Octavio about his secret amours in a manner that suggests the villainous correspondence of Lovelace with Belford.[27] Sylvia's discovery of these letters precipitates her final break with Philander.

The framework of letters is important to Mrs. Behn's narrative apart from their advantages in revealing emotions and thoughts. Letters become actors in the story. They grow longer or shorter, their style becomes inflated and rhetorical or dry and efficient according to the needs of the moment and the feelings of the writer. The circumstances of writing are interestingly detailed: one letter was torn in pieces by the agitated Sylvia, then put together and sent to Philander by Melinda, another was "writ in a Pair of Tablets," and four written in an afternoon by Philander were dated from a meadow, a grassy bank, a tree root, and his knee, echoing his approach and his agitation.[28] (Mrs. Behn explains that most of these letters were conveyed by clever pages, the maid, or the friendly farmer "Dorillus," from whose cottage Philander dates his letters when in hiding.) The discovery of a letter from Philander brings on Sylvia's downfall; she sends Foscario's letter to Philander that he may judge of his rival; and a letter smuggled to Sylvia by Dorillus in a basket of strawberries is nearly discovered by her mother, whose greediness for the fruit is sated just in time, while Sylvia watches in helpless terror.[29]

Mrs. Behn also knew the rudiments of manipulating time in fiction and realized the effectiveness of holding letters back or presenting them out of order. Just as Sylvia is on the point of yielding to Philander she gets news of his implication in Cesario's plot and pauses to lecture him on the divine right of kings and passive obedience, while the reader and Philander fidget. Vague hints reach us that all was not well on the lovers' first night together, but the details must wait for several pages. We hear of the duel from Sylvia before we have been informed that she has heard of it, but its issue is not clarified until later, when Philander gives his version of the fray. Sylvia writes Philander that "all" has been discovered, but just what she means remains vague until some time later, when the fatal epistle, "left in her hands by Monsieur her Father, in her cabinet," is produced. With Sylvia's resolution to fly comes a hiatus; the next letter is dated "After her Flight," tempting the reader to learn the details. The reader's curiosity as to what became of Philander after the second duel and Sylvia's flight is satisfied and piqued at the same time, after a suspense of several pages, by the heading "To *Sylvia*. From the *Bastill*." [30] The letters themselves are often rhetorical flights not much to the purpose, but such are always brought up sharply by an abrupt and businesslike postscript which tells what has happened or gives instructions.

At times, like Richardson, Mrs. Behn was forced to make one character tell another what he already knew. Thus, the needs of suspense assigned Sylvia the task of describing the first duel to Philander, who certainly was the more familiar with it; Mrs. Behn, therefore, had to make Sylvia give her reactions on learning of each detail of the duel and ask Philander how he could have done thus and so at the risk of his life. The same difficulty arose in the description of Philander's nervous incapacity on their first night together. [31]

All these minor distortions of the narrative give it the realism of actual events and suggest real correspondence; many of them promote suspense. Possibly, some result from the author's ineptness, but the effect on the reader is the same, whatever the cause. Mrs. Behn succeeded in investing an epistolary narrative with a liveliness and tension found before only in objective stories of intrigue; and she did it by legitimately developing the epistolary method's potentialities, widening its scope to include time, space, characters, and setting. Moreover, she powerfully stressed the epistolary foundation of her story by continually dwelling on the facts of letter writing or the relations of characters to the letters which affected them. The great and continued popularity of her experiment with the novel in letters must have made it influential on later writers, though direct influence is almost impossible to trace in "subliterature" and therefore risky to suggest. Apart from its anticipation of so much in later and better fiction, *Love-Letters Between a Nobleman and His Sister* has its own considerable merits as an epistolary novel.

Love Letters Between Polydorus the Gothick King, and Messalina, Late Queen of Albion (1689) has been attributed to Mrs. Behn, and bears some resemblance to her work; but the ascription is highly improbable.[32] The book is more likely an imitation of her manner. Polydorus is Louis XIV, Messalina is Mary of Modena; other characters are Lycogenes (James II), Anaximander (William of Orange), Father Pedro (James's Jesuit adviser Petre), and Latroon (Tyrconnel, leader of the troops in Ireland). The book was written to exploit the success of a novel called *The Amours of Messalina*, which is mentioned in its preface. It is a short work in twelve letters, dealing with Messalina's intrigues to establish the "Gothick heresy" in Albion, the defeat of Lycogenes, and Messalina's flight to the protection and later the arms of Polydorus. In spite of its ridiculous background of state scandal the story is managed with considerable skill; the letters devote much space to Messalina's amorous disquiets and agonies. They are supposedly written while the events described are taking place, and most are in a vein of extravagant rhetoric, the brief postscripts conveying necessary information. The story has several ramifications; characters say one thing and mean another. Messalina and Polydorus correspond, Messalina writes Aspasia (Tyrconnel's wife) concerning matters in Ireland and is answered; Father Pedro writes Polydorus a letter in plain prose, telling him how far the rebellion has progressed and what steps are now unsafe for him to take. Messalina escapes from Albion and reaches "the Gothick realm," whereupon Polydorus begins to besiege her virtue, Lycogenes being absent in Iberia (Ireland). The author carefully makes it plain that Polydorus is merely using the royal pair for his own purposes by the extravagance of his letters and the elaborate sophistries with which he answers Messalina's complaints. In Polydorus' first letter he asks if he shall offer rescue, but does not do so; in Letter VII he welcomes her to France but says nothing about the promised troops; later, when she demands to know if he intends to keep his promises to prevent rebellion in Ireland, he answers with a flurry of rhetoric about "cruel nymphs," and concludes:

> P.S. My lovely Queen, thou canst not be insensible how the urgency of my own affairs . . . have put some restraint on my resolutions to have equipp'd him [James].[33]

At the end of the correspondence the reader is left to surmise that Messalina's virtue will not resist Polydorus much longer. The story is greatly inferior, as a novel, to Mrs. Behn's; but it shows unusual skill in one department of the writer's craft. The reader is led into the dream world where Messalina exists within a web of delusion spun around her by Polydorus' glittering promises, a world contrasted with the undercurrent of unsavory realities. The contrast is made stronger by opposing flowery and artificial diction to the plain and forcible prose that presents the facts. (The elevated passages are nearly all written in concealed blank verse.) This effect is used for Whig propaganda, to enhance the reader's belief that Mary was duped by Louis, but its artistic value is not lessened thereby. Bad as the novel is, its technical advances could have produced a distinguished result had they been applied to better ends.

Despite their improvement in narrative mechanics, these two epistolary novels of the seventeenth century leave much to be desired in other respects. The dozen or more English epistolary novels appearing between 1700 and 1740, though their mechanics were not always so skillful, made up for that deficiency. Both Mrs. Behn's novel and *Polydorus and Messalina* are largely concerned with extravagant gallantries and have a far-away, escapist atmosphere. They ignore the facts of day-to-day existence, even though both are based on real and recent events; their vaguely defined characters are strongly redolent of the heroic romance. They present the strongest contrast to such a down-to-earth narrative as appears in Mrs. Manley's *Letters*. But later novels in letters changed milieu and material as they improved technique, and some closely anticipated the domestic novel.

The Double Captive (1718) is a curious mixture of "novel," narrative letters, and poetry. It purports to have been written by a prisoner in Newgate, a Scot who had been implicated in the Jacobite uprising of 1715. While awaiting trial he falls in love with a young lady who comes with her mother to visit his cellmate. The letters, written to "the fair Galatea," give no hint of whether she has received them or whether he is writing them merely to comfort and amuse himself. They are remarkably realistic pictures of prison life and of the feelings of a prisoner—so realistic as to make it seem possible that the story is autobiographical. The prisoner declares his love, but despairs on learning that the date of his execution has been set. He is remanded, and tells of the prisoners' behavior on that occasion. He proposes his mother as a go-between and asks Galatea for a visit. Payment of "garnish" releases him from his chains; he begins to hope for a pardon. He gives a vivid description of a prisoner's day in Newgate and relates a dream he has had of being taken to the "condemned hold." In the last letter he speaks of hopes that an amnesty may be granted and his estates restored so that he may be able to marry. Although the details of the correspondence are not filled in, the letters have unusual realism in language and in content. Throughout most of the narrative the conventional diction of love is rejected for a sardonic tone of actuality: the material of the rogue biography invades the domain of the love letter.

> *Jack Ketch* must be my Executor and Administrator . . . *Paul Lorrain* refuses to give me Absolution, unless I make him Heir to my New Suit of Black in which I received Sentence; and the Hang-man Swears and Threatens how indecently he will Butcher me in the Dissection, besides making me hang an Hour naked in the sight of the gazing Multitude, before he'll cut me down, if I pretend to give the Ghostly Father his Fees.[34]

Financial rather than aesthetic considerations helped to bring unromantic (though sensational) matter into developing epistolary fiction. At least two stories, *Love Without Artifice* (1733) and *The Jilted Bridegroom* (1706) seem to have been closely based on current events, the first clearly having been written for the notorious Edmund Curll in order to profit from a scandalous breach-of-promise suit which had just been settled. Its letters, said to have been written by the pregnant Elizabeth Leeson to the perfidious Lord William Fitz-Maurice in 1731, are enclosed in a letter to the late duchess of Monmouth by "Mary Dillon." The nine letters are realistically disjointed and lacking in grace or continunity and may indeed be authentic; the connecting passages are devoted (as they need to be) to speculating on what may be gathered from the letters about Elizabeth's state of mind and the occasions which had made her write. *The Jilted Bridegroom* ap-

pears to be written with more art, but although the characters
are called Floria and Amintor, the novel's hints that the affair
is the talk of the town may be true. A respectable young man
woos and wins a City merchant's daughter with the parents'
permission; her mother takes a realistically sudden but stub-
born aversion to him; the rather unintelligent girl is gradually
brought around to her mother's views, while the henpecked father feebly protests to all concerned. The story does not end,
but merely stops—whether from realism or the author's ineptitude cannot be determined. Floria's eight letters, confused
enough to annoy any suitor, are inserted at the proper points
in the long narrative letter which Amintor entrusts to the
good offices of the unknown friend who publishes his woeful
but shapeless tale.

Mrs. Haywood's *Irish Artifice*, which appeared in the
Female Dunciad (1728), also brought sordid and realistic
matter into epistolary fiction. Its form is conventional rather
than functional, a minor device of realism; it consists of two
long letters from "Urania," and the story is largely told in an
objective manner. Urania poses as a friend of the family:

> Tho' I have had many Reasons since to regret such Ac-
> quaintance, I once thought it the effect of my good
> Fortune to be well in the Esteem of a certain Lady, whose
> real Name I am obliged to conceal in respect to her Fam-
> ily, and shall therefore call her by the feign'd one of
> *Clarina*; she was not above Fourteen when I first saw
> her.[35]

The characters' names are the only remaining vestiges of the
trappings of romance. Aglaura, an Irish housekeeper, worms
her way into the good graces of Clarina's wealthy parents and
keeps strict watch over the foolish girl's virtue. Presently,
however, she informs Clarina that a certain Merovius is dying
for love of her and presents her with a despairing letter written
in his blood. Clarina scorns Aglaura's hypocritical warnings
and hastens to the sickbed of her unknown lover; at this point
Mrs. Haywood turns her espistolary device to the purpose of
suspense:

> But what the Consequence of this Visit was, and the
> terrible Misfortunes which this Condescention drew on
> her, must be deferr'd till another Opportunity, the Sus-

picion that your Patience, perhaps, as well as my Paper, may be at an End, obliges me to conclude for this Time,

SIR,

Your most humble
and obedient servant

URANIA.[36]

The headstrong Clarina "steals a marriage" with Merovius, fleeing with all her jewels and clothes. Merovius is revealed as Aglaura's worthless son, Clarina's parents repudiate her, and after Merovius and Aglaura have spent her money they desert her, leaving her friendless and pregnant. Clarina in despair becomes a kept mistress, and Urania hints as her second letter closes that the girl will soon become a streetwalker. The tale's unrelieved sordidness and lack of "gallantry" or romance (except to perpetrate a swindle) show that the epistolary technique was regarded by one of its most flowery and high-flown practitioners as compatible with the grimmest realism.

The Unnatural Mother and Ungrateful Wife is a similar tale, though the mechanics of fictional correspondence contribute more to its success. In three letters from one lady to another it relates the history of a family with which the recipient is slightly acquainted. The importance assumed by the affairs of the correspondents, which have the status of a subplot, gives the story additional depth and a subjective dimension. The writer reflects on events and motivations in long "asides" to her friend, and the epistolary framework is more than a device tacked on:

Madam,

    In compliance with the Request you were pleas'd to make me in your last, I intend by this to entertain you with the secret Cause of the unhappy Change, that has happen'd in Mrs. Y—'s Family, since the last Time we had the Happiness of your Company in this Country: I know you too well, to suppose, that the Misfortunes of those, you were pleas'd to honour with your Friendship, can furnish Matter of Amusement, to a Mind truly benevolent, such as I know your's to be, in an eminent Degree, or that a vain Curiosity, or the too much prevailent [sic] Itch of Scandal, could give Rise to the Desire you have to be inform'd. . . .

Madam,

　　An Accident interven'd since my last, which oblig'd
me to deferr doing myself the Pleasure of writing to you
these three Posts past, it was not other, than the Arrival
of my Brother, from making the Tour of *Europe*....
if I know any thing of his Mind, your fair Daughter had
a chief Hand in bringing him Home ... [she hopes for]
an Event that might strengthen that Amity that has so
long subsisted betwixt us, and unite two Families in
one common Interest, that are already so much cemented
in their Affections; but to my Task.[37]

The principal narrative is thoroughly realistic and completely
British. Even romantic names are abandoned:

　　Her maiden name is H—s [Hughes?], and she is the
youngest Daughter of a Farmer of middling Circumstances in Yorkshire, who rented a Farm of about one
Hundred a Year, of the unhappy Mr. Y— [Young].[38]

The characters' behavior is equally mundane. The country
wench marries the master and soon has him under her thumb,
meanwhile carrying on an intrigue with a handsome young
physician. With the doctor's connivance she conveys her husband to a private madhouse. After her husband's death she has
her stepson Dick put aboard a vessel bound for India, in the
hope of getting rid of him, and prepares to marry the doctor,
but she discovers that he has already proposed to and been
accepted by her stepdaughter, since he prefers money with
beauty to money without. The bridegroom promptly makes
life as miserable for the villainess as he can, and a few years
later her stepson Dick, who has been rescued in a Spanish port
and brought up by a distant relative, appears in England to
claim his inheritance. This conjunction of defeats causes the
"unnatural mother" to go mad and die of chagrin. Such
stories as these indicate how far a realism that led to Richardson's and Fielding's had made its way into the popular letter
fiction which new tastes in the reading public had begun to
accept before their day.

　　Epistolary tales in the old romantic vein still appeared
and became increasingly ingenious. Gildon's *The Post-Man
Robb'd of His Mail* (1719) contains a sequence of letters
called *The Lover's Sighs*, which amounts to a short novel.

The story bears an introductory Chinese puzzle of devices within devices: the letters are supposed to have been translated out of Provençal into Latin by "Gonsalvo de Mendoza" and thence into English and are included in a covering letter from "Philip Anecdot." Title pages in Latin and English are provided. These elaborate devices were no doubt designed in part to protect Gildon, since the story is a scandal-chronicle concerning George I and his Hanoverian mistresses. Alphonso the Wise, king of Castile and Aragon and earl of Provence, has a passionate Provençal mistress named Stremunia. He decides to discard her on the advice of Sacclimene, a former mistress who maintains her position by acting as procuress. Alphonso does not appear on the scene, but Stremunia writes him a series of passionate letters: first on dreaming that he has deserted her and later to complain of his neglect and voice her suspicions that she is being supplanted. Her letters are in the "Portuguese" style, but vigorous:

> But sure it cannot be; my lovely Prince, My King, my Hero, cannot be so fickle. No, my Heart be at rest, he loves me still; his Royal Office often engages his Nights as well as Days, and this has rob'd me this one Night of my Soul's Wish: the next dusky Hours will make me amends. Fly fast then glorious Sun, and come ye Shades, and bring my Sun, that gives me Light, Heat, and Motion. Oh my dear King, cou'd you have seen me last Night, beheld my Impatience, mark'd how every little Noise made my Heart bounce against my Bosom with a momentary transport of Joy. Ha! there comes my *Alphonso!* I cried often aloud; but no *Alphonso* came! I told the Hours, counted all the Minutes, and hop'd, and sigh'd, and wish'd in vain, ev'n all the livelong Night.[39]

At this juncture Stremunia receives a letter from the crafty Sacclimene. The styles of the two are carefully differentiated: Stremunia writes in the disjointed language of passion, while Sacclimene's sentences are well constructed and her arguments are hard-headed, to say the least:

> Love is an agreeable Amusement for a time; but to have that puling Passion take up all our Thoughts, especially when we once come to Woman's Estate, is a Weakness, I hope, *Stremunia* is too much a Woman to be guilty of.

Fidelity, Constancy, and the like, are the vain Day-dreams of a Green-Sickness Girl in a Country Village, and never rule in the Court, where Passions of more Consequence ought to reign; the Pursuit of Wealth and Power is what may last one all one's Life, but the Love of Man cannot hold long ev'n with the most Romantick.[40]

Stremunia falls into a fever, and the ravings of her sickbed go to Alphonso in several letters. She raves not only of her passion but of party politics; the mistress who has supplanted her, she says, is of a political complexion that may prove dangerous to the king. The story breaks off in the middle of a passionate letter, the "translator" explaining that from this point the text is defective and fragmentary. The tale is certainly a slight one; romantic passion, political sermonizing, and elements of scandal are badly mixed into it. It nevertheless shows how an epistolary tale can be strengthened by interesting plot and background, and character differentiated by means of letters.

These factors alone, however, were not enough, as is clearly demonstrated by *Passionate Love-Letters Between a Polish Princess and a Certain Chevalier*, a very similar novel of the same year, which is an absurd failure. This, too, treats of love in high places, for it purports to be the amorous correspondence of the Old Pretender (known as the Chevalier de St. George) with Princess Maria Clementina of Poland, whom he married by proxy in May 1719. Despite his promising subject, the author had not Gildon's ability and labored under a fatal defect in his material, for when the novel appeared the "lovers" had not met in person. He was obliged to show them falling into transports over one another's picture and enjoying the imaginary ecstasies of the marriage bed while hundreds of miles apart. In desperation, it would seem, he decided to have the princess abducted on her journey to France and imprisoned in a convent, where she remains as the story ends, despite attempts at escape, her new husband being unable to do more than fume impotently. The high-flown language of the letters is made all the more ridiculous by the absurdity of the situation, but the expectations aroused by the book's title no doubt assured an adequate sale.

Stories of amorous intrigue which the previous century

would have treated in conventionally romantic fashion and laid in France or Italy began to appear in British domestic settings, told in a manner which left nothing to be desired for realism and plainness. *The Fatal Amour Between a Beautiful Lady, and a Young Nobleman* (1719) is established as a "true story" by its preface, which makes it appear that the events are recent and local:

> Whether or no the following *Amour*, has run its length to a State of *Impenitency* in the fair Transgressor, we have not yet certain Intelligence, no more than what became of her Gallant.[41]

It takes the form of a long letter from an irate husband to his father-in-law, denouncing the conduct of his wife. The husband writes without romantic appellations or *beaux sentiments*; he is thoroughly British in his wrath. He has discovered several letters from his wife to her gallant and includes copies in his letter. Presently, he comes upon the guilty pair in an embrace; the lover flees through a window, sped by a shot from the husband's pistol. The shot may have proved fatal; they have learned nothing of the lover's whereabouts. The husband reproduces his wife's defense in her own words: she has shown him several letters written to him by a Frenchwoman with whom she accuses him of having had an affair. The husband protests to his father-in-law that these are forgeries and concludes by stating that he intends to seek a bill of divorcement and by asking the father-in-law's advice as to the best method of settling the matter quietly.

Epistolary technique enhances the completely matter-of-fact atmosphere of *The Fatal Amour*. The reader accompanies the husband in his discoveries, picks up hints of the liaison from the letters he finds, and also gets the points of view of the gallant and the wife from their letters. These, with the "forgeries," lead the reader to suppose that the husband is by no means so blameless as he wishes to make his wife's father believe. The quarrels of the pair get a lively presentation from the husband's point of view. He fills his letter with details of servants and tableware and provides atmosphere by his irritation and self-righteousness as he describes his discoveries, his just anger, and his efforts to control himself. *The Fatal Amour* is anonymous and brief, but its well-rounded, realistic portraiture of characters, its integration of the epistolary technique with the narrative, and its matter-of-fact domestic treatment of such a popular romantic theme as the unfaithful wife, combine to give it unusual interest.

It has become conventional among historians of fiction to emphasize the increasing influence of "middle-class" literary tastes on the growth of the novel up to the time of its first great masters.[42] It might be wiser to substitute a term such as "level-headed" for the ambiguous "middle-class." Sober, earnest, and sincerely religious readers were not confined to the ranks of Dissenting burghers; the countess of Hertford and many a literate servant might equally disapprove of most novels of the day. Defoe, Mrs. Rowe, and Richardson, on the other hand, presented at least the atmosphere of ordinary life and preached moral conduct persisted in and rewarded, immoral deeds resisted and punished. Their novels (supposedly) would not inflame the minds of the young. But the "level-headed" habit of thought could be placated as well by the absence of exotic vice as by the presence of homely (and moneygrubbing) virtue. This accounts for the success of certain early epistolary novels the contents of which were remarkable though not fantastic and which, though skating on thin ice in morals, never quite broke through.

In *The Illegal Lovers* (1728), for example, the story is outlined reflectively by a "friend of the family," with seven long letters carrying most of the narrative burden. Its opening words assert in the usual manner that it is a true and recent history; the plot, on the other hand, is rather unusual. Bellario loses his beloved wife and presently contracts a passion for her sister Lindamira, who has taken his children into her home. He first writes to her because he dares not speak of a passion that is forbidden (at least by canon law). Lindamira, though moved, begs him to travel and cure his love by diversion. Another letter chronicles Bellario's failure to moderate his feelings and announces the onset of a serious illness; he requests a last farewell. Sympathy and inclination lead Lindamira to nurse him, and pity moves her to allow "innocent liberties," with the result that the recovering Bellario "attempts" her. Horrified, she leaves, but relents when he attempts suicide, and uses his convalescence to try to reason him out of his folly. Meanwhile, people have begun to talk. Lindamira

almost wavers into agreeing to marry him, when a lecture
from a male friend reconvinces her of the deep sinfulness of
canonical incest. She commands Bellario to leave her forever;
he shoots himself, but not fatally, and she weakens to the extent of referring their case to an ecclesiastical court. A nega-
tive verdict brings a suggestion from Bellario that they turn
Catholic and seek a dispensation, but Lindamira's Protestantism is too firmly grounded. Bellario kills himself. Lindamira
has what we should call a nervous breakdown, but eventually
finds comfort in the reflection that she has preserved herself
from sin. She later marries, but will not renounce an obliga-
tion to rear Bellario's children.

Despite a plot involving suicide and incest, *The Illegal
Lovers* is not a conventional tale of passion. The suicide can
be palliated as the result of mental derangement; the never-
enacted incest, which does not involve physical consan-
guinity, is resisted by both parties. The twists and turns of
mental anguish perhaps have passion as their ultimate cause,
but the proximate cause is a Protestant conscience, and the
casuistry and scrupulousness are Levitical, not *précieux*. Such
a plot is not far from George Eliot or Thomas Hardy. It may
owe something to the general ideas behind *La Princesse de
Clèves* and its imitations, but it is clear evidence that epistolary fiction had come a long way since *Love-Letters Between
a Nobleman and His Sister*, in which a similar situation was
tossed off with amoral abandon, Sylvia's initial pratings about
the laws of God and man being quickly stifled by her
passion. Heroines who were moral and careful could play a
part in successful novels by 1728, just as they had in *The
Conscious Lovers* and similar dramas. The moral atmosphere
of *Pamela* was not seldom anticipated in earlier decades.

Such was not the case with the two very popular epistolary novels of Mary Hearne, *The Lover's Week* (1718)
and *The Female Deserters* (1719). Each is a long letter from
Amaryllis to her dear friend Emilia; both concern young
ladies who are being kept and who are enjoying it. *The
Lover's Week*, divided into six "days," deals with the progress
of Amaryllis' liking for the handsome nobleman Philander,
which culminates in her not unwilling abduction. The second
letter (*The Female Deserters*), dated from Amaryllis' country retreat, relates the amours of her similarly situated friend

Calista, who in turn tells the sad story of Isabella. The epistolary technique is not particularly ingenious or necessary to
the story, except that Mrs. Hearne doubtless thought letters
the proper setting for such intimate girlish confidences in the
first person. Amaryllis relates her story much in the manner
of Pamela, with abundant brief reflections on her feelings and
conduct. She is not given to reserve or to overnice speculation
when love conflicts with duty. The following extracts sketch
out her character:

> At length Love (as it generally does) outwent Considera-
> tion (I doubt not but you'll here blame my too easy
> complying: But, my dear *Emilia*, you know it is not in
> our Powers to act against our Inclinations, I am sure at
> least it never was in mine, not being Mistress of those
> little Arts that, in my opinion, are too much used by our
> Sex:) But to return to my Story; I writ him. . . .

> I therefore call'd for Pen and Ink, and writ him word,
> That he should certainly meet me according to his desire.
>   I know you will again reflect on me for so sudden a
> Compliance with his Request: But, dear *Emilia*, consider,
> my word was already past; neither would it have suited
> with my open free Temper, to have let anyone suffer a
> moment's Pain, that I could ease them of, out of a little
> affected Coyness of my Sex; much less would I let my
> dear *Philander* be uneasy for so foolish a thing as a Prom-
> ise of meeting him.[43]

Amaryllis is a beautiful and giddy orphan whose strict maiden
aunt watches over her virtue and her fortune. She sees and is
smitten with Philander; two days later he prevails upon her to
meet him briefly in the evening. The unsuspecting girl con-
trives an excuse, joins Philander, and is mildly horrified a few
hours later to discover that he has deceived her about the
time; it is now too late to go home without arousing her aunt's
suspicions. Philander offers to secure lodgings for her at an
inn. Too late she discovers that she is in a bagnio, and Philander procures a key to her room. Undone, Amaryllis rather
complacently accepts Philander's offer to take her into the
country, whence she writes to Emilia to explain her sudden
disappearance from town.
    The narrative's chief interest lies in the amount of de-

tailed analysis of motivation and action that arises from Amaryllis' reflections. In this respect *The Lover's Week* may be one of the most significant pieces of English fiction, outside the works of Bunyan and Defoe, produced before 1740. (*The Female Deserters* is decidedly inferior.) The plot is very simple, but it is enough to give the story structure, and Amaryllis' comments invest her actions with some depth and subtlety. She makes the reader see with great clarity how inertia, inclination, and Philander's deceptions all combine to send her to her fate, almost in spite of herself. The minor characters—the aunt, Philander, and his friend the colonel, who promotes the elopement—are not merely lay figures nor yet humor characters; Mrs. Hearne's eye for telling details, her lively conception of scenes, and her realistic dialogue give them life. The emotions and situations are never heightened with rhetoric; the style is plain, easy, and idiomatic. Amaryllis' characterization is particularly interesting because, in addition to the meticulously detailed display of her motivations, she is not made into a romantic heroine. She takes things as they come; in spite of her alarms and tremors she has no exaggerated sensibility. Her reflections are temperate. The spoiled, easygoing, pleasure-loving girl is one of the most fully presented and credible characters produced in English fiction before its maturity. *The Lover's Week* represents an ideal compromise between the excessive generalization and objectivity of "true histories" and the equally overdone subjectivity and overstressed particularities of the "Portuguese" tradition.

Four novels represent the highest development of letter fiction before Richardson. *The Perfidious P—* (1702), *Lindamira* (1702), *Olinda's Adventures* (1693, and later), and *Familiar Letters Betwixt a Gentleman and a Lady* (1725) combine highly developed epistolary technique, depth, and subtlety with realistic setting and believable plots. All are long stories, and, with the possible exception of *The Perfidious P—*, they maintain a high moral tone throughout. While not precisely edifying, they could be read by those who scorned the generality of novels as frivolous; in fact, *Lindamira* seems to have been deliberately directed toward such an audience,[44] *Olinda* abounds in moral reflections, and *The Perfidious P—*'s dedication praises the story as a solemn warning of how girls may be led astray.

The Perfidious P—, an anonymous work, tells the simple story of an amorous triangle in 133 duodecimo pages. Technically speaking, it is the best English epistolary novel before *Clarissa*. Nearly all of its fifty-three letters are written by a nobleman who calls himself Corydon and two bosom friends, Clarinda and Lucina, to one another. The essentials of the story are slight. As it opens Corydon has arranged to send his mistress Clarinda out of town to avoid scandal. Presently, her best friend Lucina writes to Corydon to know the whereabouts of the vanished Clarinda, and the two girls correspond. Corydon and Lucina arrange for Clarinda to occupy a house in Kensington, and she arrives from the north. Corydon, however, has seen too much of Lucina for Clarinda's good, and he soon declares his love to Lucina, who reproaches him harshly. An anonymous letter warns Clarinda to beware of Corydon, and she is filled with forebodings. He grows increasingly cold and neglectful to Clarinda, but continues to besiege Lucina, who remains firm. Meanwhile, the innocent Clarinda wonders what can have made both Corydon and Lucina so strangely cold toward her. She writes imploringly to both. When another anonymous letter informs her that Corydon and Lucina have been married, she forlornly retires to the consolations of religion.

The ingenious handling of the correspondence invests this rather banal tale with drama and force. The reader experiences the whole action from the point of view of each of the three principals. It begins with several rapturous letters from the happy Clarinda in retirement to Corydon in town. She reminds him in a workmanlike "flashback" of how they first fell in love, thus taking care of the exposition. Even in her happiness she has premonitions that her felicity cannot last. Lucina innocently writes Corydon in the belief that he knows where Clarinda is; her next letter is a playful one to Clarinda, beginning "Thou little thief, thou." [45] The three correspond, and we learn that Corydon visits Lucina constantly to talk of his beloved Clarinda. This information causes Clarinda some heartburnings; at length she arrives in London, only to find them both absent. Presently, she receives a letter from Corydon with a postscript in Lucina's hand. Evidently, neither amanuensis nor recipient reads this with care, for it contains a veiled declaration of Corydon's burgeoning feelings for

Lucina. But all seems to be well, and a few days later Clarinda writes Corydon as follows:

> Nothing but your dear Self cou'd be welcomer than your Epistle, which I must say we received since my *Lucina* shared it; but for my Life I can't get her to set her Fist to this; she vows she won't: she write to a Man—no, she scorns it. *My Lord*, Am not I mighty gay? Methinks I am. Ah this Sunshine! 'twill not last, there is a gloomy Fate, I fear, belongs to me. My dear *Lucina* jogs my hand, and will not let me entertain a melancholy Thought. Hold—what am I talking on? Wide of the matter: for you must know, *My Lord*, it is absolutely necessary you Dine with us to day, because there is some delicate, delicate, I won't tell you what: come and see. Make much of this Note, for I cannot tell where ever you'll have such another from ▬▬▬
>   *See what a Blot she's made as I was saying* Poor Clarinda.[46]

Next comes Corydon's avowal of love to Lucina, with the ominous postscript, "Shew this to your Friend if you dare." [47] The dramatic irony evident in the passage quoted above is intensified in the innocent Clarinda's next letter to Corydon:

> I assure you *Lucina* vows never to see your Face again; she says you are a false, perfidious, barbarous—I cannot for my heart write all the hard Words she thunders in my Ears: and this is all forsooth because you suspected [in an earlier letter] we would be such a couple of Errant Lady Errants as to pledge you in a cup of *Ratefea*.[48]

Now the emotions of the three are played off against one another in a sort of counterpoint. Clarinda, still completely ignorant of Corydon's perfidy, complains to both her correspondents of their puzzling behavior; Corydon grows increasingly cool to Clarinda and increasingly fervid toward Lucina; Lucina indignantly fends him off and at the same time is scarcely able to write anything to Clarinda in her confusion of guilt and pitying sympathy. Clarinda receives an anonymous letter, directed "To Mrs. — at *Kensington*," [49] but its warnings against Corydon are so vague that it merely puzzles Clarinda still more, and she sends it to Corydon, asking for an explanation. Corydon begins to invent all sorts of excuses for his failure to write or see Clarinda and finally breaks with her. Clarinda writes a piteous letter to Lucina; the latter sends it to Corydon to soften his heart, but agrees to see him, only, she says, to rebuke him. Clarinda passionately beseeches Corydon to return to her. He answers her with a cold letter, asking her to restrain her romantic flights. Lucina writes to Corydon, averring that she still detests him, and, to show Corydon how she despises his perfidy and how guilty she feels, encloses a copy of a letter she has sent to Clarinda. A letter from Clarinda's maid to Lucina explains that Clarinda has fallen sick and cannot write herself, but begs Lucina to explain the enclosed letter if she can for Clarinda's peace of mind. The enclosure is another letter from the anonymous friend, informing Clarinda that Corydon has married Lucina. The story closes with a letter from Miss — (Clarinda) to My Lord — (Corydon). Clarinda bids him farewell, denounces him, and betakes herself to retirement and meditation.

The letter here assumes the functions of an actor in the drama: it serves as go-between, deludes, informs, suppresses, withholds, or conceals information. But in *The Perfidious P—* the medium is given another important task as well—the differentiation of character by style and sentiment. Clarinda, innocent and romantic, wishes she were in the magic world of *The Tempest*, while the more mature Lucina playfully says, "I'll take the ghost's word for a thousand pound" in reference to a spirit (Corydon) who has informed her of Clarinda's hiding place.[50] Not only do the three principals vary their style according to their emotions, but they betray their natures by a multitude of clues which the reader understands better than they do. Thus Lucina writes Clarinda:

Hang me (*My Dear*) tho I am a Widow, if ever I heard so much of Love before as your *Corydon* fills my Ears with. 'Tis well I dote upon *Clarinda's* Name; I hear it, I am sure, perpetually; *Corydon* has got a Custom to visit me every day, only to talk of *Clarinda*. I never was a Confidant till now: but my Love to you makes your Lover's Story pleasing.

Pray hasten to us; I am sure all things are in your power: and why you should let a Passion cool that may redound so much to your Advantage, is to me a Miracle.[51]

Clarinda writes to Corydon in a flutter:

> Now advanced to Courage I write to thee; I call thee
> Life and Soul, and all those fond Words I used to blush
> to read. I prithee do not give it so harsh a Name as Chid-
> ing, when I tell my Fears. The Merchant whose rich
> Vessel is at Sea, if all his Treasure's there, does he not
> dread a Storm? You are my only Treasure . . . the serene
> Face of Beauty, or the Frowns of Power, each would
> destroy my Peace. Oh wou'd my Heroe quit the glorious
> Pomp and Dangers of the Court for my calm Harbour,
> for Solitude and me, how many various ways I'd find to
> charm! Sometimes like the *Arcadian* Nymphs, I'd range
> the Groves and Plains, whilst flow'ry Chaplets crown'd
> my flowing Hair! Sometimes! Oh Fool! this is Roman-
> tick all. . . . You are fix'd in Glory's Circle. I sunk, never
> more, I fear, to rise; no matter, give to the Ambitious
> Honour, to Church-men Luxury and Power, to Misers
> Wealth, to fighting Kings War and Conquest, to poor
> *Clarinda* your eternal Love, and my Reward exceeds all
> theirs.[52]

Clarinda reproaches Corydon on occasion for the looseness of
his style, and she has reason:

> For my part, I think the telling of this over and over, as
> some Men do their Passions, ought to be tiresome to Wo-
> men of your Nicety, and as nauseous to the Mind, as
> Meat often drest to the Stomach: for to be always in the
> high Road of making Love, a Man must Bake, Boil, Roast,
> Hash, and Mince his Love, to find Variety for his Mis-
> tress, who perhaps does not think, because 'tis brought
> warm to her, it has so often been cool'd by another, and
> only tost up again for her Palate. These common Prac-
> tices of Love ought to be below a Woman of your Sense,
> whose Delicacy shou'd relish a Plate (tho' no bigger than
> a Saucer) of something new, above those vast Dishes of
> repeated Cramb.[53]

The Perfidious P— shows in a highly sophisticated state
the approach to drama that is the essence of the epistolary
novel. Its letters assume the importance of speeches from their
frequency and their dialogue-like function of adding bits,

whose significance may be realized only later, to the mosaic of the total structure. The point of view darts from person to person; the reader receives impressions of the temperaments and feelings of all three of the participants, and at the same time is able to perceive the extent to which each controls or understands the situation. The emotional temperature of each character is balanced against and contrasted with the states of the others. Letters from the unknown friend break into the scene and change the direction of the plot; the letters copied and sent add to the complexity of the picture. The dramatic irony of Clarinda's ignorance reinforces the tension of the situation, and later she is dramatically removed from the scene when her maid writes for her. Although the cast of characters is small and the story slight, *The Perfidious P—* belongs on the technical level of *Clarissa* rather than of *Pamela*. The anonymous author's manipulation of letters gives it a richness of texture unknown in earlier epistolary fiction and rare until much later.

Lindamira, a story of considerable charm, is evidently the work of an unpracticed pen. Slips in grammar and syntax abound in its twenty-five letters, but these defects are balanced by its plain, sober English prose and its general avoidance of the high-flown terms of romance. To an unusual extent *Lindamira* shows what has been called "the sense of place," with specific details of setting, both in and out of doors, costume, furniture, and the like. The plot also is of unusual sobriety for its time. Lindamira, as the story gets under way, conventionally rids herself of a number of preposterous suitors, including Sir Formal Trifle, whose name and nature are both borrowed from Shadwell's *Virtuoso*. Colonel Harnando, who first wins her love, is a married man; this discovery drives Lindamira to a rural retreat at her grandmother's. Meanwhile, she finds a new love—Cleomidon, a barrister—but we are diverted and she is dismayed by the ridiculous suit of Parson Spintext, who pursues her while he is pursued by Xantippe, a maiden lady of mature years who tries to make Lindamira give over French romances for Seneca. Lindamira's widowed mother dies suddenly, and circumstances thwart her hopes of marrying Cleomidon. She resolutely conquers her own inclinations and his even stronger desires, forcing him to please his rich uncle by marrying an heiress, Cleodora. At this point Lindamira's cousin Doralisa comes on the scene, and a lengthy and digressive "history" of her amours at the French court breaks up the action. The improbable villainess Lyndaraxa, mother of Cleodora and now the wife of Cleomidon's uncle, attempts by elaborate intrigues including forged letters to deprive Cleomidon of his inheritance and prevent him from marrying Lindamira, his bride Cleodora having died. Lindamira, tricked, almost weds her old flame, Colonel Harnando, whose wife has previously died in childbirth; but the difficulties are solved in the nick of time and the novel ends with the lovers united and Lyndaraxa dead by her own hand.

In spite of *Lindamira*'s excellent characterization and plotting, its domestic setting and high moral tone, it is notable rather as marking a general improvement in fiction than as a milestone in the epistolary novel's development. Like *Marianne*, it is not written "to the moment," but in retrospect, in a series of letters to the confidante Indamora, after all the events have fallen into their proper perspective in Lindamira's mind. The novel is her "history" or *récit*. Writing in letters permits Lindamira to make "asides" and break the story off at suspenseful moments, but the result is essentially the first-person or autobiographical narrative in one of its more effective forms. Indeed, epistolary conventions often get *Lindamira*'s author into serious technical problems which are not resolved, and which seem scarcely to be viewed as awkward or inartistic:

> A little before the departure of Cleomidon, you, my dear Indamora, came to town. . . . It was through your persuasions I was induced to take that journey into Sussex with . . . yourself . . . you know, my aunt, Udotia's mother, sent for us up to town to be at the wedding of Doralisa, her eldest daughter. . . . But you, my Indamora, would not suffer me to indulge myself in so great a melancholy, and you argued so well against the ill effects of thinking much . . . that at last you made me sensible that we ought to submit to our lot . . . I left you then in Sussex and came to London.[54]

Olinda's Adventures: or, The Amours of a Young Lady, which first appeared in *Letters of Love and Gallantry* (1693), is similar to *Lindamira* in many ways and surpasses it in others. This novel is ascribed to the child prodigy Catherine Trotter, an accomplished poet, dramatist, and philosophical essayist (she corresponded with Locke, whose doctrines she defended).[55] In it Olinda, a very moral and reflective young lady, writes seven letters to her platonic friend Cleander. She explains the reasons for her disappearance into the country and relates the history of her past amours. An ingenious subplot varies the narrative and helps the letters to seem like genuine correspondence: Olinda is anxious to promote the marriage of Cleander and her friend Ambrisia, and at the beginning or end of each letter she advises Cleander how to proceed, encourages him in his suit, and praises Ambrisia's merits. The main plot, the tale of Olinda's own loves, is not interrupted by any digressions, as *Lindamira* is by the Doralisa episode, but proceeds steadily on its complicated way, reinforced by Olinda's reflections. Olinda as heroine is a far cry from such young ladies as Mrs. Behn's Sylvia. She lives with her mother in reduced circumstances and makes no bones about it. She is sought in marriage by Berontus, who is not a marquis but a goldsmith, and though she rejects him she censures herself for her pride:

> Her Thoughts cannot be brought so low; they tour a little above his Shop, perhaps too high for her Fortune; but she's something too young to consider that, or to prefer her Interest to her Humour.[56]

Far from abandoning herself to romantic intrigues, she commences her rather innocent story thus:

> That you may see I study nothing more in this Solitude than to oblige you; I've resolved to spend the most Part of my Time in complying with that Request you've often made me, of giving you a particular Account of all that has happen'd to me in my Life; tho' I fear I shall lose part of that Esteem which you have hitherto preserv'd for me, by acquainting you with some Passages of it, which yet, I hope, have nothing in 'em so ill, that the Kindness of a Friend mayn't find out something in the Circumstances of the Story to Excuse: For tho' perhaps I have not always been so nicely cautious as a Woman in Strictness ought, I have never gone beyond the Bounds of solid Virtue.[57]

After a number of minor suitors have been wittily disposed of, Olinda loses her heart unawares to the handsome Cloridon, on whom she has been obliged to make a business call. Cloridon is a nobleman, however, and married. He takes such a liking to Olinda that he begs her to visit him occasionally so that he may enjoy her conversation; after many misgivings she consents. The meetings are secret, to preserve both their reputations, and they are decorous until one sad day, when Cloridon embraces Olinda. The prudent Olinda promptly renounces him:

> That Love which shin'd before so pure and bright, appears now the blackest Thing in Nature; and I hate myself for not hating you; for I own (tho' I blush in owning) that I love you still; nay, I believe that I forgive you too; but I must never, never see you more: No, tho' you swear you repent, and that you would not repeat your Crime, if you were certain of Success. Would not you believe I should as easily Pardon your Breach of this Vow, as I did the last, which you made me so solemnly? Yes, you would, my Lord, and I should be betray'd to Things I never thought of yet: For all is solid, convincing Reason, that you speak; and I should soon believe any thing you would have me. Curse on that fond Credulity that first deceiv'd me into a Belief, that 'twas no Sin to love you.[58]

Cloridon departs for Flanders, and Olinda is further dismayed by an anonymous letter (later discovered to be false) which accuses him of having a mistress. She struggles hard to get the better of her inclinations:

> I cou'd expect no Remedy, for I knew not what I wou'd have. I did not continue one Moment in the same Mind; I long'd for *Cloridon's* return, and yet I reso[l]v'd not to see him, though when I thought that perhaps he would not desire it, I almost dy'd with the Fear ... I said the most violent Things I could imagine against him, and left him without the least Reluctancy; But my Rage, or Hate, was soon converted to a quiet stupid Grief, that overwhelm'd my Soul, and left me not the Power of easing it the Common Way, in Tears or Complaints.[59]

At last she succeeds (she thinks) in dismissing her charmer from her thoughts:

I find by Experience 'tis but bravely, heartily, and thoroughly resolving upon a Thing, and 'tis half done: There's no Passion, no Temptation so strong but Resolution can overcome: All is, to be able to resolve: there's the Point, for one must lose a little of the first Ardour before one can do that; and many of our Sex have ruin'd themselves for want of Time to think. 'Tis not a constant settled Purpose of Virtue will do; there must be particular Resolutions for a particular Attack. 'Tis easy enough to say, no Man shall prevail with me to do an ill Thing; the Difficulty is, such a Man shall not; he that I love; he, that 'tis Death for me to deny any thing to: There I got the better of myself, and at last attained to a calm Serenity of Mind.[60]

A new suitor, Orontes, appears on the scene. At this juncture Olinda forfeits forever her status as a romantic heroine. The voice of middle-class British realities is heard in her mother's advice:

Do you resolve to lead a single Life; I should approve of the Choice in one of a better Fortune; but you must conform your self to yours and consider that I am not able to maintain you; if you don't hate *Orontes*, I will have you marry him, he has given so great Proof of his being a good Husband, that you can't fear he will be otherwise to you; he is handsome enough, and very rich; I believe he loves you, and in fine, I think you may be as happy with him as with any Man; therefore don't be obstinately bent against your own Good,[61]

and in her reaction to it:

I had no Aversion for him, and since my Circumstances would oblige me to marry, and that I knew I could never love any Man; I thought it might as well be he, as any other; So in some Time after I yielded, and the Wedding-Day was appointed to be the Sixteenth of May last.[62]

Without heroics or spasms of sensibility Olinda stifles her inclinations and prepares to marry Orontes. Cloridon returns from Flanders, and she cannot resist the temptation of seeing him once more, but she soothes her conscience by contriving a necessary errand to bespeak a post for a relative. When

Cloridon hears of her impending marriage he promptly has Orontes kidnaped and presents him with a sinecure by way of reward for giving up his pretensions to Olinda. With her mother's consent Olinda is sequestered in the country to await the anticipated death of Cloridon's inconvenient wife so that she may marry him. As the story ends she writes that, having just heard of the wife's death from a timely attack of small-pox, she is making preparations for her return to London.

In spite of the rather ridiculous way in which the plot is huddled up at the conclusion, *Olinda's Adventures* reflects a new breadth and realism in the English novel. Olinda's mind is fully as pure as Pamela's, though like Pamela's it stresses the prudential aspect rather too much for modern tastes. Olinda is tender-hearted, but she is also moral, pious, and well-edu-cated; her thoughts move with a sober reflectiveness that is far removed from the hypersensitive flauntings of passion that formed Mrs. Haywood's stock in trade. Some of her argu-ments with herself have the sound approach of a manual of practical piety. Most of Olinda's adventures are credible, and they take place in a physical and emotional setting that is any-thing but escapist, though her matrimonial triumph is remark-able, to say the least. Moreover, like Lindamira, Olinda com-bines a non-Pameloid sense of humor with her other vir-tues. She reflects wryly on her own conduct and salts her narrative with amusing portraits of ridiculous people. The transfer of emphasis from action to agent is as great in *Olin-da's Adventures* as it is in most other early epistolary novels, but here the agent is a real person instead of a mass of unco-ordinated, exaggerated feelings. The various elements of the story are smoothly welded together; the epistolary technique, both in the frame-letters and the inserted epistles, is appropri-ate, useful, and well developed.

Mrs. Mary Davys' *Familiar Letters Betwixt a Gentle-man and a Lady* is a domestic novel in twenty-two letters which appeared in her collected *Works* (1725). The letters, dated from November 1 to January 25, constitute a "scrib-bling treaty" between Artander, who is in the country set-tling his estate, and Berina, who remains in town. The two are "platonic friends" who furnish one another with all the amus-ing stories and gossip they can accumulate. They try dis-cussing politics for a while, but since Berina is a "new woman" and a violent Whig and Artander is a Tory, they cannot agree and give over the subject. Artander's letters grow warmer, and presently he declares his love. Berina laughs at him, feigning to suppose that he is only teasing her, but her laughter grows fainter as the correspondence ends with his approaching return to town, and the reader is left to assume that a marriage will take place.

Unlike a good many of her contemporaries in the field of letter fiction, Mrs. Davys possessed a sense of humor and an eye for physical detail. A pair of correspondents like Artander and Berina, who manage to be witty instead of passionate while conveying the impression that they entertain tender feelings for one another, is a refreshing innovation. Artander wryly describes the rewards of courtesy:

> I being very ceremonious and full of Compliment at the Stairshead, with an unlucky turn of my Foot, struck it against her prodigious Hoop-petticoat, and threw both her and myself down stairs. The Hoop, like Bladders ty'd under the Arms in swimming, kept her from danger, but I am nothing but Pain and Plaister. You Ladies are very dangerous Company, for if you can't break a Man's Heart with your Eyes, you'll break his Neck with your Dress.[63]

Later he tells of a visit he has paid to a gentlewoman of the neighborhood:

> After I had paid my Compliment, receiv'd hers, and gaz'd a while at the Charms of her Dress and Person, I made bold to fancy she was a little craz'd; and turn'd to take a Survey of the Room and Furniture, which was no way inferiour to herself: Upon her Tea-Table, instead of a Set of China, stood a Paste-board, with a piece of fat Bacon upon it; and on the Seat of the Sash-window, a red earthen Pan, half-full of Pease-pudding, which I guess'd to be the Remains of her Dinner.... However, as I was walking to and fro, watching the Cobwebs that they did not fall into my Wig, I slid over a piece of Bacon-Swerd, which threw me directly into the Lady's Lap, and overset her Cricket: She grew very merry at the Accident, and I very much out of Countenance.[64]

The letters continually refer to the physical process of writing and to the surroundings of the writers, so that the image of a real correspondence is constantly but unobtrusively kept before the reader's eye. (The two have agreed, in the interest of brevity and wit, to restrict each letter to a single sheet of paper.) Berina reveals her feelings for Artander in spite of herself, even as she scorns Artander's protestations of love:

> But since I came home, I have heard another cause of [an acquaintance's] implacable Aversion: they say she loves *Artander*, and has often made violent signs that way, to an insensible—as you are. However, I bear all the Brunt, and am, it seems, thought the sole cause of your Indifference; which, if true, I shou'd be sorry for, because I wou'd not play the Dog in the Manger. I cou'd be very glad to know the Truth, but am sure you are too generous to confess. I intend to let her know I will be her Advocate, and use my Interest in her behalf: say, *Artander*, will you give her Hopes, and send the welcome News by me? Or must she despair of your Love, to preserve your Friendship for
>
> Berina.

> I'll swear, *Artander*, I was never so merry in my Life, as at the reading of your last Letter; I don't believe there's a Man in the World, that defies Love as you do, cou'd ever assume the Lover like you: Why, you mimick it as naturally as if you had serv'd an Apprenticeship to its God: Methinks the very Paper whines, 'tis writ in such a beseeching Stile. I declare, I thought you had been in Earnest, and was going to contrive some Way to comfort you ... you over-act your Part: the next time you put on the Lover, do it with an easier Air; 'tis quite out of Fashion to talk of Dying, and Sighing, and Killing Eyes, and such Stuff; you shou'd say, Damn it, Madam, you are a tolerable sort of a Woman, and, if you are willing, I don't much care if I do you the Honour to marry you. That's the modern Way of Courtship. ... But tell me how I shou'd have brought myself off, had I been a Woman, whose Heart was susceptible of Love? ... You seem to hint, as if you were to be in Town soon. I confess I cou'd wish that part of your Letter true.[65]

The very lack of stress on conventional passion in the let-ters, combined with their playful tone and the brief references to everything under the sun which establish them on solid ground, makes them perhaps the most realistic letters in early English fiction. The plot conveyed by the correspondence is negligible; but the deficiency is made up by the richness of character portrayal and the breezy humor of the letters them-selves. Artander and Berina are clearly Thomas and Jane; and as a portrait of two very real people exchanging ideas, *Famil-iar Letters* is a true epistolary novel, a humble foreshadowing of the approach to fiction improved by Fanny Burney and perfected by Jane Austen.[66]

These last epistolary narratives are works of exceptional merit when measured against any fiction of their era, and compared with the primitive stories in letters mentioned in the early part of this chapter, most of which they follow in time, they show notable progress. Epistolary fiction, as well as other types of fiction in the early eighteenth century, indi-cates that authors were beginning to take the trouble to think a story through. They had begun to organize it around a firm structure of plot, enrich its texture with significant details, place it in a realistic contemporary setting, and elaborate its technique in a manner which bore on its total effect. They were also experimenting with improved methods of character-ization and conceiving personages and plots consonant with life as they and their readers experienced it. The result was a steady improvement in their stories, which sometimes rivaled the mature fiction of the midcentury and after.

The weakness of these early epistolary novels lay in their uneven development. The excellent technique of Mrs. Behn's *Love-Letters* was offset by her failure to sustain it through the novel's three parts, her poor characterization, and her rather absurd romantic conception of the story. *The Perfidious P—,* which has technique and a well-conceived plot but lacks detailed setting, is of slight stature as a novel from its very brevity and the plot's simplicity. Mrs. Davys' *Familiar Letters* is rich in characterization and technique, but its "plot" is nei-ther complex nor of wide scope. *Lindamira* and *Olinda's Ad-ventures* approach the ideal of the epistolary novel in many ways, but they are autobiographies first and epistolary fiction second. Thus, before Richardson's emergence as a writer all the elements of the genre which he brought to maturity were present in English fiction and had already been developed to a degree which he certainly reached but did not often surpass. What the earlier epistolary novels lacked was the simultaneous presence of all these elements combined into an organic whole and sustained through a long narrative of significance and depth. The epistolary novels of Richardson's predecessors, though highly promising experimental works, were fragmentary and tentative.

CHAPTER IX

Before Richardson, and After

[*Pamela*] might possibly introduce a new species of writing.
—Samuel Richardson (to Aaron Hill)

It would be pleasing to be able to suggest that the elements of
the epistolary novel, scattered and waiting in various literary
genres, gradually assembled themselves after the Restoration,
and that once they had cohered in a recognizable form the
form steadily developed and matured until it was ready, so to
speak, for Richardson. This was not what happened. The examples of letter fiction discussed in the preceding pages form
a very large and heterogeneous collection; a statement that
neatly labels some few of them may be absurd when applied
to the others. To look for development or evolution in this
era of English fiction shows an ill-considered rage for order.
Fiction was too amorphous and was written too haphazardly
to develop as a literary form does when it has acquired prestige, become canonical, and is turned out by "schools."
Writers like Mrs. Haywood, who produced much fiction,
improved with practice; some writers had far greater advantages than others in education, income, or talent, and their
work was proportionately better. But we need not restrict
ourselves to epistolary fiction, or even exclude the output of
such a writer as Defoe, when we say that English fiction developed irregularly before 1740 and that notable works appeared sporadically, with little evidence of what is usually
meant by literary influence.

Writers who hit upon something that "took," like the formula of Mrs. Haywood's early romances, exploited that formula as long as it sold, but they veered with the wind. Mrs. Haywood herself is an excellent example: she successively imitated Mrs. Behn, Defoe, Mrs. Manley, Mrs. Penelope Aubin, Addison, Richardson, and Fielding in the course of her long career.[1] But few Mrs. Haywoods arose, and the novel that a lady wrote as a youthful sally or that a hack ground out at a bookseller's suggestion might never be repeated or come to the eye of another writer who could imitate or improve it. Thus, nothing technically comparable to Mrs. Behn's *Love-Letters Between a Nobleman and His Sister* was written in the twenty years after it appeared. Tales with letters interpolated and miscellanies of letters, which varied from essays, gossip, or portraits to short stories, appeared side by side with well-developed novels in letters. Writers did not study to improve their technique when they were scarcely conscious of possessing such a thing.

Public demand, however, seems to have made fiction in letters harden into several forms, especially after 1700. Shapeless works like the duchess of Newcastle's *CCXI Sociable Letters*, or *Loves Missives to Virtue*, were seen less often; epistolary fiction appeared either as a novel, a collection of stories, or a tale interspersed with letters. Romantic gallantry waned, while plots grew firmer and setting more realistic. Ingenuities in depicting character or in manipulating a fairly complicated exchange of letters became more and more frequent after the seventeenth century. There appears to have been a "boom" in fiction in the 1720's, with a subsequent decline in production and a greater insistence on moral sobriety in the novel; these forces affected all kinds of fiction alike.[2] Whether we speak of fiction in general or letter fiction in particular, the first four decades of the eighteenth century had effected a change. More fiction, and of better quality, had appeared than at any comparable period since the reign of Elizabeth.

Among all the pre-Richardsonian epistolary forms the novel was obviously the most significant and was endowed with the greatest potential for growth. The miscellany of amusing letters, too closely allied to essays for independent development, had only a dead end ahead; its epistolary form was a mere convention of the age. The heroid or complaint letter could be repeated—until the situation palled—but not developed. The series of spy letters, though invested with plot and psychology in Montesquieu's *Persian Letters*, was pulled in two directions at the same time—toward the central plot and the centrifugal comment or satire. If either were overdeveloped the form was lost, and the result was a novel in letters or a collection of essays. Travel letters or histories related to a friend were not letters in essence, but journals. The short story in a few letters, however, which became a novel if lengthened and developed, contained the core of dramatic conflict necessary for a novel and used the epistolary method as an integral part of its technique to lift the narrative from the pictorial level to the dramatic.

True novels in letters appeared seldom, and as it were suddenly, showing no clear connection with more primitive forms of fiction. *The Perfidious P—* and *Love-Letters Between a Nobleman and His Sister,* or Mrs. Davys' *Familiar Letters,* are technically far in advance of anything closely contemporary with them. How may we account for the rare, isolated appearances of these superior pieces of fiction, which seem to have been created *ex nihilo?* A genuinely new literary form is almost unheard of; some source or earlier tradition is nearly always behind what at first seems to be an innovation. Was there not some kind of literature to which these early novels in letters owed the larger elements of their structure? The idea of using letters in narrative would have been obvious enough, since primitive fiction in that form was abundant in various popular works, but the technique of handling groups of characters and lengthy or complicated plots had to come from elsewhere. Among the possible sources, the drama at once suggests itself.

The early epistolary novels grew in intimacy and immediacy—"writing to the moment"—as their technique improved over the years. In all respects they approached the method of the drama: the story was shown completely in the present, with the future always indefinite and events distorted in value because they were seen without the ordering process of retrospect. Making characters work out a story by exchanging letters was technically similar to making them do it by exchanging speeches, as the drama did. If the author did not introduce characters, describe setting, give exposition, or summarize action in his own person, a kind of closet drama resulted, complete with "scenes." This was Richardson's method, and he recognized his novels as dramas no less than his critics have done.[3] The same can be said of the epistolary novels written by his uncritical predecessors.

The fact that a modern critic or a thoughtful writer is aware of a literary similarity does not, of course, indicate that it was recognized or had an important function when it existed. But before dismissing a connection between plays and novels as too hypothetical to consider, we should bear in mind the seldom-remembered importance which playbooks had in the literary situation of the early eighteenth century. For every denunciation of the effect of novels and romances on women and the young, we find one or more scathing references to the reading of plays. The beau or the fine lady of Augustan times did not have to be an inveterate playgoer to be thoroughly familiar with what was on the stage. And plays were devoured not only by the Biddy Tipkins, but by persons of intellectual stature. When Lady Mary Wortley Montagu went into "exile" in 1739, she took along a library of about five hundred titles; this included the Latin and Greek classics, grammars, and dictionaries, but it also contained romances, novels, fifty-one bound volumes of plays, and nine single plays.[4] The playbook and the novel catered to the same tastes, and it has been remarked that the novel was ready to fill the vacuum caused by the decline of the drama early in the eighteenth century.[5] The milieu of the emerging epistolary novel, for author or reader, was one in which the drama bulked large.

The known authors of early letter fiction were never far from the stage. Mrs. Behn, Mrs. Manley, Mrs. Haywood, Mrs. Trotter, and Mrs. Davys all wrote plays before, while, or shortly after they were working in fiction, and important borrowings from plays have been found in the novels of Mrs. Behn and Mrs. Haywood, in the anonymous *Lindamira*, and in Mrs. Davys' works.[6] The drama has long been recognized as one of the most important influences on Richardson.[7]

The drama, then, shared authors, readers, booksellers, and in a sense form and structure, with early letter fiction. If we agree that epistolary fiction comes very close to the dramatic method, we should be able to reverse the proposition

and suggest that in an age when fiction was decidedly informal, writers who had had some experience as playwrights
and who turned to fiction when the stage was denied them
wrote fiction that departed as little as possible from the dramatic conventions they knew. In short, it seems likely that the
earliest English epistolary novels may have evolved from the
drama. This is a repetition—no less logical—of the statement
that they were progressing toward it. To cast a novel into
semidramatic form, using letters as the closest available approximation to speeches and thinking of the tale in a series of
loosely conceived scenes, is a far less drastic step for a dramatist to take than writing a novel in the objective mode. Such a
task would force the author to compose descriptions of setting and action, rather than leaving the whole story in speech-
like discourse. Further, the long and inflated speeches of
heroic plays and sentimental tragedies, far removed from
brisk stichomythic dialogue, fitted admirably into the conventions of the typical ranting letter in the "Portuguese" mode.

Because of its nature and the probable circumstances of
its composition, *Love-Letters Between a Nobleman and His
Sister* serves as an excellent "laboratory specimen" for testing
such a theory. If Mrs. Behn wrote it, as is generally agreed,
she must have begun work immediately after her abandon-
ment of the theater in 1682 and before she had written (or at
least published) any other fiction.[8] Fifteen of her plays had
been produced and published; she was a veteran playwright
and skilled in her craft. The general resemblance of the
novel's structure to that of a play is sufficiently obvious. The
story begins with a dialogue in which Philander seeks to seduce Sylvia. Offstage events—the duels, Philander's escape
from Sylvia's house in disguise, and Sylvia's discovery and
imprisonment—are reported as they would be in speeches.
Minor characters enter briefly. After Sylvia's flight and Philander's second duel, the dialogue combines reporting with
planning. More interesting still, the attentive reader quickly
notes that long passages in Part I (written when Mrs. Behn
was fresh from the stage), though printed as prose, are actually a loose kind of blank verse. As their first night of love approaches, Sylvia begins a letter to Philander with the following apostrophe (suspiciously like Juliet's "Gallop apace, you
fiery-footed steeds"):

Approach, approach, you sacred Queen of Night,/ and bring *Philander* veil'd from all eyes but mine;/ approach at a fond Lover's Call, behold/ how I lie panting with Expectation,/ tir'd out with/ your tedious Ceremony to the God of Day;/ be kind, oh lovely Night, and let the Deity descend/ to his beloved *Thetis's* Arms, and I to my *Philander's;*/ the Sun and I must snatch our Joys in the same happy Hours;/ favour'd by thee, oh sacred silent Night!/ See, see, the enamour'd Sun is hasting on apace/ to his expecting Mistress,/ while thou dull Night art slowly lingering yet./ Advance, my Friend! my Goddess! and my Confident!/ hide all my Blushes, all my soft Confusions,/ my Tremblings, Transports, and Eyes all Languishing.⁹

Many similar examples occur; and the same kind of blank verse is found in many of the more agitated passages of the second and third parts of the novel.¹⁰ One might argue that this resemblance to blank verse is not close enough to be significant, since prose writers often develop the vicious habit of falling into blank-verse rhythms (Dickens and Thomas Wolfe are famous examples), but this loose blank verse is precisely the medium which Mrs. Behn was using for the stage. One of her last plays before she left the theater was *The Roundheads: or, The Good Old Cause* (produced December 1681), which was a comedy printed as prose in its early quarto and in subsequent editions. But the prose contains the same kind of concealed and loose blank verse found in the novel:

L[ady]. *Des*[bro]. By what strange Miracle, my dearest *Freeman,*/ wert thou set at liberty?

Free. On the zealous Parole of *Rabbie Ananias;*/ that Rhetorick that can convert whole Congregations/ of well-meaning Blockheads to errant Knaves,/ has now mollify'd my Keeper;/ I'm to be render'd back within this Hour:/ let's not, my dear Maria, lose the precious minutes/ this Reverend Hypocrite has given us.

L. *Des.* Are you in earnest, Freeman? and wou'd you take/ what Honour will not suffer me to grant?

Free. With all my Heart, Honour's a poor Excuse./ Your Heart and Vows (your better part) are mine;/ you've only let your Body out to one/ whom you call Husband, and whom Heaven has mark'd/ for Cuckoldom./ Nay, 'tis an Act of honest Loyalty,/ so to revenge our cause;/ whilst you were only mine, my honest Love/ thought it a Sin to press these Favours from you;/ 'twas injuring my self as well as thee;/ but now we only give and take our Right.[11]

Mrs. Behn's earlier plays showed the same metrical license, even though they were printed as poetry. In a passage from *Abdelazer*, chosen at random, we find:

Abd. I made her too betray the credulous Cardinal,
And having then no further use of her,
Satiated with her Lust,
I set *Roderigo* on to murder her.
Thy Death had next succeeded; and thy Crown
I wou'd have laid at *Leonora's* Feet.[12]

With this evidence of structure and style at hand, we may assert that the first fiction Mrs. Behn wrote bore a strong resemblance to the plays she had just been writing. The resemblance is strong enough to suggest that a combination of dramatic technique and of the method of the *Portuguese Letters* was sufficient for her purposes and was in fact all the material she used to tell her scandalous tale.

Love Letters Between Polydorus . . . and Messalina is another example of the use of blank verse in fiction.[13] The letters of the two principals (as distinguished from the postscripts and the purely practical letters of Father Pedro and Aspasia) amount to speeches, a sort of dramatic debate between lust and virtue, or between the villain and the injured queen whom he is trying to entrap through her helplessness and her obligations to him. The novel is the dramatic exposition of a simple situation. Blank verse is often found in the more intense moments of Mrs. Haywood's novels and in her epistolary sequences. In *Lindamira* and *Olinda's Adventures*, the debt to drama is merely structural (*Lindamira* owes much to Shadwell's *Virtuoso*), since their idiom is plain prose. *The Perfidious P—*, however, is pure drama; like the earlier novels it uses concealed blank verse.[14] But this is restricted to the letters of the mistreated heroine Clarinda, for Corydon writes prose. It is probable that the blank verse, reserved for

Clarinda, is supposed to elevate her in the reader's eyes, to make her a nobler and more passionate character than her perfidious lover. One might compare the use of blank verse and prose in these novels to its use in the earlier drama, where for the most part heroes and fine ladies spoke poetry while fools, peasants, madmen, and low characters talked in prose. An illuminating parallel is furnished by a letter from "Lysander" to "Eugenia" in *Familiar Letters of Rochester* (1697). Lysander, who has been writing plain prose, launches into a passage of blank verse. He then draws himself up and remarks:

> Madame, tho' I design'd these Thoughts in down-right Prose, yet in the Ardor of writing they run into Blank Verse, whether I would or no.[15]

The modulation of prose rhythms into blank verse was evidently considered to be a genuine symptom of "Ardor," a connection which is logical from the theatrical history of the medium.

The same splitting of discourse between plain prose and theatrical rant has been observed in *Clarissa*, in which a simple, downright style, approved in Lovelace by the heroine, whether in speech or writing, is a mask. When carried away by ardor, or when playing the part of the libertine with Belford, Lovelace uses the flamboyant style of "academy rhetoric" which Clarissa despises and fears. Likewise, Clarissa herself, who early in the novel writes and speaks bluntly though with delicate expressions, assumes the rant of the stage, of a Belvidera or a Calista, in the "high scenes," especially after the rape—and Richardson is clearly conscious that she is doing so.[16]

We unfortunately have no direct evidence in letter or essay to show that the author of an early letter novel was working deliberately from the drama. Fielding, classically educated and also beginning his novels from nothing, so to speak, published his defense of the Cervantic comic epic in prose, but he had the ancient epic with its position at the head of the genres to back him up, and he had an educated audience to win over. Furthermore, critics have passed from acceptance of his professed intentions to some doubt, and to re-acceptance in the light of careful comparison of his works with their classical models.[17] If this last method is valid and if we consider the status of the drama among those who read and wrote early epistolary fiction, we are justified in looking to the drama as the chief "source" of the eighteenth-century epistolary novel. Certainly, to say that these novels were imitations of the drama is a better explanation for their existence and high quality, especially in the absence of a well-formed tradition, than to suppose, as some have, that they grew up on the model of such earlier forms as letters in miscellanies, *portugaises*, or spy letters. Some of their features must have come from these sources, it is clear, but the drama seems to be the only literary form that accounts for the complexities which a few of these novels attained.

The various shortcomings of early epistolary fiction have been noted at some length. The later novels of Richardson and his followers, however, also had obvious faults in spite of their general superiority. Their defects may be divided into two categories: the limitations of the epistolary method as a narrative device, no matter how masterfully handled, and the difficulties of presenting a fictional correspondence effectively and credibly. The latter can be overcome by various methods (at least in portions of the novel), but they are inseparable from the epistolary novel as Richardson handled it.[18] The latter difficulties were recognized by Richardson's early critics. Mrs. Donnellan wrote him:

> The epistolary style is yours, 'tis speaking, 'tis painting; but I think there must be a friend to tell some things that a man can't tell of himself, for I am very delicate on the subject of self-praise, and think it should be as much avoided as possible; but when the scenes represented are passionate, they must come from the persons concerned, or they lose their spirit.[19]

Lady Mary Wortley Montagu commented acidly in one of her letters to the countess of Bute: "This letter is as long and dull as any of Richardson's." [20] In the early nineteenth century Mrs. Anna Barbauld and Sir Walter Scott analyzed the epistolary technique in Richardson; they were well aware of its failings:

> That letters should be written at all times, and upon every occasion in life, that those letters should be preserved, and altogether form a connected story, it requires much

art to render specious. It introduces . . . the necessity of having an insipid confidant to tell the circumstances that an author cannot relate in any other way. It obliges a man to tell of himself, what perhaps no man would tell; and sometimes to repeat compliments which modesty would lead him to suppress; and when a long conversation is repeated, supposes a memory more exact than is generally found.[21]

[The advantage of having several characters comment on the same matter] is at least partly balanced, by arresting the progress of the story, which stands still while the characters show all their paces. . . . In order that all may be written, which must be known for the purpose of the narrative, characters must frequently write, when it would be more natural for them to be acting—must frequently write what it is not natural to write at all—and must at all times write a great deal oftener, and a great deal more, than one would think human life had time for.[22]

These comments lead to the conclusion that Richardson was putting a greater strain on the epistolary method than it could bear. His novels bore two opposing stresses: the need to explore the minutest corners of a situation in detail and the simultaneous need to create a believable epistolary situation and believable letters. The former requirement compelled him to make characters write with inhuman prolixity and speed, note down details and conversations with inhuman accuracy, speak about themselves with an unnatural priggishness or frankness, and record rapid action which they could not possibly have got on paper. To exhibit all the possible reactions to an event, characters had to tell one another what they already knew. Their letters went on to amazing lengths from the necessity of telling all—lengths not explained away by coy references to "always scribbling." Sometimes, Richardson was so carried away as to write pure drama, forgetting that his characters were sending epistles. His epistolary method required to sustain it a confidant, who might be as well-developed as Anna Howe or quite colorless. Protagonist and confidant, though never so intimate, by hook or by crook had to be always kept apart and under the necessity of communicating by letter. And it imposed the absurd fiction of the "editor" to give the letters the status of a true story.

All the requirements of the mature and fully discoursed novel in letters militated against realism. If it had been admitted that the story was a romance, or romantically conceived, the lack of realism would have been less important. But Richardson would not admit, and perhaps did not even recognize, the essentially romantic elements in the adventures of Pamela (Part I), Clarissa, and Harriet Byron. He wrote to two correspondents with considerable vehemence:

> I hate so much the French Marvellous and all un-natural Machinery, and have so often been disgusted with that sort of Management of those Pieces, that I am contented to give up my Profit, if I can but Instruct.[23]

> I must own I am so great an enemy to the French Marvellous, that I only aimed to give the Piece such a Variety, as should be consistent with Probability, and the general Tenor of a genteel Married Life.[24]

The general tenor of genteel married life, however, does not include duels, ravishments, or paragons of virtue and vice any more than it includes people who confide their inmost thoughts to their friends at enormous length and appear to devote most of their waking hours to the task. Inasmuch as Richardson was trying to be faithful to the everyday realities of life, the excesses of the epistolary method sometimes betrayed him. Ordinary people do not write letters very frequently or at great length, nor are they apt to have confidants of the kind required in epistolary novels, nor to reveal their thoughts and feelings so indiscriminately. These defects are perhaps not readily apparent to the average reader, who concentrates on the single page before him. But they were plain to critics who studied literature in a much more casual manner than do textual analysts of the present day. Furthermore, flaws which can be pardoned in Richardson because of the abundant compensation his novels afford can less easily be overlooked as they were repeated *ad nauseam* in the hundreds of epistolary novels that followed Richardson's success.

It is instructive to consider epistolary novels written before 1740 with reference to these faults. Many of them do not occur, and the effect of others is minimized. Letters in the earlier novels were nearly all of believable length, a page or so, when the author was trying to give the impression of correspondence. In autobiographical relations such as *Lindamira*, *Marianne*, and *Olinda's Adventures* they grew much longer than single letters could ordinarily be, but these were "histories" like Pamela's journal, supposedly worked at in odd moments and dispatched when the writer came to a stopping place or when the "pacquet" reached a convenient size. Letters conveyed by means of pages or other servants (as Richardson had the letters sent to and from Miss Howe during Clarissa's captivity) could be sent off and received several times a day with much more probability than letters which presumably required the post. Mrs. Davys in her *Familiar Letters* and Mrs. Manley in her *Letters* made sure that the epistles were dated at proper intervals (five to twelve days for Mrs. Davys, one to two for Mrs. Manley), and Mrs. Manley dated them from stages on the road to Exeter.[25] Letters such as those in *The Perfidious P—* were not only of realistic length, but were not more analytical than the reader might expect genuine letters to be. They concentrated on the problem of the moment, but with none of the endless balancing of pros and cons that makes parts of *Clarissa* such heavy going.

The crudely conceived stories, the romantic atmosphere, the casual treatment, and the plots of intrigue in the immature epistolary novels enabled them to avoid many traps into which greater novels fell. Though psychological tales and *portugaises* tore a passion to shreds, casuistic dissection of feeling was all that was expected of them. They were sufficiently new to be eagerly bought and read; readers apparently did not complain of the scanty plot and barrenness of setting. Authors who did not see so far into the implications of their stories as Richardson did could turn out artistically satisfying works (*The Perfidious P—* is an example) without exploring so deeply or writing at such great length as was necessary for him. Plots of romantic intrigue permitted heroines to be imprisoned or abducted and heroes to be banished or kidnaped, so that they had to correspond. The domestic and realistic novel which came later was reduced in its resources to journeys for health and pleasure (as in *Humphry Clinker*), an expedient easily worn threadbare. These journeys had to be accounted for and minutely described, sometimes with loss of concentration on the central effect; a character of Mrs. Haywood or Mrs. Davys could be dispatched to the country in a few words to settle an estate or merely to go into retirement, and there was an end of it. Romantic plots also kept the protagonists frequently involved in one harrowing accident after another, a series of dangers, "distresses," and agonies of the heart that gave them plenty to write about and very good reasons to write. They were not constrained to prattle about minor matters, and the pressure of events did not encourage them to digress or sermonize as Pamela did in her exalted state.

Characters in a shallowly conceived story had no need to write about more than the simplest and most obvious facts of a situation, or to look far into the past or future. The crude novel carried with it the circumscription of its material. The only relevant feelings and comments in *The Perfidious P—*, for example, are those which relate directly to the love triangle. If these were adequately presented—and they were examined with some subtlety—enough material had been brought into the story to assure its completeness as a short and simple novel. There was no need to develop or even to mention antecedent circumstances other than the beginning of love between Corydon and Clarinda, which was introduced in a short flashback. Much the same may be said of other simple epistolary novels. Their scope was so limited and their canvas so small that nonessentials might be eliminated, and would in fact have been out of place. The result was complete, even if it was not very significant.

Such mechanical devices for starting an epistolary tale as the fiction of a packet of letters discovered and published, or the "editing" of a collection of letters, presented few difficulties to the authors and readers of pre-Richardsonian fiction. By the time Richardson assumed the "editorship" of his three series of letters, the novelty of the device had been exhausted. Readers grew more and more critical; as Richardson's followers poured out their imitations, the pose of editorship became a vestigial absurdity. The situation had been rather different earlier, when readers were more ingenuous, less used to the new form of fiction, and less educated in its ways. No doubt a larger part of the earlier public was credulous. "Editorship" had both novelty and the reader's desire for a true story to recommend it. Employed with great ingenuity and inventiveness, because of the fictional requirements of the day, it had importance to the stories it introduced.

To point out that epistolary fiction before Richardson's escaped many of his structural flaws is not to contend that it was artistically superior. It merely had the virtues of its defects. Neither pressure from readers nor authors' aims required the early novels to cope with problems inescapable for larger and better-developed works of fiction. Clearly, they were more realistic as correspondence; they certainly avoided the fatal prolixity of Richardson and must have been easier for impatient readers to take.[26] The few good novels in letters written by Richardson's precursors were concentrated and slight rather than large and discursive, but they were often as successful in what they tried to accomplish as Richardson's were in their different way.

Pamela caused a sensation. Its appearance greatly increased the size of the reading public for fiction, and with *Clarissa* and *Grandison* it assured the epistolary novel's prestige. Where Richardson's absolute importance is concerned, what his contemporaries were doing is perhaps neither here nor there. But the fiction we have examined brings up several questions concerning this literary upheaval. Was *Pamela* really something new, and if it was, in what way? Did Richardson know earlier epistolary works, English and French, and did he borrow from them? If earlier authors wrote good epistolary novels, must not Richardson's place in the history of English fiction be reconsidered? What was the precise nature of his contribution to the novel?

Richardson's own statements concerning the sources of *Pamela* are well known. The plot he says he elaborated from an anecdote told him by a deceased friend; the epistolary method suggested itself to him as he worked on his book of familiar letters, interrupted while the novel was being written. From all the available evidence, there seems to be no good reason why these statements should not be largely true. Several attempts have been made to show that Richardson was indebted to *Marianne* for his plot and method of writing, but resemblance does not prove influence, and he stated categorically that he knew nothing of French or of French novels. The similarities of the two plots are not striking, and other equally good parallels for *Pamela* can be found both in the actual events and the fiction of the time. He could have read part of *Marianne* in English, but it seems unlikely that he made use of the novel and doubtful that he had read it. As to his general knowledge of French fiction, the preface Warburton wrote for the fourth volume of *Clarissa,* containing the suggestion that he had followed the plan of French writers, called forth a letter asserting Richardson's complete ignorance of the French language or literature. It is true that he called himself "an enemy to the French Marvellous," but he could have gained such a vague knowledge of the characteristics of French fiction as that statement implies merely from conversation, without having read a French novel. A very probable explanation is that some of the books Richardson read in his youth to the young ladies at their work were translations of French romances.[27] Such fiction was devoured by genteel young ladies during Richardson's youth and long after, and the word "marvellous" fits romances better than the realistic novels which followed them.

All we know of Richardson's life and character indicates that his knowledge of English novels written in his earlier years must have been sketchy and slight. As an industrious and priggish youth, as a hardworking young printer and a self-made businessman, he would have scorned novels as wasteful of precious time, frivolous, and downright wicked. He might have read fictional pieces with a pious purpose, such as Bunyan's, or with a thick coating of improving morals, such as Defoe's; but mere fiction was probably in very dubious standing for him and his early associates. That he had considerable knowledge of contemporary plays, derived from reading or seeing them in his relatively giddier youth, has been deduced from references in his novels and letters; he read and commented on various novels in his leisurely later years. But plays, bad as their reputation was, occupied a higher position than did novels. Richardson knew the *Tatler* and *Spectator,* but evidence for his early knowledge of fiction is so slight and vague that theorizing on it is purposeless.[28]

We need not suppose that Richardson needed to know earlier fiction in order to write *Pamela.* The accounts we have of his life indicate that writing letters—including very long letters, copies, and letters to persons living under his own roof—was as natural to him as breathing.[29] Letters, for business, pleasure, or art, were a very important part of his life. There is no reason why writing a story in letters should not have seemed both obvious and very congenial to him. The volume of familiar letters into which he plunged with such loving ardor contains several sequences, technically simple, but of some length; and in fact stories which might be considered sketches for the novels are found among its letters.[30] *Familiar Letters* shows considerable talent in presenting character, setting, situation, and similar elements of fiction. *Pamela*, too, is a simple story, technically speaking. Its epistolary method shows no remarkable ingenuity; the exchanges are not developed to any complexity, much of the story is journal, more is a monologue by Pamela without the introduction of other points of view. Part II tends to become a conduct book, a series of miscellaneous essays on domestic problems. *Pamela* is technically inferior to several of its predecessors; if Richardson worked from models it seems incredible that he imitated them so clumsily. He surpassed all previous epistolary fiction in *Clarissa*, but *Clarissa* represented years of loving labor and experiment, the amazingly painstaking expansion of a simple story, and the elevation of the epistolary technique to an indispensable importance for the texture of the narrative.[31] *Clarissa* cannot be explained in terms of borrowing from other writers, while *Pamela* is too obviously Richardson feeling his way to be the product of purposeful reading in earlier fiction. *Pamela* is not unlike earlier letter novels, as we have seen, but this suggests that both story and technique were waiting to be used. Earlier authors dealt with the story of Pamela, it might be said, while Richardson wrote the novel *Pamela*. Other explanations are possible, but unnecessary. Given the time and the man, *Pamela* was not an astonishing production. It was a crystallization of many tendencies of its age.

 Pamela became the rage, while its forerunners more or less quickly dropped out of sight. But among the often underestimated factors in its success were the advertising and promotion that Richardson, as a printer and influential businessman, was able to give it, the verbal puffing it received from Aaron Hill and other literary friends of the author, Dr. Slocock's famous sermon, the book's impressive bulk, and its

combination of "warm scenes" and moral preaching.[32] The
last factor was of the greatest importance. In our day this
formula makes runaway best-sellers; in Richardson's it opened
up a new section of the public to *Pamela*. Not only the young
and frivolous, who read romances, plays, and novels, but also
prosperous and sober persons, could read this new work with
its parade of moral instruction. They could enjoy its romantic
theme of the maid marrying the master and its "inflaming descriptions" while they salved their consciences with its general
sobriety, its rewarding of "vartue," and its preaching. The
appeal of Pamela was much the same as the appeal of Reynolds' *Gods Revenge Against Murther* a century earlier.

The form in which *Pamela* was cast seems to have caused
little surprise. One reviewer commented:

> The Manner in which we come to the Knowledge of
> them [the incidents in Pamela's story] is very singular.
> The Narrative is all of her own relating, in a Series of
> Letters to her Father and Mother, jointly for the most
> part, and in a few Instances to the latter alone,[33]

but readers in general apparently found nothing curious in the
epistolary presentation of the novel. Richardson did not refer
to his technique until later, and the flood of eulogistic criticism which poured in on him after 1740 was at first concerned only with praising the morality and value of the
piece.[34] Not until the time of *Clarissa* did he and his correspondents become much interested in the niceties of putting
fiction into letters. Certainly, the general reader of 1740 was
sufficiently habituated to familiar letters in and out of fiction
to find nothing very surprising in the method of *Pamela*.

Richardson and his friends did comment on what they
found to be new in *Pamela*—the plain language, the relatively
unromantic story, and the moralizing. *Pamela* was something
new in fiction, a novel which one need not be ashamed of
reading. More importantly, though this was seldom commented on in Richardson's time, *Pamela* carried the technique
of "discoursing" to far greater lengths than had any previous
piece of original English fiction. Its only parallels in that respect were the novels of Boursault, Marivaux, and Crébillon.
The story was of the simplest in plot and action. Earlier writers would have found it suitable for treatment in fifty pages at

the most; indeed, a very similar tale (which has been suggested as a source for *Pamela*) was told in a single *Spectator* by John Hughes.[35] But Richardson expanded his story to two and then four volumes. He expanded it not by complicating the plot and introducing new action or (in *Pamela I*) by digressions not to the purpose, but by making it move with unprecedented slowness, while each tiny step was reflected upon, turned in all directions, and painstakingly examined by Pamela's active brain. *Pamela* included a multitude of details not essential to the story, but all bearing on it and increasing the richness of its total effect.[36] The uncompromising particularity of Richardson's mind led him to do something new with old materials. The novelty of *Pamela* lay not in the technical materials Richardson used, but in the extent to which he developed them.

When Richardson turned to writing novels he was in an enviable and indeed unique position, compared to earlier English writers of fiction. He enjoyed financial security and was exempted from writing for bread. As early as 1738 he was living in a suburban villa, in prosperous semiretirement. A well-established businessman, Richardson was in a situation which even Fielding, Smollett, and Sterne were unable to enjoy. He could take as much time as he wanted to write a novel, and he was able to plan its outline, expand details, and work it over with minute care until he was satisfied. The writing of *Clarissa* from 1743 to 1747 is an illustration. In his later years he was able to profit from constant (if adulatory) criticism. The contrast between his lot as a writer and that of earlier novelists is clear and striking. As a printer with influential connections among the booksellers, he was able to extract from the publication of his works profits which enormously exceeded anything an ordinary novelist might expect. Richardson was the first modern English novelist to have the opportunity to work as a craftsman and as an artist.

All the money and time in the world, however, could not have produced his novels if he had lacked ability. His first novel may be of questionable value, but *Clarissa* shows the artistic growth he had undergone as a result of hard work and technical experimentation. *Pamela* could have been an "accident"; but Richardson's progress from *Pamela* to *Clarissa* is indisputable proof of his unique artistic abilities. The tech-

nical elaboration and integration of Richardson's masterpiece
were distinctly his own. He brought to English fiction an
artistic endowment greater than had been devoted to it since
Bunyan.

These combined factors of time, devotion, and talent enabled Richardson to make his essential contribution to the
English novel. The previous eighty years had seen the use of
letters in fiction develop to where its technical possibilities
had been exploited to their fullest extent—but one by one. All
stages in the growth of epistolary fiction had been represented, from scattered letters hardly to be called fiction to
true epistolary novels. If improvement was to be made in the
epistolary genre it could not be by fresh innovation, but
rather by a new mastery of existing techniques. Richardson
used nothing—epistolary technique, moral purpose, dramatic
devices, "discoursing"—that others had not used before him.
But he developed all the fictional methods exploited only fit-
fully and tentatively by earlier writers, used them simultane-
ously, and integrated them into long and important works.
The biological maxim that "ontogeny recapitulates phylog-
eny" is very applicable to Richardson's use of the epistolary
method. In progressing from the *Familiar Letters* to *Clarissa*
and to the less intense but even more complex structure of
Grandison, he recapitulated in his own work all the evolu-
tionary developments of his precursors and went beyond
them. His long and meticulous labors and his superior abilities
gave his novels a greater total effect than those of any of his
literary ancestors, because he brought together what had been
scattered. Richardson was a new and better kind of writer;
for this reason he produced a new and better kind of novel.

To show that earlier fiction had anticipated Richardson's
novels in all but their total effect is by no means to minimize
his claims to be the father of the modern English novel; it is
rather to elucidate them. Most of the literary phenomena
which have commonly been associated only with the novels
of Richardson and his followers had existed much earlier. But
the fact of their previous existence makes the impact of Richardson on the English novel all the more impressive. The nature of that impact is precisely described by André Gide's
phrase, "gradations, gradations—and then a sudden leap." The
excellence of Richardson's novels appears more to advantage

in contrast with these early attempts than it does in a literary void. Richardson was not the first to invent or use the materials of the novel in letters; but in a very real sense he created the epistolary novel as we think of it today.

Notes

NOTES TO CHAPTER I

1. *Anatomy of Criticism* (Princeton, 1957), pp. 303–4.

2. The first figure (all fiction) is based on an estimate made from the entries in the Chester Noyes Greenough catalogue of English prose fiction, an unpublished list on cards in the Harvard College Library. Although probably the most comprehensive listing extant, this catalogue needs to be used with caution, since it is derived from the work of a number of contributors and its entries vary in reliability and completeness. The second figure (epistolary fiction) is derived from the information assembled to form the basis of the present study. For the proportion of epistolary fiction to fiction as a whole from 1740 to 1800 (one to six) see Frank G. Black, "The Technique of Letter Fiction in English from 1740 to 1800," *Harvard Studies and Notes in Philology and Literature*, XV (1933), 291.

3. Quoted from an autograph letter now in the British Museum, in Alpheus W. Smith, "Collections and Notes of Prose Fiction in England, 1660–1714" (unpublished Harvard dissertation, 1930), p. xli.

4. See Queenie D. Leavis, *Fiction and the Reading Public* (London, 1932), p. 130; Alan D. McKillop, *Samuel Richardson, Printer and Novelist* (Chapel Hill, N.C., 1936), p. 20; James R. Foster, *A History of the Pre-Romantic Novel in England* (New York, 1949), p. 22.

5. These are chiefly: Charlotte Morgan, *The Rise of the Novel of Manners* (New York, 1911); Godfrey F. Singer, *The Epistolary Novel* (Philadelphia, 1933); Bridget G. MacCarthy, "The Epistolary Form Prior to 1740," in *Women Writers... 1621–1744* (Cork, 1944); and Helen S. Hughes, "English Epistolary Fiction before *Pamela*," *The Manley Anniversary Studies*

in Language and Literature (Chicago, 1923), pp. 156–69. The last is the pioneering work on the subject.

6. These are: Sterg O'Dell, *A Chronological List of Prose Fiction in English . . . 1475–1640* (Cambridge, Mass., 1954); Charles C. Mish, *English Prose Fiction, 1600–1700* (Charlottesville, Va., 1952); William H. McBurney, *A Checklist of English Prose Fiction, 1700–1739* (Cambridge, Mass., 1960).

7. Thus, McBurney does not include sketches, periodical fiction, or pamphlets, for example (see p. ix). The Greenough catalogue mentioned in note 1 is much more comprehensive in its listing. See Appendices B and C, for notes on the contents of periodicals and miscellanies; and the works of Mayo and Wiles cited in note 1, chapter V. Esdaile's *List of English Tales and Prose Romances* (London, 1912), usually given as the standard bibliography, has been superseded by the works mentioned here.

8. New York, 1958 (Everyman paperback), p. 16.

9. An example of this uncertainty is furnished by the history of Mrs Aphra Behn's *Life and Memoirs*, which has been viewed by various writers as pure fact, pure fiction, and, in various proportions, a combination of both. See note 34, chapter IV; and Ernest Bernbaum, *The Mary Carleton Narratives* (Cambridge, Mass., 1914).

10. Shakespeare Head Edition (Oxford, 1929–31), I, xiv.

11. See the discussion of this point in chapter IX. These early novels were often, perhaps usually, read aloud to a group (as in Richardson's well-known account of his reading to the young ladies at their work), and this practice doubtless offered considerable scope for amateur histrionics.

12. By far the best discussion is Alan D. McKillop, "Epistolary Technique in Richardson's Novels," *Rice Institute Pamphlet*, XXXVIII (1951), 36–54.

NOTES TO CHAPTER II

1. For general discussions of most of the works dealt with in this chapter, the reader is referred to the following: Charles E. Kany, *The Beginnings of the Epistolary Novel in France, Italy, and Spain* (Berkeley, Calif., 1937); Rudolph Schevill, *Ovid and the Renascence in Spain* (Berkeley, Calif., 1913); René Pruvost, *Matteo Bandello and Elizabethan Fiction* (Paris, 1937); Thomas P. Haviland, *The Roman de Longue Haleine on English Soil* (Philadelphia, 1931); Samuel L. Wolff, *The Greek Romances in Elizabethan Prose Fiction* (New York, 1912); Ernest A. Baker, *The History of the English Novel* (10 vols., London, 1924–39), II, III; Dale Randall, *The Golden Tapestry* (Durham, N.C., 1963); Margaret Schlauch, *The Early English Novel* (London, 1963).

The successive editions in which these works appeared in England are recorded in O'Dell, *A Chronological List of Prose Fiction in English . . . 1475–1640;* and Mish, *English Prose Fiction, 1600–1700.*

2. This last is the *Collection des papiers de Barluze,* in the Bibliothèque Nationale. Of medieval romances using letters, the most notable were *Amadis de Gaule* and, of course, *Troilus and Criseyde.*

3. Grant Showerman, tr. and ed., *Ovid: Heroides and Amores,* Loeb Classical Library (New York, 1914), pp. 157–59; 281; 293–95.

4. See Morris P. Tilley, "*Euphues* and Ovid's Heroical Epistles," *MLN,* XLV (1930), 301–8.

5. "Prefatory Discourse," pp. iii-vii. He also quotes Scaliger and Heinsius on Ovid and the heroid.

6. Sig. G2ᵛ (edition of 1540).

7. *The Pretie and Wittie Historie of Arnalt & Lucenda* (1575), sigs. C 1–C 1ᵛ; M3ᵛ. I have expanded words abbreviated in the text. This novel appears in the 1575 version as a phrase book, with facing pages in English and Italian, the translation being by "Claudius Hollyband" (Claude Desainliens).

8. For a general discussion, see Howard J. Savage, "The Beginning of Italian Influence in English Prose Fiction," *PMLA,* XXXII (1917), 1–21. The original work, written in 1444, may be regarded as the first scandal novel, since it dealt with an actual amour of Count Schlick, who came to Siena in 1432 in the train of the Emperor Sigismund. Piccolomini was at the time a member of the emperor's suite.

9. Samuel Putnam, tr. (2 vols., New York, 1949), I, 276 (ch. XXXII).

10. Frederick J. Furnivall, ed., *Robert Laneham's Letter,* New Shakespeare Society Publications, Series VI, No. 14 (London, 1887), p. 30.

11. See George B. Parks, "Before *Euphues,*" *Joseph Quincy Adams Memorial Studies,* ed. James G. McManaway et al. (Washington, D.C., 1948), pp. 475–93.

12. R. Warwick Bond, ed., *The Complete Works of John Lyly* (3 vols., Oxford, 1902), I, 142, 161.

13. Henry H. Gibbs, ed., *The Historie of Plasidas,* a collation of the three earliest editions of *Eurialus* (London, 1873), pp. 142–43; Morris W. Croll and Harry Clemons, eds., *Euphues* (New York, 1916), pp. 342–46.

14. See Alexander B. Grosart, ed., *The Life and Complete Works of Robert Greene* (15 vols., 1881–86), II, 102–3; Croll and Clemons, p. 360.

15. From Whetstone's *Heptameron of Civil Discourses* (1582), sig. K1.

16. Part I, pp. 73–82.

17. Paul Dottin, ed., *Robinson Crusoe Examin'd and Criticiz'd* (London and Paris, 1923), pp. 71–72.

18. For a brief discussion see Charles C. Mish, ed., *Short Fiction of the Seventeenth Century* (New York, Anchor, 1963), pp. 195–97. *Gods Revenge* grew larger and more interesting. In 1661 it was pirated as *Blood for Blood;* the "Sixth Edition" of 1679 incorporated a new section of ten histories dealing with the punishment of adulterers; in 1685 a section called *The Triumphs of Chastity*, by Thomas Wright, was added. By 1688 the work had become *The Glory of God's Revenge Against the ... Sins of Murther and Adultery.... To Which Are Annexed, The Triumphs of Friendship and Chastity.... The Whole Illustrated with about Fifty Elegant Epistles, Relating to Love and Gallantry.*

19. *The Triumphs of God's Revenge* (1670), p. 332.

20. *Ibid.*, sig. b1.

21. See Pepys's diary entries for December 7, 1660, and May 12, 1666; *Spectator*, No. 37 on "Leonora's Library"; Scott's Note VI to *Old Mortality;* and *The Works of Mrs. Chapone* (4 vols., Boston, 1809), I, 25–26.

22. See Haviland, pp. 50–54, 152–78. *Cléopâtre* has 22 histories; *Ibrahim*, 15; *Pharamond*, 20; *Clélie*, 15; *Le Grand Cyrus*, 32. An example of how a French "history" might become an English "novel" is furnished by *Lindamira* (1702), in which the episode of the jealous Octavius is adapted from the history of Leontidas in *Artamenes; or, The Grand Cyrus* (1690–91). See Benjamin Boyce, ed., *The Adventures of Lindamira* (Minneapolis, 1949), p. viii.

23. D'Urfé's *Astrée* in the French edition of 1638. *Astrée* contains 129 letters, *Cyrus* 117, *Clélie* 121, and *Almahide* 116.

24. See Louis B. Wright, *Middle-Class Culture in Elizabethan England* (Chapel Hill, N.C., 1935), pp. 105–20.

25. For a survey of changes in prose fiction in general, see Benjamin Boyce, "The Effect of the Restoration on Prose Fiction," *Tennessee Studies in Literature*, VI (1961), 77–83.

NOTES TO CHAPTER III

1. We should perhaps except the epistolary *Tatlers* and *Spectators*.

2. *The Modern World Disrob'd* (1708), p. 16.

3. Wing L 1115; preface, pages unnumbered.

4. Wing L 40; preface, pages unnumbered.

5. These were Mme Ferrand's *Lettres de Cléante et de Bélise,* Boursault's *Lettres de Babet* and *Treize lettres amoureuses,* and the anonymous *Commerce galant.* For a general discussion of these see Kany, pp. 117–26.

6. For this estimate see William H. McBurney, "Formative Influences on the English Novel, 1700–1740" (unpublished Harvard dissertation, 1948), p. 37.

7. Sig. A8.

8. In *The History of Hypolitus, Earl of Douglas* (1741), sig. O 10.

9. *Letters Writ by a Turkish Spy* (8 vols., 1753), VI, sigs. A4–A4^v.

10. From the second edition, reissued in Mrs. Haywood's *Works* (1724), pp. iv–v.

11. The most notable discussion of the subject at this time was Dryden's famous prefatory essay to *Ovid's Epistles* (1680).

12. See Benjamin Boyce, *Tom Brown of Facetious Memory* (Cambridge, Mass., 1939), p. 94, for this and other examples.

13. *The Works of Mr. Thomas Brown* (4 vols., 1719–20), I, 192.

14. See Nos. 18, 21, and 26 in Appendix A.

15. See Antonio G. Rodrigues, *Marianna Alcoforado: História e crítica de uma fraude literária* (Coimbra, 1943), pp. 131–49, for a census of editions.

16. See Nos. 43 and 101 in Appendix A.

17. For discussions of the history, criticism, and influence of the *Lettres,* see Rodrigues; Kany; Max von Waldberg, *Der empfindsame Roman in Frankreich* (Strassburg and Berlin, 1906), ch. 2; Frederick C. Green, "Who Was the Author of the 'Lettres Portugaises'?" *MLR,* XXI (1926), 159–67, and my article, "Madame d'Aulnoy on the *Lettres Portugaises,*" *MLN,* LXVII (1952), 544–46.

18. Page 74.

19. *Five Love-Letters from a Nun to a Cavalier, with the Cavalier's Answers* (1714), pp. 32–41, *passim.*

20. Examples of such comments are given in Chapter VI.

21. See Rodrigues, pp. 67–69; he postulates that the *Lettres* may ultimately have been based on actual ones.

22. *Five Love-Letters,* pp. 53, 72.

23. See Charlotte Charrier, *Héloïse dans l'histoire et dans la légende* (Paris, 1933), p. 446.

24. Honnor Morten, ed., *The Love Letters of Abelard and Heloise* (London, 1937; a reprint of the edition of 1722), pp. 34, 35, 37, 60, 76.

25. Morten, ed., *Abelard and Heloise*, p. 84.

26. See his preface to Hughes's *Poems on Several Occasions* (1735), p. xxxiii.

27. It has been persuasively argued that Marana is the author of the entire work, the MS of Vols. II–VIII having been procured directly from him, translated by Bradshaw, and issued for the first time as an English translation in London. See William H. McBurney, "The Authorship of the *Turkish Spy*," *PMLA*, LXXII (1957), 915–35; Joseph E. Tucker, "On the Authorship of the *Turkish Spy: An État Présent*," *PBSA*, LII (1958), 34–47. The Greenough catalogue records seventeen appearances of the work in part or complete before 1740, for eight different booksellers. Some of the changes in booksellers may represent the legal transfer of copy, but the *Spy*'s popularity and the relaxed state of the copyright laws make it unlikely that they all do.

28. *Letters Writ by a Turkish Spy* (8 vols., 1753), I, i–iii.

29. See John R. Moore, *A Checklist of the Writings of Daniel Defoe* (Bloomington, Ind., 1960), Item No. 406. Defoe's *Letters*, ed. G. H. Healey (Oxford, 1955), p. 38, has a passage indicating more than a slight knowledge of the book, in a letter to Harley.

30. See Nos. 44, 110, 113, 192, 200, and 201 in Appendix A.

31. R. Foulché-Delbosc, ed., *Madame d'Aulnoy: Travels into Spain* (London, 1930), pp. 51, 55–56. (General discussion of the work, with a reprint of the English translation of 1692.)

32. See Paul B. Anderson, "Mary Delariviere Manley, a Cavalier's Daughter in Grub Street" (unpublished Harvard dissertation, 1931), pp. 144–45.

33. *Letters, Written by Mrs. Manley* (1713), p. 29.

34. *Loves Empire* (English translation of 1682), pp. 25 ff.

35. *Ibid.*, p. 79.

36. W. Moy Thomas, ed., *The Letters and Works of Lady Mary Wortley Montagu* (2 vols., New York, 1893), I, 144, 151.

37. *Letters from a Lady at Paris to a Lady at Avignon* (1716), sig. A3.

38. *Letters of the Marchioness de M*** to the Count de R**** (1735), p. 303.

NOTES TO CHAPTER IV

1. *In Miscellanies . . . by the Honourable Lady Margaret Pennyman* (1740).

2. See, for example, John Chamberlayne, *Magnae Britanniae Notitia* (1673), p. 188.

3. See Nos. 65, 68, 88, and 112 in Appendix B. For general information on epistolary manuals and on the place of letter

writing in English literature, see Katherine G. Hornbeak, "The Complete Letter-Writer in English, 1568–1800," *Smith College Studies in Modern Languages*, XV (1934), 1–150; Jean Robertson, *The Art of Letter Writing* (London, 1942); William H. Irving, *The Providence of Wit in the English Letter Writers* (Durham, N.C., 1955).

4. See Boyce, *Tom Brown*, p. 91, and Nos. 88 and 123 in Appendix B.

5. *A Poste*, in Alexander B. Grosart, ed., *The Works in Verse and Prose of Nicholas Breton* (2 vols., London, 1879), II [4].

6. John Massinger, tr., *The Secretary in Fashion* (1640), sigs. a2–a2ᵛ.

7. *A Poste*, pp. 49–50. (Bk. II, Letters 59 and 60.)

8. *Ibid.*, pp. 19–20 (I, 53, 54); pp. 25–26 (I, 78–81); p. 7.

9. Reprinted in Alan D. McKillop, *The Early Masters of English Fiction* (Lawrence, Kansas, 1962), pp. 47–51 (see p. 50).

10. Such are Letters 15–21, 91–93, 54–55, 51–52, 1–6, 105–8, and 161–65.

11. See McKillop, *Samuel Richardson*, p. 21.

12. *The Quakers Art of Courtship* (issue of 1710), p. 131.

13. *Ibid.*, pp. 45, 137; p. 37; p. 44.

14. *Brutes Turn'd Criticks* (1695), p. 7; p. 9; p. 13.

15. *Loves Missives to Virtue* (1660), sigs. A1ᵛ–A3ᵛ.

16. *Ibid.*, pp. 24, 27, 32.

17. *CCXI Sociable Letters* (1664), sigs. C2–C2ᵛ.

18. *Ibid.*, p. 142.

19. *Ibid.*, sig. C2. For a general discussion of the work, see Henry T. Perry, *The First Duchess of Newcastle* (Boston, 1918), pp. 248–51.

20. *Coll. H. Marten's Familiar Letters* (1662), p. 8.

21. See the articles on Marten and Gayton in *DNB*.

22. *Works* (4 vols., 1719–20), II, 58–62, 39–40, 151–52, 296–302, and 302–11; and see Boyce, *Tom Brown*, pp. 153–69.

23. See Nos. 57, 65, 70, and 112 in Appendix B.

24. *Athenian Mercury*, VIII, No. 18 (Oct. 29, 1692).

25. *The Post-Boy Rob'd of his Mail* (1706), pp. 391, 474.

26. *Ibid.*, pp. 392–410, 474–86.

27. See Charles Stonehill, ed., *The Complete Works of George Farquhar* (2 vols., London, 1930), I, xxi–xxii; John W. Bowyer, *The Celebrated Mrs. Centlivre* (Durham, N.C., 1952), pp. 15–31, for further details on Farquhar's letters.

28. *The Post-Boy Rob'd*, p. 330.

29. *Familiar Letters of Love, Gallantry, and Several Occasions* (2 vols., 1724), I, 172.

30. *The Post-Boy Rob'd*, pp. 332, 334, 325, 482.

31. See Paul B. Anderson, "Mary Delariviere Manley," pp. 144–57; "Mistress Delariviere Manley's Biography," *MP*, XXXIII (1935–36), 270–72.

32. See Paul B. Anderson, "Delariviere Manley's Prose Fiction," *PQ*, XIII (1934), 170. The first twenty-four letters were bound up with Mme d'Aulnoy's *Memoirs of the Court of England*, the remainder with the same lady's *History of the Earl of Warwick*. In 1711 all forty-one letters appeared, pirated, as *Court Intrigues*.

33. *The Lady's Pacquet Broke Open* (1707), Letters 23, 34–37. Letter 34 refers to Steele's *Christian Hero* as just completed.

34. The most up-to-date account of the *Life and Memoirs* (though its conclusion on the authorship differs from the above) is in W. J. Cameron, *New Light on Aphra Behn* (Auckland, 1961), pp. 87–100.

35. See No. 119 in Appendix B.

36. "I know not how it is, but this Collection seems to me far beyond that which I gave the Town with Success some Years ago under the Name of . . . *The Post-Boy Rob'd of his Mail*." (*The Post-Man Robb'd* [1719], p. xiv.)

37. The convention of the familiar letter dominated periodicals as well, from the *Gentleman's Journal* (1692–94), which was "by way of letter to a gentleman in the country," to the innumerable periodicals of the 1720's and later, with their letters to the editor. A large proportion of these letters were, of course, not authentic, and many were of high quality as fiction, the *Tatler* and *Spectator* containing notable examples. See Appendix C for a selection of representative pieces of epistolary fiction in periodicals; see also the discussions in Richmond P. Bond, *Studies in the Early English Periodical* (Chapel Hill, N.C., 1957), and Natascha Würzbach, *Die Struktur des Briefromans und seine Entstehung in England* (Munich, 1964), pp. 109–36.

NOTES TO CHAPTER V

1. The reader is referred to the following works, in which some of the general information summarized in this chapter is discussed in detail: Marjorie Plant, *The English Book Trade* (London, 1939); John Ashton, *Social Life in the Reign of Queen Anne* (London, 1883); James R. Sutherland, "The Circulation of Newspapers and Literary Periodicals, 1700–1730," *The Library*, Fourth Series, XV (1934–35), 110–24; Arthur S. Collins, *Authorship in the Days of Johnson* (London, 1927); Harry Ransom, "The Rewards of Authorship in the Eighteenth Century," *University of Texas Studies in English* (1938), pp. 47–66; Roy M. Wiles, *Serial Publication in England before 1750* (Cambridge,

1957), and "Prose Fiction in English Periodicals before 1750" (unpublished Harvard dissertation, 1933); McBurney, "Formative Influences on the English Novel," ch. I; Ralph Straus, *The Unspeakable Curll* (London, 1927); Robert D. Mayo, *The English Novel in the Magazines, 1740–1815* (Evanston, Ill., 1962), ch. I; Alexandre Beljame, *Men of Letters and the English Public in the Eighteenth Century*, ed. Dobrée (London, 1948).

2. See Collins, pp. 234, 240; Sutherland, pp. 111–13.

3. This estimate takes into account, among other things, that women might be more likely than men to read novels and less likely to buy them, and that the public for fiction and for nonfiction was by no means the same.

4. The following prices (per part or per volume) for works of epistolary fiction have been found in the books examined. Five items are listed at 6*d.*, thirty-three at 1*s.*, nineteen at 1*s.* 6*d.*, twelve at 2*s.*, fourteen at 2*s.* 6*d.*, eight at 3*s.*, one at 3*s.* 6*d.*, seven at 4*s.*, eleven at 5*s.*, and four at 6*s.* Many of the items carry no indication of price whatever, and fuller information might change the picture. Bound volumes seem in general to have cost 6*d.* more than the same volumes sewed.

5. This was *The Weekly Novelist*, started in 1735 by J. Watson, a printer.

6. *The Visions of Quevedo* (1677), p. 188.

7. Vol. IV (1734), 489. The letter is reprinted from the *Grub-Street Journal*, No. 247 (September 1734).

8. See Mayo, pp. 60–66; Wiles, "Prose Fiction," p. 41. The parts of Mrs. Behn's book came out every Monday at 4*d.*, "four sheets in Folio, stitch'd in Blue Paper."

9. See Wiles, "Prose Fiction," bibliography, and Appendix C.

10. *Letters and Works*, II, 200.

11. See George F. Whicher, *The Life and Romances of Mrs. Eliza Haywood* (New York, 1915), p. 191.

12. Among those listed were Aaron Hill, Mrs. Jane Barker the novelist, George Bubb (later Dodington), Osborne (the bookseller?), and an undersecretary of state, Charles De La Faye. The book cost them 3*s.* in quires and 5*s.* bound.

13. A copy of this undated pamphlet is in the Harvard College Library. Mrs. Boyd's novel appeared in 1732; subscribers paid half-a-crown down and an equal amount on delivery of the book in sheets.

14. Shaftesbury sarcastically mentioned "our favourite novels: those dear, sweet, natural pieces, writ most of them by the fair sex themselves." See *Characteristics*, ed., J. M. Robertson (2 vols., London, 1900), II, 11; I, 222–25. Swift knew Mrs. Manley well from their work on the *Examiner*, and as a scandal novelist,

whether or not he read her novels; Pope's remarks on Mrs. Haywood in the *Dunciad* indicate at least a general familiarity with her novels. There is no reason to suppose that men of wit necessarily refrained from dipping into works of which they did not approve.

15. A copy of the sale catalogue of Defoe's library is in the British Museum.

16. He also liked Voiture's letters, Farquhar's epistolary *Love and Business*, and the *Turkish Spy*. See William Matthews, ed., *The Diary of Dudley Ryder: 1715–1716* (London, 1939), pp. 209–11, 44, 47, 290, 125, 164, 168.

17. See Benjamin Boyce, "Pope, Gildon, and Salamanders," *N&Q*, CXCIV (1949), 14.

18. These poems are most conveniently accessible as quoted in Whicher, pp. 16–17.

19. No. 139 (Feb. 28, 1710).

20. No. 128 (July 27, 1711).

21. Quoted in Helen S. Hughes, *The Gentle Hertford* (New York, 1940), p. 142.

22. She is the author of the five letters signed "Cleora" in Mrs. Rowe's *Letters Moral and Entertaining* (1729–33).

23. *Letters and Works*, I, 144–46, 151, 264; II, 205.

24. These were so highly regarded that selections from them went into Arthur Masson's *A Collection of Prose and Verse*, widely used as a grammar-school reader. See Joyce Hemlow, *The History of Fanny Burney* (Oxford, 1958), pp. 18–19.

25. The information on which these conclusions are based relates mostly to the early eighteenth century. The public of the late seventeenth century probably did not differ greatly, but must have been somewhat smaller, more closely centered around London and the court, and less moralistic.

26. See Plant, p. 94. A total of about five hundred editions or issues can be traced for epistolary fiction in the period covered by this study.

27. For example, a tribute to the power of Mrs. Haywood came in 1727 with the appearance of a chapbook called *The Pleasant and Delightful History of Gillian of Croydon*, which was eye-catchingly described on its title page as being "done much after the same Method, as those celebrated Novels, By Mrs. ELIZA HAYWOOD."

28. About 1730 the production of novels in general declined rather rapidly; the public also seems to have changed its tastes suddenly at this time, preferring fiction more moralistic and decorous than before. See note 2, Chapter IX. (A possible alternative explanation is that Mrs. Haywood, as Mrs. Manley had done, "went into keeping.")

29. Mrs. Manley's first two plays failed in 1696; Mrs. Haywood more or less gave up writing for the stage in 1720. Mrs. Behn's epilogue to *Romulus and Hersilia* (1682) caused her arrest, but whether any action was taken against her is unknown. However, in the early 1680's a serious decline in the production of new plays took place, perhaps because attendance at the theaters was falling off. See Alfred Harbage, *Annals of English Drama* (Philadelphia, 1940), pp. 144–47.

30. See the preface to Mrs. Davys' *Works* (1725), and Eu. Hood, "Literary Contracts," *Gentleman's Magazine*, XCIV (1824), 318, 410.

31. See Collins, p. 244.

32. Ashton, p. 305.

33. See the *Tatler*, No. 101; George Woodcock, *The Incomparable Aphra* (London, 1948), p. 169 (quoting a letter from Mrs. Behn in 1684, begging the bookseller Tonson for better terms); Whicher, pp. 21–22; and Anderson, "Mary Delariviere Manley," p. 274, quoting a letter to Harley.

34. Anderson, "Mistress Delariviere Manley's Biography," p. 269.

35. Dedication to *The Fatal Secret* (1724).

36. See the articles on Elizabeth Rowe and Catherine (Trotter) Cockburn in *DNB*.

37. See the introduction to *The Adventures of Lindamira*, ed. Boyce, on the hypothetical author (or translator). Mrs. Trotter sometimes lived in genteel poverty with her widowed mother, but the success of her play *Agnes de Castro* (1696) must have helped her considerably, and there is no evidence that she worked as a hack. Mrs. Davys kept a coffeehouse in Cambridge, and all her works were published by subscription; the widow of the Rev. Peter Davys, a friend of Swift's, she was long acquainted with Swift, who sometimes helped her financially. See William H. McBurney, "Mrs. Mary Davys, Forerunner of Fielding," *PMLA*, LXXIV (1959), 348–55.

NOTES TO CHAPTER VI

1. Dryden briefly mentions "the novels of Boccace" in the preface to the *Fables* and the dedication of the *Aeneis*. Congreve's preface to his novel *Incognita*, though of value, is more of an apology for writing fiction than a critical essay.

2. See Joseph B. Heidler, *The History, from 1700 to 1800, of English Criticism of Prose Fiction*, University of Illinois Studies in Language and Literature, XIII, No. 2 (Urbana, 1928); and Arthur J. Tieje, "The Expressed Aim of the Long Prose Fiction from 1579 to 1740," *JEGP*, XI (1912), 402–32; "A Peculiar Phase of the Theory of Realism in Pre-Richardsonian Fiction," *PMLA*,

XXVIII (1913), 213–52; *The Theory of Characterization in Prose Fiction Prior to 1740*, University of Minnesota Studies in Language and Literature, V (Minneapolis, 1916).

3. Samuel Croxall's *A Select Collection of Novels* (6 vols., 1722), I, A7ᵛ–A8. The *Essai sur l'origine des romans* (1670) of the learned Bishop Huet of Avranches, which prefaces Croxall's collection, may be called the pioneering critical work on prose fiction. Translated anonymously into English in 1672 and by Stephen Lewis in 1715, it was highly regarded throughout the eighteenth century.

4. Advertisement for Mrs. Rowe's *Friendship in Death* and *Letters Moral and Entertaining*, listed under "Books just Published for T. Worrall" in *Friendship in Death* (4th ed.; 1733).

5. See Tieje, *Theory of Characterization*, pp. 39, 42, 61–63.

6. Several of Mrs. Haywood's nonepistolary works, and novels of her contemporaries and followers, do contain passages in which some attempt is made to describe the thoughts or feelings of a character in a crisis at length and in a detailed, analytical manner. Infrequent, brief, and poorly done, these do not command the important place in the work as a whole which inserted letters assume. The same observation may be made of similar passages in the works of Defoe, if the purely religious and moralizing elements of a distressed character's thoughts are removed.

7. While Richardson may not have read frivolous novels, such a busy printer could not have been unaware of the commoner fictional techniques of the day. See Alan D. McKillop, "Supplementary Notes on Richardson as a Printer," *Studies in Bibliography*, XII (1959), 214–18, and William M. Sale, Jr., *Samuel Richardson: Master Printer* (Ithaca, N.Y., 1950), pp. 145–250.

8. As in *Love-Letters Between a Nobleman and His Sister*, *Letters from the Marchioness de M*** to the Count de R****, *The King of Pirates*, and *The Secret History of White-Hall*.

9. Thus, Mrs. Behn was Astrea, Mrs. Martha Fowke Clio, Mrs. Elizabeth Thomas Corinna, Katherine Philips Orinda, Mrs. Centlivre Astrea; their gallants were Lycidus, Lysander, Strephon, Pylades, Poliarchus, Celadon, and so forth.

10. Page 1.

11. Sigs. A3ᵛ, A5, A7–A7ᵛ.

12. *Ibid.*, pp. 84–87.

13. *Ibid.*, p. 100.

14. *Ibid.*, p. 103.

15. It appeared in the *London Gazette*, December 2–6, 1703. The letter from Leeuwenhoek was taken from the *Philosophical Transactions*, as Defoe is careful to acknowledge.

16. *The Post-Boy Rob'd of his Mail* (1692), sigs. A6–A6ᵛ.

17. *The Post-Boy Rob'd*, sigs. A4ʳ–A5.

18. The advertisement is quoted above.

19. *Memoirs of the Court of England* (1707), preface (unnumbered).

20. *Love-Letters Between a Nobleman and His Sister* ("Seventh Edition," 2 vols., 1759), I, A6ᵛ. Similar elaborate accounts of finding letters or taking copies are in *An Account of the Secret Services of M. de Vernay* (1683) and *The Cabinet Open'd* (1690), supposedly the stolen letters of Mme de Maintenon, as well as *Love Letters . . . Mr. Wilson* (1723).

21. *Letters Writ by a Turkish Spy* (13th ed.; 8 vols., 1753), I, a4.

22. *Ibid.*, III, A5ᵛ–A6. The same device is found in other novels, notably *Love-Letters Between Polydorus . . . and Messalina* (1689), p. 19.

23. *Ibid.*, I, xvi.

24. Sigs. A3, A3ᵛ–A5ᵛ, A6ᵛ.

25. *Ibid.*, sig. A6. "History," it must be remembered, means "true account, accurate reporting."

26. Sig. A3.

27. The "letter," entitled *A New Vision of the Lady Gr—s* [Grey's], appeared in 1682. A footnote in the *Monthly Review*, I (1749), 394, ascribes the book to Mrs. Behn as a matter of common knowledge. On Lord Grey see the recent biography *Cold Caleb* by Cecil Price (London, 1956).

28. From *The Postmaster*, No. 219 (March 26, 1725).

29. See Boyce, ed., *Lindamira*, pp. xii–xiii.

30. *Letters from a Lady at Paris to a Lady at Avignon* (1716), sigs. A2–A3.

31. *The Life of Marianne* (1735), sig. B1.

32. *The Secret History of Queen Zarah* (1705), sigs. A5ᵛ–a3.

33. *Ibid.*, sigs. a2ᵛ–a3ᵛ; a5–a5ᵛ.

34. *Five Love-Letters from a Nun to a Cavalier, with the Cavalier's Answers* ("Third Edition," 1714), sig. A2ᵛ.

35. *The Post-Boy Rob'd of His Mail* (1706), p. 410; *The Compleat Library* (July 1692).

36. *Love-Letters from King Henry VIII to Anne Boleyn* (1714), p. xiii.

37. Page viii.

38. *Familiar Letters of Love, Gallantry, and Several Occasions* (2 vols., 1724), I, 218. The translation is ascribed here to L'Estrange, and differs considerably from John Hughes's more correct version. It had appeared in Vol. II of *Letters of Love and Gallantry* (1694), and figured on the title page as "the Nun's Letter to a Monk."

39. *Letters of Abelard and Heloise* (1713), sigs. A3–A5ᵛ. It should be remembered that this version had been altered into pseudofiction; the reader would have found it little different from the ordinary "true history" in letters.

40. *Ibid.*, pp. 129, 155, 175.

41. Pages xiv–xv.

42. Pages 6–7, 13–15 of "Discourse." The poem Mrs. Haywood had read somewhere was probably the anonymous "In Praise of LETTERS" in Mrs. Jane Barker's *Poetical Recreations* (1688), pp. 131–33. It had been composed by lifting lines from the poem by Howell quoted above and transposing them, with a few couplets added.

43. *Ibid.*, pp. 7, 10 of text.

44. *Love-Letters Between a Nobleman and His Sister*, I, 229, 284, 314.

45. *The Fair Concubine* (1732), p. 38.

46. *The British Recluse*, in Mrs. Haywood's *Secret Histories, Novels, and Poems* (4th ed.; 4 vols., 1742), II, 49.

47. *Memoirs of the Court of England* (1707), p. 371. "Those" are the letters of the Portuguese Nun.

48. *Spectator*, No. 397 (June 5, 1712).

49. *Tatler*, No. 87 (Oct. 29, 1709). See also his comments on the moving qualities of letters in No. 82 (Oct. 18, 1709) and *Spectator*, No. 322 (March 10, 1712).

50. *Familiar Letters of Love, Gallantry, and Several Occasions*, I, 99.

51. *Tatler*, No. 30 (June 18, 1709).

52. Notable examples are Richardson's own preface to the 1759 edition of *Clarissa;* Warburton's preface, printed in the fourth volume of the first edition; and Mrs. Donellan's letter to Richardson of September 25, 1750, in *The Correspondence of Samuel Richardson*, ed. Anna L. Barbauld (6 vols., London, 1804), IV, 32.

53. "Journ. Liter." apparently refers to the *Journal littéraire*, published at the Hague, 1729–36. The "Chevalier de Her—" is Fontenelle.

54. *Letters from the Marchioness de M**** (1735), sigs. A2–A4.

55. *Ibid.*, pp. 1–3.

56. Leavis, pp. 104–5.

57. See the plot summaries of letter novels in the following chapters.

58. Paul van Tieghem, "La Sensibilité et la passion dans le roman européen au XVIIIᵉ siècle," *RLC*, VI (1926), 424–35.

59. The phrase is Lady Mary Wortley Montagu's (*Letters and Works*, II, 285).

60. *Seven Portuguese Letters* (1681), p. 37.

61. *Letters from a Lady of Quality*, p. 9 of "Discourse."

62. On Richardson's successors see Frank G. Black, *The Epistolary Novel in the Late Eighteenth Century* (Eugene, Ore., 1940).

63. See Joyce M. Horner, *The English Women Novelists and Their Connection with the Feminist Movement, Smith College Studies in Modern Languages*, XI, Nos. 1–3 (Northampton, Mass., 1929–30); Bridget G. MacCarthy, *Women Writers . . . 1621–1744;* Ian Watt, *The Rise of the Novel* (London, 1957), pp. 298–99, 151–52.

64. For similar findings in other literary areas, see Raymond D. Havens, "Romantic Aspects of the Age of Pope," *PMLA*, XXVII (1912), 297–324; Helen S. Hughes, "A Romantic Correspondence of the Year 1729," *MP*, XXXVII (1939–40), 187–200; Harko G. De Maar, *A History of Modern English Romanticism* (1924; repr. New York, 1964).

NOTES TO CHAPTER VII

1. *Lucres* (discussed above) became *The Art of Love: or, The Amours of Count Schlick* (1708). *Euphues* appeared as *Euphues and Lucilla* (1716) and *The False Friend and Inconstant Mistress* (1718 and later).

2. *The Countess of Salisbury* (translated in 1683 by Ferrand Spence from a French *nouvelle historique*) is an example of the characteristic use of letters in plotting. Edward III, in love with the countess, arranges a truce so that her husband may visit her and writes a letter explaining the noble disinterest of his love. The earl finds this letter and suspects an intrigue. The jealous countess of Stafford drops a forged letter to herself from the king, saying that the countess of Salisbury means nothing to him, where she can see it. Meanwhile, the king writes to Salisbury again, regretting that he cannot visit her. The forgery is finally revealed, and everyone is happy. Though letters are so important to the plot, there are only three in the story.

3. The heroine of Mrs. Haywood's *Philidore and Placentia* (1727) fears to declare her love to the hero because she believes him to be a servant. Since "paper cannot blush," as Mrs. Haywood had observed, Placentia resorts to letters.

4. See McKillop, "Epistolary Technique in Richardson's Novels," pp. 46–47, for additional discussion of this point. Feminine curiosity and the lending of files of letters inevitably gen-

erate less tension and reader interest than the attempts of an imprisoned heroine to communicate with the outside world and secure help and advice.

5. *The Court of Caramania* (1727), pp. 79–80. A manuscript "key" identifies Marmillio in the Harvard University copy.

6. Timante, the hero, enters Araminte's bedroom as she is about to have a "Glister," her maid having been called away, and administers it himself without reflecting on the consequences.

7. *Love-Letters Between a Nobleman and His Sister* ("Seventh Edition," 2 vols., 1759), I, 116, 260–74.

8. Of particular interest are Mrs. Behn's *The Unfortunate Bride, The Lucky Mistake, The Nun: or The Perjur'd Beauty,* and Mrs. Haywood's *Cleomelia.* In this last, at least half of which is in letters, the narrative of seduction, betrayal, disgrace, return of the abandoned but still faithful Heartlove to Cleomelia, the death of her betrayer, and her eventual happy marriage, is told twice over; once briskly and objectively in the narrative skeleton, and once emotionally and subjectively in the passionate letters of Cleomelia and Heartlove. Moreover, Cleomelia forces Heartlove to write her letters which falsify his real feelings, so that she may show them about as evidence.

9. For example, *Alexis and Sylvia,* the second novel in Costeker's *The Constant Lovers* (1731), an extremely dull and inept story of distressed lovers, contains thirty-three letters scattered through it at intervals of a few pages. They have little to do with the story and seem to have been inserted quite mechanically in deference to convention.

10. Of course there were exceptions. Nashe's *Unfortunate Traveller,* Mrs. Behn's *Oroonoko,* and the novels of Defoe are well-known examples of early fiction whose texture is unified in this manner.

11. This lack of realistic dialogue is also strikingly apparent when the pages of the earlier novels are compared with those of Fielding, Smollett, or even Richardson, all of whom make frequent use of short speeches and animated scenes.

12. *Secret Histories, Novels, and Poems* (4th ed.; 4 vols., 1742), I, 73. Note the easy nonchalance with which D'Elmont and Mrs. Haywood shrug off one set of emotions and take up another.

13. *Philidore and Placentia* (1727), p. 29.

14. See Whicher, pp. 53–55, 49–52; Baker, *History of the English Novel,* III, 98; Anderson, "Delariviere Manley's Prose Fiction," pp. 175–88. Even in such analytical passages letters sometimes had considerable importance. The passage in *The Fatal Secret* discussed by Whicher (*Secret Histories,* III, 209–23) is

devoted to analysis of the alteration in the heroine Anadea's feelings toward the handsome De Blessure; it includes three pairs of letters. De Blessure fervently pleads his cause, while the burden of Anadea's letters changes from hostile rejection to reluctant acceptance. Her feelings when writing and receiving the letters are described in detail.

15. Mrs. Haywood's title page claims that the stories in the book were originally written in Spanish [sic] by "Ban Dello." The plot of this story does not resemble the argument of any of Bandello's tales.

16. *The Power of Love* (1720), pp. 183–84. The story is the forty-second in Painter, the fifth in Boaistuau, to whose version Mrs. Manley's text is closer.

17. *The Disguis'd Prince* (1728), p. 5. Here Mrs. Haywood renders Préchac's sense accurately, but amplifies his wording.

18. It seems to have been a weapon used in Mrs. Haywood's feud with Swift and Pope. See my article, "An Anonymous Attack on Swift," *N&Q*, CC (1955), 530–32, and John R. Elwood, "Swift's 'Corinna,' " *ibid.*, pp. 529–30.

19. *Some Memoirs of the Amours . . .* (1730), p. 31.

20. *Ibid.*, pp. 47–59.

21. *Cleomelia: or, The Generous Mistress* (1727), p. 21.

22. *A Patch-Work Screen for the Ladies* (1723), sigs. a1–a1ᵛ.

23. *Some Memoirs of the Amours*, pp. 44–45.

24. *Ibid.*, p. 46.

25. It is quoted below.

26. *Some Memoirs of the Amours*, p. 34.

27. See Parks, "Before *Euphues*," p. 490. Specifically, Pettie's collection was so described.

28. *God's Revenge Against . . . Adultery* (London, 1821), p. 92.

29. *Memoirs of a Certain Island* (2 vols., 1726), I, 140–42. A manuscript "key" identifies Bellario as Budgell in the copy at Harvard University.

30. See Lawrence E. Bowling, "What Is the Stream of Consciousness Technique?," *PMLA*, LXV (1950), 338–39; Parks, p. 478; McKillop, *Samuel Richardson*, pp. 37–38.

31. *Secret Histories*, I, 193–94. Note that Mrs. Haywood frequently lapses into rough blank verse in this passage. This failing, very often found in her letters, strongly suggests that she is associating them with the ranting speeches of the stage; see below. The proportion of letters increases as this story progresses: Part I has only four, used for plotting; Part II has six; Part III has twenty.

32. *Some Memoirs of the Amours*, p. 41.

33. *Ibid.*, pp. 32–34, 70–71.

34. See Black, "The Technique of Letter Fiction in English from 1740 to 1800," pp. 297–98; and the letter of the Marchioness de M*** quoted above. Compare also Sterne's celebrated account of the death of Le Fever in *Tristram Shandy*. (Sterne owned Crébillon's work, as the sale catalogue of his library indicates.)

35. *Stories Moral and Comical* (1706), p. 186. The story is the thirty-fifth novel of the fourth day in the *Heptameron*; it later furnished Mrs. Centlivre with the plot for her farce, *A Wife Well Manag'd;* see Bowyer, p. 165.

36. *Ibid.*, p. 190. The original merely says that the husband was vexed on reading the letter.

37. *The Works of Mrs. Davys* (2 vols., 1725), I, 219. A similar revelatory letter is found in *The Prude* (1724), pp. 31–32. These letters invite comparison with the blunt business letter in which Gamaliel Pickle proposes to Miss Sally Appleby in the third chapter of *Peregrine Pickle*.

38. *The Post-Boy Rob'd of His Mail* (1706), pp. 63–65.

39. *Secret Histories*, III, 273–74.

40. *Memoirs of the Court of England* (1707), pp. 157–58.

41. *Love upon Tick* (1724), pp. xii–xiii.

42. See the *DNB* article on Edward Wilson (d. 1694). See also Mrs. Manley's account of Wilson, discussed below.

43. The volume is a translation of Mme d'Aulnoy's *Mémoires de la cour de l'Espagne* (1690); it appeared again in 1698, and in her *Works* (1707 and later).

NOTES TO CHAPTER VIII

1. Most of these references are scattered through the fourth and fifth letters (as originally arranged).

2. *Five Love-Letters . . . with the Cavalier's Answers* (1714), p. 54.

3. *Love's Posie* (1686), p. 96.

4. *Letters from a Lady of Quality to a Chevalier* (1724), pp. 22, 11, 31–32.

5. *The Post-Boy Rob'd of His Mail* (1692), Letter CIII; *The Post-Man Robb'd of His Mail* (1719), Book III, Letters I and II. The bawd's letter is a translation.

6. *A Spy upon the Conjurer* ("Campbell" ed., 1724), p. 198.

7. See the *DNB* article on Elizabeth Rowe; and Helen S. Hughes, "Elizabeth Rowe and the Countess of Hertford," *PMLA*, LIX (1944), 726–46.

8. As in the story of Rosalinda, one of Mrs. Rowe's better narratives, *Letters Moral and Entertaining* (1733), Part II, pp. 1–18. It has a sequel in Part III.

9. *Letters Moral and Entertaining*, Part III, pp. 102–3. The tale covers pp. 101–29.

10. See David Daiches, "The Identity of Burns," *Restoration and Eighteenth-Century Literature: Essays in Honor of Alan Dugald McKillop* (Chicago, 1963), p. 324.

11. See note 32 to Chapter IV.

12. His career was differently explained in another work; see the discussion above.

13. They are fully discussed in Anderson, "Delariviere Manley's Prose Fiction," pp. 175–77.

14. Letter LV, for example, is informatively titled, "The unfortunate *Lysetta* to the neglectful, but still most dearly belov'd *Lyonides:* On having been debauch'd by him with a Promise of Marriage."

15. *Love-Letters on All Occasions* (1730), p. 84.

16. *The Post-Boy Rob'd of His Mail* (1706), p. vi.

17. A possible exception is Mrs. Mary Davys' *The Fugitive* (1705), appearing as *The Merry Wanderer* in her *Works* (1725).

18. *Letters Written by Mrs Manley* (1713), pp. 6, 27–28.

19. See Anderson, "Delariviere Manley's Prose Fiction," pp. 173–74.

20. Another variety of French epistolary fiction, the scandalous story told in letters (as in Mme du Noyer's *Lettres historiques et galantes* [1704]), was less frequently imitated in England. The best example is Mrs. Haywood's lively *Bath-Intrigues* (1725); others of interest are her *Letters from the Palace of Fame* (1727), and parts of Mrs. Manley's *Court Intrigues*.

21. The novel was almost universally ascribed to Mrs. Behn in the eighteenth century. It appeared at least twelve times before 1740, was issued in parts, was versified, and was published as late as 1759. A long scene in a cave in Part III, probably borrowed from *Macbeth*, can scarcely be distinguished in atmosphere from a typical "Gothic" scene in later fiction. The best modern account (though inaccurate) is in Baker, *The History of the English Novel*, III, 83–84; and see Price, *Cold Caleb*, pp. 142–46.

22. *Love-Letters Between a Nobleman and His Sister* (2 vols., 1759), I, A2, 41, 83.

23. *Ibid.*, I, 64–67, 79, 94–96, 107.

24. *Ibid.*, I, 110.

25. *Ibid.*, I, 122.

26. *Ibid.*, I, 116.

27. *Ibid.*, I, 162–316, *passim.*

28. *Ibid.*, I, 64, 127, 59, 43, 45, 67–70.

29. *Ibid.*, I, 114–16, 107–8, 39–40.

30. *Ibid.*, I, 48–54, 99–105, 114–16, 120.

31. *Ibid.*, I, 70–71, 87.

32. See my article, "Love Letters Between Polydorus . . . and Messalina," *Seventeenth-Century News*, XIV (1956), 11.

33. *Love Letters Between Polydorus . . . and Messalina* (1689), p. 38.

34. *The Double Captive* (1718), p. 61. Since the book's title page describes it as printed for the benefit of the author, it is possible that someone imprisoned in Newgate had arranged to have his miscellaneous writings printed to relieve his wants or satisfy his creditors.

35. *The Female Dunciad* (1728), p. 19.

36. *Ibid.*, p. 30.

37. *The Unnatural Mother and Ungrateful Wife*, pp. 1–2, 30–31. The book is undated, but all authorities list it as before 1740. Internal evidence dates it after the Peace of Utrecht. Mrs. Dodd, one of the three booksellers listed on the title page, flourished 1726–43.

38. *Ibid.*, p. 3. Mr. Y— is elsewhere referred to as "Mr. Y—g"; and the villainess as "Miss Nelly." Her conduct may have been influenced by the fact that Mr. Young's former wife had come upon her in bed with Mr. Young and beaten her with a poker before dying of grief.

39. *The Post-Man Robb'd of His Mail* (1719), p. 165. Sacclimene and Stremunia are presumably Madame von Kielmannsegge and Madame von Platen.

40. *Ibid.*, pp. 170–71.

41. *The Fatal Amour* (1719), p. 30. This book was printed with *The Secret History of the Prince of the Nazarenes*, and is paged continuously with it.

42. Perhaps the best of the many discussions of the subject, since it is heavily documented and cautiously avoids hasty generalizations, is in Watt, *The Rise of the Novel*, pp. 35–59.

43. *The Lover's Week* (1718), pp. 6–7, 13–14. This and its sequel, *The Female Deserters*, appeared later as *Honour the Victory and Love the Prize* (1720). It is dedicated to Mrs. Manley, and the "hero" is a reader of Mrs. Behn (p. 17).

44. See Boyce, ed., *Lindamira*, p. xi.

45. *The Perfidious P—* (1702), p. 19.

46. *Ibid.*, pp. 49–50.

47. *Ibid.*, p. 53.

48. *Ibid.*, pp. 54–55. "Ratefea," usually spelled "ratafia," is flavored brandy.

49. *Ibid.*, 56–57. The salutation introduces a note of reality. To the outside world Clarinda is Mrs. —; and the reader was to suppose that the "editor" had deleted the name of an actual person.

50. *The Perfidious P—*, pp. 22, 18.

51. *Ibid.*, p. 34.

52. *Ibid.*, pp. 21–22.

53. *Ibid.*, p. 13.

54. See Boyce, ed., *Lindamira*, pp. 85–86. It is well to remember that by 1702 "writing to the moment," one of Richardson's proudest boasts and most important achievements, was by no means rare in epistolary fiction. Of course all *portugaises* are written as they are thought; but realistic references to external events as they occur are found in the letters of Mrs. Behn's Philander and Sylvia, Polydorus and Messalina, and the enamored Teresa, to name a few, quite in the Richardsonian manner. (On the last see above.)

55. *Olinda* appeared five times altogether in the miscellanies published by Samuel Briscoe between 1693 and 1724; the ascription was first made in 1718. It is true that if Catherine Trotter wrote *Olinda* she did it at fourteen; but she wrote a successful tragedy at sixteen, and Lady Mary Wortley Montagu wrote an effective imitation of *Lindamira* (unpublished) at fourteen. See Robert Halsband, *The Life of Lady Mary Wortley Montagu* (Oxford, 1956), p. 6. On Catherine Trotter Cockburn see Alison Fleming, "Catherine Trotter—'the Scots Sappho,'" *Scots Magazine*, XXXIII (1940), 305–14. *Olinda* seems to have been the only letter fiction of its day to reverse a trend; it was translated into French in 1695 as *Les Amours d'une belle angloise*. The volume is in the Arsenal Library in Paris.

56. *Familiar Letters of Love, Gallantry, and Several Occasions* (2 vols., 1724), II, 126.

57. *Ibid.*, II, 122.

58. *Ibid.*, II, 185. This letter to Cloridon is enclosed in the last of Olinda's letters to Cleander as proof of the intensity of her feelings.

59. *Ibid.*, II, 153, 168.

60. *Ibid.*, II, 170.

61. *Ibid.*, II, 177.

62. *Ibid.*

63. *The Works of Mrs. Davys* (2 vols., 1725), II, 271. A photographic reproduction of this novel is available in the Augustan Reprint Society's Publication No. 54 (Los Angeles, 1955), with my introduction and a bibliography of epistolary fiction.

64. *Ibid.*, II, 275–76.

65. *Ibid.*, II, 293, 306–7. On p. 296 Berina artlessly relates that she dreamed of seeing Artander blind, and "when I wou'd have led him, he pull'd out my Eyes, too."

66. The very incongruity of the names in this novel is sig-

nificant; evidently even Mrs. Davys found it impossible to disengage herself from the outworn tradition of the French romance, typified by Ferrand Spence in the preface to his translated *Countess of Salisbury* (1683): he explains "the giving the Countess... a Romantick Appellation [Philenia], whereas her True Name was *Joan*.... I fancied any thing in the least allied to *Joan* would be apt to give but scurvy fulsom Ideas" (sig. A6).

NOTES TO CHAPTER IX

1. See Whicher, pp. 201–4; the chronological list of her works given there illustrates her amazing fertility and the variety of authors and styles she imitated.

2. The best account of these trends is in McBurney, "Formative Influences on the English Novel," pp. 257–74.

3. See Brian W. Downs, *Richardson* (London, 1928), p. 97; Wilhelm Dibelius, *Englische Romankunst* (2 vols., Berlin, 1910), I, 83–84; Percy Lubbock, *The Craft of Fiction* (London, 1921), pp. 142–46, 153, 271–72.

4. Halsband, p. 180.

5. Singer, *The Epistolary Novel*, pp. 61–62.

6. After quitting the stage in 1682 Mrs. Behn produced *The Luckey Chance* and *The Emperor of the Moon* in 1686 and 1687; Mrs. Manley produced a tragedy, *Lucius*, in 1720; Mrs. Haywood had a comedy, a tragedy, and a burlesque opera acted in 1723, 1729, and 1733. On borrowings see Boyce, ed., *Lindamira*, pp. x, xiii; Baker, *The History of the English Novel*, III, 89–90; Whicher, pp. 35–38; McBurney, "Mrs Mary Davys," pp. 348–55.

7. On this point see McKillop, *Samuel Richardson*, pp. 41, 140–54; George Sherburn, "Samuel Richardson's Novels and the Theatre: A Theory Sketched," *PQ*, XLI (1962), 325–29, and "Writing to the Moment: One Aspect," *Restoration and Eighteenth-Century Literature: Essays in Honor of Alan Dugald McKillop* (Chicago, 1963), pp. 201–9; Leo Hughes, "Theatrical Convention in Richardson: Some Observations on a Novelist's Technique," *ibid.*, pp. 239–50.

8. The incident of Mrs. Behn's disastrous anti-Whig prologue to *Romulus and Hersilia* occurred in August 1682; Lord Grey eloped in the same month and fled to Holland a year later; the first part of the novel appeared in November 1683.

9. *Love-Letters Between a Nobleman and His Sister* (2 vols., 1759), I, 46.

10. *Ibid.*, I, 71, 215, 237–39, 294–312, *passim*, 313, 317–22, *passim*. These are only the most striking examples.

11. Act IV, scene 1, in *The Works of Aphra Behn*, ed. Montague Summers (6 vols., London, 1915), I, 388–89.

12. Act V, scene 3, in *Works*, II, 96.

13. The following passage (p. 16) is typical of the style of a large portion of the book: "Oh! wretched *Messalina*, say no more;/ forgive me *Polydorus*, for I rave,/ and my blind Fears suggest impossibilitys;/ Greatness has double Splendor in Distress,/ as Roses double sweetness when in Tears;/ and *Polydorus* Soul is far above/ that gilded Pageantry that fills and reigns/ in mean Desires; 'Tis true thy Messalina/ comes like the poor Shipwrac'd Mariner from the devouring Sea,/ not stock'd with all the Riches of the East,/ as when I parted from thy Bouteeous Land..."

14. See Whicher, pp. 37–38, and the letters quoted above, for blank verse in Mrs. Haywood; *The Perfidious P—* (1702), particularly pp. 10–18, *passim*. Blank verse is also notable in *The Lover's Sighs* and *The Illegal Lovers*, and can be found in many examples of letter fiction. Mrs. Boyd's *The Female Page* (1732) is almost entirely written in this cadenced prose.

15. II, 199.

16. See William J. Farrell, "The Style and Action in *Clarissa*," *SEL*, III (1963), 365–75. A rant of Belvidera which is quoted on p. 373, though printed as prose, is in the same kind of loose blank verse under discussion here.

17. See Watt, *The Rise of the Novel*, pp. 239–59; and as an example of the method of close comparison, Maurice Johnson, "The Noble Model," in *Fielding's Art of Fiction* (Philadelphia, 1961), pp. 139–56.

18. See Dibelius, I, 80–84; Lubbock, 142–55, 271–72; Black, "The Technique of Letter Fiction in English from 1740 to 1800," pp. 291–312; Paul Dottin, "Samuel Richardson et le roman épistolaire," *Revue anglo-américaine*, XIII (1935–36), 481–99.

19. Barbauld, ed., *The Correspondence of Samuel Richardson*, IV, 32 (Letter of Sept. 25, 1750).

20. *Letters and Works*, II, 284 (Letter of Sept. 22, 1755).

21. *Correspondence*, I, xxvii.

22. Sir Walter Scott, ed., *The Novels of Samuel Richardson, Esq.* (3 vols., Edinburgh, 1824), I, xliv–xlv.

23. Forster MS (Victoria and Albert Museum), XVI (48E10), part 1, fol. 74. (Letter to Stephen Duck.)

24. *Ibid.*, fol. 58.

25. Mrs. Manley dated her first four letters June 24, 23, 24, and 25 (unless the error is the printer's). The use of postscripts, blots, "torn" or "imperfect" letters, and so on, was more frequent in pre-Richardsonian fiction.

26. Shenstone wrote to a friend that *Pamela* would have made one good volume (we should remember that Part I appeared

in two duodecimo volumes and the whole work in four, then in two volumes octavo), and that he was surprised at Richardson's failure to perceive this fact. See his *Letters,* ed., Marjorie Williams (Oxford, 1939), p. 82, and pp. 262, 271, 393 for other complaints of Richardson's discursiveness.

27. See McKillop, *Samuel Richardson,* pp. 16, 25–39, and the letter to Stinstra (reprinted in *The Early Masters of English Fiction,* pp. 47–51).

28. See McKillop, *Samuel Richardson,* pp. 169–89, and his article cited in note 7 to chapter VI, above. Pamela mentions Philips' *Distrest Mother* at length; Charles Johnson's play *Caelia* (1733) may have contributed plot material to *Clarissa;* Rowe's *The Fair Penitent* and Otway's *Orphan* are mentioned in it. Richardson referred to *The Princess of Cleves,* but in a manner that makes it uncertain whether he had read it. See *The History of Sir Charles Grandison* (Shakespeare Head edition, 6 vols., Oxford, 1930), VI, 225–26.

29. See Downs, p. 167.

30. See note 10, chapter IV.

31. For an account of the time and labor involved in the composition of *Clarissa,* see McKillop, *Samuel Richardson,* pp. 120–26.

32. See Paul Dottin, "L'Accueil fait à *Pamela,*" *Revue anglo-américaine,* VII (1929–30), 505–19; McKillop, *Samuel Richardson,* pp. 43–57.

33. *The History of the Works of the Learned* (2 vols., 1740), II, 439. (Issue for December 1740.) It is significant that a notice of *Pamela* in a journal of this caliber could be secured.

34. Probably the first important notice of Richardson's epistolary technique was taken by the French critic Desfontaines in the *Bibliothèque britannique,* XXIX (1742), 70–71, 193–214.

35. *Spectator* No. 375 (May, 10, 1712).

36. This elaboration of detail did not go down with all readers. The author of *The Life of Pamela* (1741) said (p. 185) that a gentleman had expressed his wonder that "the Author had not told the exact Number of Pins *Pamela* had about her when she set out for Lincolnshire, and how many Rows of those Pins she bought for a Penny." Feminine readers, however, would have been likely to enjoy just such domestic details. See Watt, p. 153.

A Chronological List of English
Letter Fiction 1660-1740

This is a condensed version of the list originally prepared as a basis for this study, which attempted to list every recorded appearance in England from the Restoration through 1740 of works which might be reasonably regarded as letter fiction, excepting those in periodicals; it included information on price, format, printer, and bookseller, subsequent editions or issues within the period, location in libraries, and the like. It was based on the Chester Noyes Greenough card catalogue of English prose fiction, 1475–1830, in the Harvard University Library, supplemented and corrected from various general and specialized bibliographies in print and in manuscript, and by examination of works available for study in several libraries.

Since the original compilation, however, the Wing short-title catalogue of English printed books through 1700, Charles C. Mish's *English Prose Fiction, 1661–1700*, and William H. McBurney's *Chronological Check List of English Prose Fiction, 1700–1739* have appeared in print and are readily available. Through reference to these works it has been possible to condense and simplify the listing considerably. The reader should bear in mind that a very broad definition of "prose fiction" has been followed (see Chapter I) and that many of the works listed are not exclusively in the form of letters, nor are most of them what we should now classify as novels. Although the list has been extensively checked, it claims only reasonable completeness and accuracy. At many points considerations of space have dictated the deletion of authorities for including an item, notes of minor interest, information on modern reprints, and similar material.

The listing uses the abbreviations "pr" for "printed," "TC" for Arber's *Term Catalogues*, "tr" for "translator," "Translated," and "Greenough" for an entry in the Greenough card file. Authorities given are listed in brief form, since they are mentioned in the text. "Moore" for Defoe items indicates entries in John R. Moore, *A Checklist of the Writings of Daniel Defoe* (Bloomington, Ind., 1960).

The works that follow are arranged in chronological order, according to the year in which they first appeared in English after 1660, regardless of the date of the original work, English or Continental. Within the chronological order they are arranged alphabetically by English author or translator, anonymous works appearing first. The following information is generally given:

1. Author or translator, bracketed if doubtful.

2. Title. Most have been greatly condensed; capitalization has been uniformly restricted to the first words of titles and alternate titles, and to proper names.

3. Date or dates. The year of the first reliably recorded edition is given, followed (unless the work is listed in McBurney) by years through 1740 in which subsequent editions or issues appeared or are recorded. If a work appeared more than once in a given year, the date is followed by the appropriate number (as 2, 3) in parentheses.

4. Printer and bookseller of the first edition recorded if the work is not listed by Mish, Wing, or McBurney.

5. Price or prices of various editions, when known, unless the work is listed in McBurney.

6. Format, if the work is not listed elsewhere.

7. Location, when necessary, if known, according to the library symbols used in Wing.

8. Wing number (the first for a given work), preceded by an asterisk if the work is listed in Mish, for items through 1700, indicated thus: *R1303.

9. Reference to entry number in McBurney for works from 1700, indicated thus: M-94.

10. Indication of a translated work's source, when appropriate; indication of its technical characteristics, if it has been available for examination; in some instances, brief reference to a work in which it is discussed.

1. BEAUMONT, ROBERT. Loves missives to virtue. 1660. B1629. A series of letters to a lady, with a slight narrative element.

2. BRETON, NICHOLAS. A poste with a packet of madde letters. 1660, 1669, 1678, 1685. B4388. A miscellany or fictionalized letter-manual; letters with replies and in sequences.

3. F[ORDE], T[HOMAS]. Foenestra in pectore, or, Familiar letters. 1660, 1661. F1549. A series of essay-like and narrative letters from one person to several others.

4. S., T., tr. Arnaldo, or, The injur'd lover. 1660. *B5241. Tr. of an expanded Italian version, by Brusoni, of San Pedro's *Arnalte y Lucenda* (ca. 1492), a late medieval romance with numerous inserted letters.

5. REYNOLDS, JOHN. Blood for blood: or Murthers revenged (*Gods Revenge Against Murther*). 1661, 1662, 1663, 1669, 1670, 1679, 1682, 1685, 1686, 1687, 1688, 1691, 1704, 1708 (in various versions, and with additions). *R1303. Short tales with letters inserted, serving important narrative functions.

6. [GAYTON, EDMUND.] "Edmundus de Speciosa Villa." Coll[onel]: Henry Marten's familiar letters to his lady of delight. 1662, 1663, 1685. M819. An attack on Marten which incorporates his actual letters and adds spurious "heroical epistles."

7. C., W. The history of the most renowned Fragosa king of Aragon. 1663, 1664. *C155. A romance with inserted letters.

8. BULTEEL, JOHN. Birinthea, a romance. 1664. *B5454. A version of Xenophon's *Cyropaedia*, with inserted letters.

9. CAVENDISH, MARGARET, Duchess of Newcastle. CCXI sociable letters. 1664, 1718. N872. An imitated correspondence between two women, with faint narrative elements and colloquial manner; domestic setting.

10. BOYLE, ROGER, Earl of Orrery. Parthenissa. 1669,

1676. *0494. An imitation of the French romances, with inserted letters.

11. L'Estrange, Sir Roger, tr. The gentleman apothecary. 1670, 1677, 1678, 1693, 1726, 1736, 1739, 1740 (2). Price 1 shilling. *V390. Tr. from de Villiers, *L'Apoticaire de qualité* (1670). A short witty tale with a number of letters important to plot and characterization.

12. Anonymous. A letter concerning the . . . country of Muley Arxid, King of Teleletta. 1671. Entry doubtful; see Morgan, *Novel of Manners*.

13. Anonymous. News from Jamaica in a letter . . . by the German Princess. 1671. NN. A satirical "letter" of advice and news from the transported swindler Mary Carleton.

14. Anonymous, tr. The novels of Dom Francisco de Quevedo Villegas. 1671, 1707, 1709. *Q192. One novel, "The Retentive Knight," consists of twenty-three characteristic letters from a miser, Quevedo's *Cartas del caballero de la tenaza* (1625). It also appeared with *The Life of Buscon* (1657ff.) tr. by John Davies of Kidwelly.

15. [Head, Richard?] O-Brazile, or The inchanted island. 1675 (3). *H1269. A "tall story" in a letter, perhaps a burlesque on travelers' tales.

16. Porter, P., tr. The memoires of the duchess Mazarine. 1676 (2), 1690, 1713, 1714, 1728, 1732. *S355. Tr. from St-Réal, *Mémoires de Mme. la Duchesse de Mazarin* (1675). Supposedly the duchess' own memoirs, with letters.

17. P., W., Gent. The wit's academy; or, The muses' delight. 1677, 1682, 1684, 1696, 1699. P 139. The miscellaneous contents include ninety fictional letters, in the manner of Breton's *Poste with a Packet*.

18. L'Estrange, Sir Roger, tr. Five love-letters from a nun to a cavalier. 1678, 1680, 1686, 1689, 1693, 1701 (2), 1702 (bilingual), 1705, 1714, 1716. Price, 1s. 6d. *A889. Tr. from Guilleraques [?], *Lettres portugaises* (1669). Entirely in epistolary form, the *locus classicus* of psychological-epistolary fiction.

19. P., W., Gent. A flying post. 1678. Entry doubtful; see Robertson, *Letter Writing*, pp. 36–37.

20. Anonymous. The penitent hermit, or The fruits of

jealousie. 1679. Price, 1 shilling. *P1233. The full title suggests an autobiographical narrative divided into "letters."

21. ANONYMOUS, tr. Seven Portuguese letters. 1681, 1693. *A893. Tr. from a work also titled *Lettres portugaises* (1669), a sequel to the original five, by "une femme du monde."

22. ANONYMOUS. A new vision of the Lady Gr[ay']s ...in a letter. 1682. N791. A broadside, purporting to be a narrative letter from the wife of Forde, Lord Grey of Werk.

23. ANONYMOUS, tr. The novells of Loredano. 1682. *L3068. Tr. from Giovanni Loredano, *Novelle amorose* (1656), romantic stories with numerous inserted letters.

24. H., R., tr. Loves empire; or, The amours of the French court. 1682. *L3264a. Tr. from Bussy-Rabutin, *Histoire amoureuse des Gaules* (1665), the pioneering scandal novel; many single letters and series integrated with the narrative.

25. ANONYMOUS, tr. An account of the secret services of M. de Vernay...by way of letters. 1683. L57. Probably a translation of a "nouvelle historique"; a letter from "S.L." containing seven supposedly authentic letters, some in cipher.

26. ANONYMOUS, tr. Five love-letters written by a cavalier. 1683, 1694, 1701, 1714, 1716. *F1110. Tr. from the anonymous *Réponse aux lettres portugaises* (1669), supposed to be the Cavalier's answers to the letters of the Portuguese Nun.

27. BEHN, MRS. APHRA. Love-letters between a nobleman and his sister. 1683 (Pt. I), 1685 (Pt. II), 1687 (Pt. III), 1684, 1693 (2), 1694, 1701, 1707, 1708, 1712, 1714, 1721, 1734 (versified), 1735 (2; one sold in parts), 1736. *B1740. Pt. I is the first original piece of long fiction in English entirely in letters. See Wiles, *English Periodical Publication*, pp. 69, 297.

28. DUNTON, JOHN. The informer's doom...[a] letter from Utopia. 1683. *D2629. Topical satire in the form of a letter.

29. G., D. A Sundays adventure, or Walk to Hackney. 1683. *G9. Autobiographical wooing-narrative; exchanges of letters involved in plot.

30. SHURLY, J., Gent. The compleat courtier: or, Cupids academy. 1683. S3503. Collection of fictional letters in the manner of Breton.

31. SPENCE, FERRAND, tr. The Countess of Salisbury. 1683, 1692. *A3630. Tr. from d'Argens, *La comtesse de Salisbury* (1682), a *nouvelle historique* with inserted letters importantly involved in the plot.

32. ANONYMOUS. Wits cabinet: or, A companion for young men and ladies. 1684, 1686, 1689, 1697, 1703, 1731, 1737. W3216. In part a collection of fictional love letters in pairs and sequences.

33. ANONYMOUS, tr. The amours of Count Teckeli. 1686. Price, 1 shilling. *P3203. Tr. (probably) from Préchac, *Le Comte de Tekely* (1686). A "historical novel" with inserted letters figuring in the intrigue.

34. ANONYMOUS, tr. Loves posie. 1686. *L3281. Tr. from the anonymous *Commerce galant* (1682). A long letter containing an exchange of 27 letters that tell a love story.

35. BEHN, MRS. APHRA, tr. La montre: or, The lover's watch. 1686, 1692, 1696ff (in *Histories and Novels*). B3595c. Tr. (loosely) from Bonnecorse, *La montre* (1666), a *carte du tendre* that includes an amorous correspondence.

36. [BRADSHAW, WILLIAM, and MIDGLEY, ROBERT, trs?] Letters writ by a Turkish spy. 1687 (Vol. I), 1691–94 (Vols. I–VIII, several eds.), 1703, 1707, 1730, 1732, 1734. Price (complete set), 12s. and 18s. *M565B. Tr. from Marana, *L'espion turc* (1684–6). The original of the extremely popular "spy" letters. A loose narrative, entirely in letters, mixing current history, gossip, travel, and traces of plot.

37. BEHN, MRS. APHRA, tr. Lycidus, or The lover in fashion. 1688. *T129. Tr. from Tallemant, *Le second voyage de l'isle d'amour, à Licidas* (1664). A fantasy in the form of a letter, with slight fictional elements.

38. ANONYMOUS. Love letters between Polydorus, the Gothick king, and Messalina, late queen of Albion. 1689. *B1743. An epistolary novel, purporting to be the correspondence of Louis XIV and Mary of Modena.

39. ANONYMOUS. The Quakers art of courtship. 1689, 1710, 1719, 1733, 1737. Price, 1 shilling. Q14. A simultaneous parody of Quaker forms of address and of epistolary manuals, with single narrative letters and exchanges.

40. BEHN, MRS. APHRA. The lucky mistake. 1689, 1692, 1696ff (in *Histories and Novels*). *B1745. A novel of intrigue, with inserted letters important to the plot.

41. ANONYMOUS, tr. The cabinet open'd: or, The secret history of the amours of Madam de Maintenon. 1690, 1692. *C190. Tr. from Lenoble, *La cassette ouverte* (1690). Scandal novel with letters, supposedly by Mme de Maintenon, figuring in the plot.

42. ANONYMOUS, tr. The frauds of Romish monks and priests. 1690, 1691 (3), 1704 (2), 1706, 1725, 1726. G390. Tr. from Gavin, *Histoire des tromperies des prestres* (1690). Autobiographical journey-letters recounting anticlerical anecdotes.

43. ANONYMOUS, tr. The ingenious and diverting letters of the Lady ——'s travels into Spain. 1691–92 (3 pts., 2 eds.), 1697 (2), 1705 (2), 1707, 1708, 1717, 1722, 1726 (2, one in a periodical), 1735, 1736, 1740. *B2038. Tr. from d'Aulnoy, *Relation du voyage d'Espagne* (1691). The original of a popular type, the travel-journal.

44. GILDON, CHARLES. The post-boy rob'd of his mail. 1692, 1693, 1694, 1705, 1706, 1709. *G735A. Tr. in part from and the remainder based on Pallavicino, *Il corriere svaligiato* (1643), via Préchac, *La valize ouverte* (1680). A large, colorful miscellany, using the device of the rifled post-bag for authenticity; single letters and pairs.

45. ANONYMOUS. Letters of love and gallantry and other occasions. 1693, 1694, 1697. L1784. A two-volume miscellany with a great variety of epistolary forms, including *Olinda's Adventures*, an epistolary novel.

46. ANONYMOUS. The player's tragedy, or, Fatal love. 1693. *P2418. A realistic novel of intrigue, dealing with an amour of "Bracilla" (Mrs. Bracegirdle). Inserted letters figure in the plot.

47. P., J., tr. The present court of Spain. 1693, 1698. *A4223. Tr. from Mme d'Aulnoy, *Mémoires de la cour d'Espagne* (1690). Several novels, one of which, "The Enamored Teresa," told both in seventy-five letters and in autobiographical narrative, was reprinted, 1707ff. See No. 87, below, and M-27.

48. ANONYMOUS, tr. Scarron incens'd. 1694. *S838. Tr. from the anonymous *Scarron apparu à Mme. de Maintenon* (1694). Scandal novel with supposedly authentic letters concerning Scarron, the former husband of Louis XIV's mistress.

49. ANONYMOUS [Mrs. Mary Manley?] The unhappy

lovers, or The timorous fair one. 1694. *U67. Romantic love story told in a letter, with inserted letters.

50. GILDON, CHARLES. Miscellaneous letters and essays on several subjects. 1694, 1696, 1697, 1702. G732. This collection includes narrative sequences in letter form.

51. C., J., tr. Memoires on [sic] the court of England. 1695, 1707, 1708, 1710. Greenough. See M-28. MH (ed. of 1707), ICN. Tr. from Mme d'Aulnoy, *Mémoires de la cour d'Angleterre* (1695). Romantic account of Restoration amours, with numerous letters in sequences, or involved in plot.

52. SAVAGE, JO., tr. Brutes turn'd criticks, or, Mankind moraliz'd by beasts. 1695. M2851. Tr. from Moscheni, *Lettere . . . delle bestie* (1672). Sixty letters in satirical exchanges, in which animals typify human failings.

53. BEHN, MRS. APHRA. The histories and novels. 1696 (2), 1697, 1698, 1699, 1700, 1702, 1705, 1711, 1714, 1718, 1722, 1725, 1735. *B1711. In this posthumous collection, made by Gildon, some of the novels, and the "memoirs" of Mrs. Behn, are partly epistolary.

54. MANLEY, MRS. MARY. Letters, written by Mrs. Manley. 1696, 1713, 1725 (2; as *A Stage-Coach Journey to Exeter*), 1735 (2, one in Vol. III of *Mr. Pope's Literary Correspondence*), 1736. Prices, 1 shilling, 2s. 6d., 5s. (in collections). *M434. A sprightly series of travel letters and epistolary narratives, with a *portugaise* by "Col. Pack."

55. PIX, MRS. MARY. The inhumane cardinal: or, Innocence betray'd. 1696. pr for John Harding and Richard Wilkin. 12mo. ICN. Tale of intrigue and corruption at Rome; inserted letters used in plotting.

56. ANONYMOUS. Letters of religion and virtue. 1697. L1786. A pious parody in opposition to the letters of the Restoration wits (see No. 57, below). Narrative exchange between two persons.

57. BROWN, THOMAS, and GILDON, CHARLES, eds. Familiar letters: written by the . . . Earl of Rochester. 1697 (2), 1699, 1705 (2), 1714. Price 5s. R1743. A miscellany of English and translated letters, including epistolary narratives.

58. [DUNTON, JOHN.] "Philaret." The challenge sent by a young lady to Sir Thomas: or, The female warr. 1697.

C1796. Exchange between a man and a woman, with elements both of essay and fiction.

59. JONES, DAVID, Gent. The secret history of White-Hall. 1697 (2), 1717, 1722. J934. Purports to be a collection of secret letters revealing the inside story of English Restoration diplomacy.

60. BEHN, Mrs. APHRA. The unfortunate bride: or, The blind lady a beauty. 1698, 1700. *B1772. Posthumous intrigue novel; letters contribute to plot.

61. BROWN, THOMAS. A collection of miscellany poems, letters, &c. 1699, 1700, 1711ff (in *Works*). B5052. Contains narratives and sketches in epistolary form.

62. S——CY, ED. The country gentleman's vade mecum. 1699, 1700, 1702, 1730, 1731, 1732. Price, 1 shilling. C6533. Eighteen letters of advice, with satirical narratives and sketches of city cheats.

63. ANONYMOUS [Edward Ward?] The English nun, or, A comical description of a nunnery. 1700. M-X1. Apparently, one or more descriptive "familiar letters," according to Greenough. See Troyer, *Ned Ward*, p. 237.

64. ANONYMOUS. Youth's pleasant recreation, or Merry pastime. 1700, 1704. TC. Greenough lists as partly epistolary.

65. BROWN, THOMAS, tr. and ed. Familiar and courtly letters, written by Monsieur Voiture [et al.]. 1700, 1701, 1704, 1705, 1736. Price, 4s. (per volume of 2). V862. Original English and translated letters; many include fictional elements.

66. CR——D, D., Gent. Several letters; containing the amours of: I. The unfortunate dutchess; or, The lucky gamester. II. Love after enjoyment; or, Fatal constancy. III. The unhappy mistake; or, The fate of cross'd loves. 1700. pr for Job Austin. 8vo. CU. Each novel is a letter, with inserted letters; I and II were reprinted; see No. 202, below, and M-333, M-X39.

67. ANONYMOUS. The female critick: or, Letters in drollery. 1701. Satire on fashionable love-letters; see McKillop, *Samuel Richardson*, p. 19.

68. [BOYER, ABEL, ed.] Letters of wit, politicks, and morality. 1701. pr for F. Hartley, W. Turner, and Tho. Hodgson. 8vo. MH. Collection of English and translated letters, some forming narrative sequences.

69. [GILDON, CHARLES, tr.?] The French convert. 1701. Greenough. ICN (ed. of 1704). Autobiographical narrative of a noble Frenchwoman converted to Protestantism, in a letter; several inserted letters figure in plot.

70. WARD, EDWARD [and others]. A pacquet from Will's. 1701, 1705. pr for Sam. Briscoe. 8vo. MH. A miscellany of several narrative types of letters, mostly humorous; also appeared as part of No. 65, above.

71. ANONYMOUS, tr. An historical account of the amours of the Emperor of Morocco . . . Writ by way of letters. 1702. M-X4. A translated scandal novel with inserted letters.

72. ANONYMOUS. Love's various chances. 1702. pr for E. Harris. L. Greenough. Full title indicates that this consists of six novels interspersed with letters.

73. ANONYMOUS. The perfidious P—. 1702. M-9. A short but fully developed epistolary novel of high quality.

74. ANONYMOUS [ed. by Thomas Brown?]. The adventures of Lindamira. 1702. M-7. An excellent epistolary novel of some length.

75. BROWN, THOMAS. Certamen epistolare. 1702, 1703, 1705, 1709ff (in *Works*). A humorous exchange in eight letters "between an attorney and a dead parson."

76. BROWN, THOMAS. Letters from the dead to the living. 1702 (2), 1703, 1707, 1708, 1709ff (in *Works*). Miscellaneous letters, some translated, in the satirical genre established in England by Brown.

77. FARQUHAR, GEORGE. Love and business. 1702ff. (See *Works*, ed. Stonehill.) Farquhar's correspondence with several ladies, modified into semifiction.

78. ANONYMOUS. Letters from the living to the living. 1703. Imitation of Brown's letters; see Boyce, *Tom Brown*, p. 165.

79. BROWN, THOMAS. A continuation or second part of the letters from the dead to the living. 1703, 1705, 1707ff (in eds. of No. 76, above).

80. ANONYMOUS. England's jests refin'd and improv'd. 1704. pr for J. Sprint. TC, Greenough. This edition, called the fourth, is said to contain fictional letters.

81. ANONYMOUS [William Pittis]. A letter from the dead

Thomas Brown to the living Heraclitus. 1704. See Boyce, *Tom Brown*, p. 167. Pittis is "Heraclitus."

82. ANONYMOUS, tr. Secretaria di Apollo: or, Letters from Apollo. 1704. pr for R. Smith. 8vo. MH. Tr. from Boccalini, *La secretaria di Apollo* (1654). Satirical letters in the tradition of "letters from the dead."

83. DEFOE, DANIEL. The storm. 1704. Moore 81. A wide variety of letters, mostly narrative, which Defoe claims to be entirely authentic.

84. ANONYMOUS, tr. Memoirs of the adventures of a French lady of quality ... at Venice. 1705. M-X7. A narrative in the form of a letter, perhaps tr. from the anonymous *Mémoires curieux et galans* (1699).

85. ANONYMOUS. The jilted bridegroom, or, The London coquet. 1706. M-20. Realistic domestic novel with important use of inserted letters.

86. D'URFEY, THOMAS. Stories, moral and comical. 1706, 1719. Sold by Isaac Cleave. 8vo. MH. The "second comick story," "The Prudent Husband," tr. from Novel 35 of the *Heptameron*, has been adapted by the use of letters.

87. ANONYMOUS, tr. The diverting works of the Countess D'Anois. 1707. M-27. The third section consists of "The Enamored Teresa"; see No. 47, above.

88. BROWN, THOMAS. The works of Mr. Thomas Brown. 1707, 1708, 1709, 1711, 1712, 1715, 1720, 1723, 1730. pr for Sam. Briscoe and sold by B. Bragg. Price, 10*s* (4 vols., 1720). 8vo. MH. Contains all of Brown's epistolary works.

89. MANLEY, MRS. MARY. The lady's pacquet of letters. 1707. M-26 (see M-28, 29). Forty-one letters of several kinds, including Mrs. Manley's own correspondence; some of high quality as narrative.

90. ANONYMOUS, tr. The art of love, or The amours of Count Schlick. 1708. M-35. Tr. of Aeneas Sylvius' semiepistolary romance of 1444, doubtless through an intermediate version.

91. ANONYMOUS. A voyage to the new island Fonseca. 1708. M-34. Two imaginary voyages in letters from the West Indies by a "Turkish sailor" and a "French renegado;" some satire on English politics and manners.

92. [PLAYFORD, HENRY?] The island of content: or, A new paradise discover'd. In a letter. 1709. M-42. Full title indicates that this is also topical satire.

93. WEAVER, JOHN, tr. Secret memoirs, historical and galant. Collected from the French. 1709. pr for W. Taylor. 4to. CU. M-X10. Four narrative letters, exchanged by two persons, compiled from materials in Mme Du Noyer's *Lettres historiques et galantes* (1704). Amorous intrigues, scandal.

94. ANONYMOUS. Advice from the shades below. 1710. An imitation of Tom Brown's satirical letters. See Boyce, "News from Hell," *PMLA*, LVII (1943), 402ff.

95. ANONYMOUS. Advice from the shades below. No. 2. 1710. See No. 94, above.

96. ANONYMOUS. Serious and comical essays ... with ingenious letters, amorous and gallant. 1710. pr and sold by J. King. 8vo. ICN. Contains a miscellany of twenty-five short letters in the Bretonian manner, rather bawdy in tone.

97. [TOLAND, JOHN?] The description of Epsom ... in a letter to Eudoxa. 1711. pr for A. Baldwin. 4to. Price, 6d. ICN. A narrative letter with pictures of fashionable life, scenery, gossip.

98. The infernal congress: or, News from below. 1713. pr for J. Baker. 8vo. MH. Satire: from "the late comedian, Dick Estcourt, to the Spectator."

99. ANONYMOUS. A new voyage to the island of fools ... in letters. 1713. M-63. Satire on English habits and politics in five letters. Almost certainly by Ned Ward, on evidence of style and similarity to his "rambles through the town" in content and conduct.

100. ANONYMOUS. The present state of Fairy-land in several letters from Esquire Hush. 1713. M-64. Anti-Tory satire in four letters; the king of Slave-onia (Louis XIV) is ironically assured that matters in England are going as well as he could wish. Very possibly by Walpole; see J. H. Plumb, *Sir Robert Walpole.*

101. HUGHES, JOHN, tr. Letters of Abelard and Heloise. 1713, 1714, 1718 (2), 1720, 1722, 1728, 1734-35 (in the periodical *Weekly Amusement*), 1737. pr for J. Watts et al. Prices, 1s. 6d., 5s., 6s. (for various formats differing in binding). 12mo. (1st ed.). MB. Tr. from DuBois, *Histoire des*

amours et infortunes d'Abélard et d'Héloïse (5th ed., 1711), a fictional account of the lovers with the letters much modified.

102. [HEARNE, THOMAS, ed.?] Love-letters from King Henry VIII to Anne Boleyn. 1714, 1720, 1736 (3). pr for J. Churchill. Prices, 1 shilling, 5s. MH. These letters are not fictional, but are presented in a manner that makes them indistinguishable from a "historical novel" of the period.

103. ANONYMOUS, [tr.?] The fatal effects of arbitrary power. 1715. M-X12. 8vo. ICN. A supposed memoir of the intrigues of Philip II's court by "Antonio Perez." Numerous letters and documents inserted as authenticating devices.

104. ANONYMOUS. The German Atalantis. 1715. M-76. Autobiographical narrative with important use of inserted letters; court scandal.

105. ANONYMOUS. The history of Menuthia . . . in a letter. 1715. M–77. Full title indicates that this is probably political satire masked as an account of foreign parts.

106. OZELL, JOHN, tr. Letters of gallantry. By M. de Fontenelle. 1715. pr for Jonas Brown and John Watts. 12mo. MH. Tr. from Fontenelle, *Lettres galantes* (1685); many brief narratives, and a sequence with elements of plot.

107. SMITH, CAPT. ALEXANDER. The secret history of the lives of the most celebrated beauties. 1715. M-80. Brief fictionalized biographies of royal mistresses, often with correspondence significant to plot.

108. ANONYMOUS, tr. Letters from a lady at Paris to a lady at Avignon. 1716. M-86. Mme DuNoyer's famous series; exchange of letters between two ladies, with plot line, short narratives, comment, satire.

109. LYLY, JOHN. Euphues and Lucilla: or The false friend and inconstant mistress. 1716, 1718 (2), 1720, 1732. Sold by J. Noon and T. Sharpey. 4to. O, ICN. A "modernized" version of Lyly's novel; epistolary elements enlarged and emphasized.

110. [DEFOE, DANIEL] "Kora Selym Oglan." The conduct of Christians made the sport of infidels. 1717. M-87; Moore 381. Single letter using the "spy" device; topical satire.

111. ANONYMOUS. The double captive, or Chains upon

chains. 1718. pr by J. Churchill. 8vo. MH. An amorous correspondence with a realistic account of life in Newgate.

112. MISCELLANEOUS. Familiar letters of love, gallantry, and other occasions. 1718, 1720, 1724. pr for Sam. Briscoe and others. 8vo. Price, 5s (2 vols.). L. A collection of extremely varied contents; includes authentic letters, plus *Olinda's Adventures* and other contents of No. 45, above.

113. DEFOE, DANIEL. A continuation of letters written by a Turkish spy at Paris. 1718. Moore 406. Defoe's employment of the "spy" device.

114. HEARNE, MRS. MARY. The lover's week. 1718. M-90 (see M-114). A realistic tale of amorous adventure, in letters.

115. ANONYMOUS. The amorous pedant; or, The schoolmaster's love-letter to his mistress. 1719. Greenough. The situation indicated by the title is a commonplace in letter fiction.

116. ANONYMOUS. The fatal amour between a beautiful lady, and a young nobleman. 1719. M-94. Excellent domestic-realistic story in a letter, containing letters.

117. ANONYMOUS. Passionate love-letters between a Polish princess and a certain chevalier. 1719. M-105. A "novel" entirely in letters; the purported correspondence of the Old Pretender and his bride, Maria Clementina of Poland.

118. DEFOE, DANIEL. The king of pirates. 1719, 1720. Moore 424. The adventures of Captain Avery, told in two autobiographical letters.

119. [GILDON, CHARLES] "Sir Roger de Whimsey." The post-man robb'd of his mail: or, The packet broke open. 1719 (2). M-102. A miscellany like G's earlier *Post-Boy Rob'd*, but showing the influence of the *Spectator*. Contains *The Lover's Sighs*, an epistolary scandal-novel of good quality.

120. HAYWOOD, MRS. ELIZA. Love in excess; or, The fatal enquiry. 1719. M-103. Romance with heavy employment of interpolated letters, significant to plot.

121. HEARNE, MRS. MARY. The female deserters. 1719. M-104. A sequel to *The Lover's Week*, later printed with it as *Honour the Victory and Love the Prize;* of inferior quality.

122. ANONYMOUS. Miscellanea aurea, or, The golden medley. 1720 (2). pr for A. Bettesworth and J. Pemberton. Price, 3s. 8vo. MH. Very miscellaneous contents, some by Gildon; see Appendix B.

123. BROWN, THOMAS. The remains of Mr. Tho. Brown. 1720, 1721. pr for Sam. Briscoe and others. 8vo. MH. A miscellany of narrative and satirical letters, most printed earlier.

124. FOWKE, MRS. MARTHA, and BOND, WILLIAM. The epistles of Clio and Strephon. 1720, 1728 (2), 1729, 1732 (2), 1740. pr for J. Hooke and others. 8vo. Prices, 1 shilling and 2*s.* 6*d.* MH. A hybrid of the letter novel and the Ovidian elegy. Exchanges in prose and verse depict the progress of a Platonic love affair.

125. MANLEY, MRS. MARY. The power of love: in seven novels. 1720. M-115. Bandello, perhaps via Painter, is the source of these tales, three of which make important use of letters.

126. HAYWOOD, MRS. ELIZA, tr. Letters from a lady of quality to a chevalier. 1721. M-122. A sentimental novel entirely in letters by Boursault, freely translated, with a prefatory essay on writings of this kind.

127. HAYWOOD, MRS. ELIZA. The British recluse. 1722. M-131. Sentimental-realistic novel with numerous letters.

128. OZELL, JOHN, tr. Persian letters. 1722. M-136. Montesquieu's *Lettres persanes* (1721); satire, elementary plot.

129. ANONYMOUS. Love-letters between a certain late nobleman and the famous Mr. Wilson. 1723. M-138. The career of Beau Wilson is "explained" in a story told twice (confusingly), once in supposedly authentic letters.

130. BARKER, MRS. JANE. A patchwork-screen for the ladies. 1723. M-141. One of the "novels" in this collection is largely epistolary—"The Heroick Cavalier."

131. HAYWOOD, MRS. ELIZA. Idalia: or, The unfortunate mistress. 1723. M-142. Novel of intrigue with numerous inserted letters.

132. WALKER, CAPT. CHARLES. Authentick memoirs of the life . . . of the celebrated Sally Salisbury. 1723. M-146. The famous London courtesan is depicted in fifteen lively letters from her customers and acquaintances.

133. ANONYMOUS [Mrs. Mary Manley?]. Love upon tick: or, Implicit gallantry. 1724. M-150. Satirical novel of a coxcomb duped by letters, which form the bulk of the work. Internal evidence suggests Mrs. Manley's authorship.

134. A., MA. The prude. A novel. 1724. M-153. Real-

istic tale of a prude who is a secret libertine; many inserted letters figure importantly in plot.

135. DAVYS, MRS. MARY. The reform'd coquet. A novel. 1724. M-154. Sentimental-realistic story in domestic setting; a large proportion in the form of inserted letters.

136. DEFOE, DANIEL. The history of the remarkable life of John Sheppard. 1724 (3). Moore 468. Rogue biography with letters.

137. DEFOE, DANIEL. A narrative of all the robberies, escapes, &c., of John Sheppard. 1724. M-151, Moore 461. Purports to be an "open letter" or confession from Sheppard.

138. E., G. Authentick memoirs of the life and adventures of John Sheppard. . . . By way of familiar letters from a gentleman in town, to his friend and correspondent in the country. 1724. M-156.

139. HAYWOOD, MRS. ELIZA. The fatal secret; or, Constancy in distress. 1724. M-158. Short tale of intrigue; high proportion of inserted letters.

140. HAYWOOD, MRS. ELIZA. The masqueraders; or, Fatal curiosity. 1724. M-159. Sentimental tale with very high proportion of inserted letters.

141. HAYWOOD, MRS. ELIZA. The rash resolve: or, The untimely discovery. 1724. M-160. Same type as No. 140.

142. HAYWOOD, MRS. ELIZA. A spy upon the conjurer. 1724. M-161. A long narrative letter by "Justicia," followed by a collection of characteristic letters supposed to be written to Duncan Campbell, the "dumb seer."

143. HAYWOOD, MRS. ELIZA. The works of Mrs. Eliza Haywood. 1724. M-163. Contains most of her works already listed; four volumes.

144. ANONYMOUS [Samuel Humphreys?], tr. The amorous history of the Gauls. 1725. M-184. This differs from the seventeenth-century translation of Bussy-Rabutin (see No. 24).

145. DAVYS, MRS. MARY. The works of Mrs. Davys. 1725. M-171. Published by subscription in two volumes, this includes an excellent letter-novel, *Familiar Letters Betwixt a Gentleman and a Lady*.

146. HAYWOOD, MRS. ELIZA. Bath-intrigues: in four letters to a friend in London. 1725. M-172. "J. B." writes "Will" a lively account of disgraceful amours at Bath, including his own.

147. HAYWOOD, MRS. ELIZA. The dumb projector. 1725. M-173. An epistolary account of Duncan Campbell's adventures in Holland. See Whicher, *Eliza Haywood*.

148. HAYWOOD, MRS. ELIZA. Fantomina: or, Love in a maze. 1725. M-174. Humorous tale of intrigue; letters important to plot.

149. HAYWOOD, MRS. ELIZA. Memoirs of a certain island. 1725. M-178. Scandal-chronicle in the *Atalantis* tradition; many inserted letters.

150. HAYWOOD, MRS. ELIZA. Secret histories, novels, and poems. 1725. M-179. Contains most of her works already listed.

151. HAYWOOD, MRS. ELIZA. Reflections on the various effects of love. 1726. M-197. Short accounts of ancient and modern amours, interspersed with ranting letters.

152. SIMMONDS, EDWARD. The genuine letters of Mary Queen of Scots. 1726, 1735 (2). Pr by A. Campbell for J. Millan. Prices, 1 shilling and 4s. 8vo. Greenough (adv.). Apparently, a romanticized account of the Bothwell episode, with translations of the "casket letters" inserted.

153. MISCELLANEOUS. Atterburyana. 1727. M-206. A collection made by Curll, which includes a miscellany of original and translated letters, narrative, satirical, and amorous, and two short novels containing letters.

154. HAYWOOD, MRS. ELIZA. Cleomelia: or, The generous mistress. 1727. M-208. Tale of sentiment and passion, with a high proportion of inserted letters.

155. HAYWOOD, MRS. ELIZA. Letters from the palace of fame. 1727. M-210. Epistolary scandal-chronicle with reflections on political figures.

156. HAYWOOD, MRS. ELIZA. Love in its variety. 1727. M-220. Tales of intrigue, including letters; said to be translated from Bandello, but almost certainly original.

157. HAYWOOD, MRS. ELIZA. The perplex'd dutchess: or, Treachery rewarded. 1727. M-211. Tale of intrigue in a letter

"from a *Sicilian* Nobleman"; inserted letters important to plot; no connection with Webster's play, though it deals with "the Court of *Malfy*."

158. HAYWOOD, MRS. ELIZA. Philidore and Placentia: or, L'amour trop delicat. 1727. M-212. Short romance of passion with numerous inserted letters.

159. HAYWOOD, MRS. ELIZA. The secret history of the present intrigues of the court of Caramania. 1727. M-213. Scandal-chronicle with some letters used in plotting.

160. HAYWOOD, MRS. ELIZA. Secret histories, novels, &c. 1727. M-214. Contains Nos. 140, 146, 155, 157.

161. ANONYMOUS. The adventures of Melinthus. 1728. M-235. Romance with inserted letters; said to be a translation from the French, but this is doubtful.

162. ANONYMOUS. The illegal lovers; a true secret history. 1728, 1734. pr for W. Trott. Price, 1 shilling. 8vo. L. A psychological novel of merit; numerous inserted letters important both to plot and characterization.

163. ANONYMOUS. Sarah, the Quaker, to Lothario, lately deceased. 1728 (2). A "letter to the dead"; see Boyce, "News from Hell."

164. ANONYMOUS [Mrs. Eliza Haywood]. Some memoirs of the amours and intrigues of a certain Irish dean... with the gallantries of two Berkshire ladies. 1728. M-225. A scandalous tale about Swift, Stella, Vanessa, and the Blount sisters, much of which consists of passionate letters.

165. HAYWOOD, MRS. ELIZA. The agreeable Caledonian. 1728. M-231. Novel of amorous intrigue, with inserted letters.

166. HAYWOOD, MRS. ELIZA, tr. The disguis'd prince: or, The beautiful Parisian. 1728. M-238. A translation and adaptation of a partly epistolary novel by Préchac.

167. HAYWOOD, MRS. ELIZA. Irish artifice; or, The history of Clarina. 1728. M-232. A realistic story of intrigue in a domestic setting, told in two letters.

168. ROWE, MRS. ELIZABETH. Friendship in death: In twenty letters from the dead to the living. 1728. M-234. Tom Brown's device turned to moral instruction; single letters and sequences.

169. ROWE, MRS. ELIZABETH. Letters, moral and enter-

taining. 1729. M-234. Similar to No. 168, but showing improvement in narrative technique; includes a set of letters by the countess of Hertford.

170. ANONYMOUS. The brothers: or, Treachery punish'd. 1730. M-247. Romance of love and adventure in a Spanish setting with inserted letters.

171. ANONYMOUS [John Campbell?]. The polite correspondence: or, Rational amusement. 1730? [date uncertain] pr and sold by John Atkinson, etc. 8vo. L. Six series of letters: one is an exchange of travel letters, one a novel in twenty-nine letters, of realistic-domestic love intrigues, with an elaborately complicated plot.

172. ANONYMOUS. The unnatural mother and ungrateful wife. 1730? [date uncertain]. pr for J. Jefferies, Mrs. Dod, and Mrs. Windbush. Price, 1 shilling. 8vo. L. Domestic-realistic tale of treachery, in three letters with inserted letters.

173. HAYWOOD, MRS. ELIZA. Love-letters on all occasions lately passed between persons of distinction. 1730. M-249. Collection ranging in scope from single narrative letters to short letter novels.

174. L., S. The amours of Philario and Olinda: or The intrigues of Windsor. 1730. M-246. A short romance in a domestic setting, with inserted letters.

175. ANONYMOUS, tr. The adventures of the celebrated Madam de Muci. 1731. M-266. In a letter from the lady's companion to her betrothed; story of adventures and love-intrigues; inserted letters important to plot.

176. ANONYMOUS, tr. Winter evenings tales. 1731. M-261. Seventeen brisk anecdotal tales, supposedly told by a company of ladies and gentlemen. Several employ letters; the last is semiepistolary.

177. COSTEKER, JOHN LITTLETON, Gent. The constant lovers. 1731. M-257. Two novels, the second, "Alexis and Sylvia," making considerable use of inserted letters.

178. GWINNETT, RICHARD, and THOMAS, MRS. ELIZABETH. Pylades and Corinna. 1731. M-259. A fictionalized biography of the two, with letters said to be their correspondence over a period of years.

179. [MOORE, JAMES?] Original letters, from Japhet

Crook, alias Sir Peter Stranger, Bart. 1731. Greenough (advertised in No. 180).

180. MOORE, JAMES. The unparallel'd impostor: or, The whole life . . . of Japhet Crook. 1731. M-255. Rogue biography with various letters for authentication, with eleven supposedly by Crook, illiterate in spelling and style.

181. ANONYMOUS. The fair concubine; or, The secret history of the beautiful Vanella. 1732. M-267. Scandal-chronicle of Miss Vane, mistress of Prince Frederick, making use of several letters in plotting.

182. BOYD, MRS. ELIZABETH. The happy-unfortunate: or, The female page. 1732. M-275. A romantic story using letters for plotting and characterization.

183. [HAYWOOD, MRS. ELIZA?] Secret memoirs of the late Mr. Duncan Campbell. 1732. M-273. Consists in part of a series of letters supposed to be written to Campbell.

184. ANONYMOUS. A compleat and genuine account of the life and actions of Joseph Powis. 1732. pr and sold by J. Applebee, A. Dodd, and E. Nutt. 8vo. L. A rogue biography with a collection of letters supposedly by Powis.

185. ANONYMOUS. Authentic memoirs of that exquisitely villainous Jesuit, Father Richard Walpole. Being the copy of a letter. 1733. 8vo. L. The "familiar letter" as an authenticating device.

186. ANONYMOUS. Love without artifice: or, The disappointed peer. 1733. M-279. The story of a sensational contemporary breach of promise suit, in a realistic letter from a friend of the principals, containing their correspondence.

187. ANONYMOUS. The statesman's progress. 1733. pr by R. James. Greenough. Evidently, an epistolary satire on Sir Robert Walpole.

188. MADDEN, SAMUEL. Memoirs of the twentieth century. Being original letters of state, under George the Sixth. 1733. M-284. Twenty-odd letters, supposedly from ambassadors, etc. General satire on all aspects of English and European life; attack on Walpole. Six volumes projected, but five suppressed.

189. ANONYMOUS. Letters historical and critical, from a gentleman in Constantinople to his friend in London. 1735. pr for G. Sparan. Greenough. Apparently an imitation of the *Turkish Spy*.

190. ANONYMOUS. The Persian letters, continued. 1735. M-297. Imitation of No. 192. Satire on England.

191. HUMPHREYS, SAMUEL, tr. Letters from the Marchioness de M*** to the Count de R***. 1735. M-304. The psychological epistolary novel of Crébillon *fils;* technically advanced.

192. LYTTELTON, GEORGE, Baron. Letters from a Persian in England, to his friend at Ispahan. 1735. M-299. A distinguished imitation of the *Lettres persanes.*

193. ANONYMOUS. Letters from a Moor at London to his friends at Tunis. 1736. M-309. Twenty-four "spy" letters, which combine a travelogue with mild satire on English laws and customs.

194. ANONYMOUS, tr. The life of Marianne: or, The adventures of the Countess of ****. 1736. M-318. The first three parts of Marivaux' famous epistolary novel.

195. ANONYMOUS. Post-office intelligence: or, Universal gallantry. 1736, 1740. pr for E. Curll. Price, 3*s.* 8vo. L. A miscellany of love letters, mostly fictional.

196. MUSGRAVE, WILLIAM, tr. Lettres Moscovites: or, Muscovian letters. 1736. M-317. Eleven long letters of travel and adventure in Russia; accounts of the state of the nation.

197. ANONYMOUS. A letter from Mrs. Jane Jones, alias Jenny Diver. 1737. pr for A. Dodd. 8vo. L. A long letter of advice from the famous prostitute to one of her sisters in infamy; ironical self-satire; enclosed in a letter from "C. E." with an account of finding the letter after Jenny's death.

198. ANONYMOUS, tr. French novels. 1738. M-261c. New translations of the first, seventeenth, and twelfth stories of *Winter Evenings Tales* (see No. 176, above); the first two are largely epistolary.

199. LEDIARD, THOMAS, tr. and ed. The German spy, in familiar letters. 1738. M-326. Forty-eight letters of travel and adventure, partly amorous. Perhaps partly a translation, but much is clearly autobiographical.

200. ANONYMOUS, tr. Chinese letters. 1739. pr for D. Browne and R. Hett. 12mo. MH. Letters exchanged among members of a group. Tr. from the Marquis d'Argens' *Lettres chinoises* (1736–38). A Chinese "spy" in Paris.

201. ANONYMOUS, tr. The Jewish spy. 1739. M-337. Let-

ters among members of a group; another use of the "spy" device by D'Argens.

202. ANONYMOUS. The unfortunate dutchess. 1739. M-333. A narrative letter containing several inserted letters. Romantic intrigue; this is the first story in *Several Letters* (1700); see No. 66.

203. RICHARDSON, SAMUEL. Pamela, or, Virtue rewarded. In a series of familiar letters from a beautiful young damsel to her parents. pr for C. Rivington and J. Osborn. 2 vols., 12mo.

Notes on Epistolary Miscellanies

In addition to letter fiction published in the form of "novels" or "histories" and in periodicals, the late seventeenth and early eighteenth centuries produced a number of miscellanies of letters. It is clear that these owe their existence more to the bookseller than to the *épistolier*. Equipped with catchpenny titles, they usually begin with the witty familiar epistles of So-and-So, but more often than not these occupy only a few pages and are succeeded by a hodgepodge of everything the bookseller could lay his hands on in the way of letters, English or translated. These epistolary grab-bags often contain much fiction or semifiction, whose existence is not indicated by the title.

The miscellanies, which evidently were highly popular, present a bibliographical tangle: piracies, reissues with new titles, and reissues concealed in partly new works are the rule. Their importance to the history of epistolary fiction makes it desirable to describe them in some detail, but their size and the variety of matter they contain have required discussions too lengthy to be inserted in the Chronological List. Ten of the miscellanies listed in Appendix A are here described.

THE POST-BOY ROB'D OF HIS MAIL (No. 44).

The edition of 1706 (two volumes in one) is somewhat altered from that of 1692–93; at least the order of letters in Vol. I has been changed, and deletions and additions have been made. (I have not seen the 1693 edition of Vol. II.) Vol. I contains

129 letters in 1692, 94 in 1706. Vol. II contains 88 letters in 1706. Each volume is supposed to be a single letter to a friend, giving a circumstantial account of how a party of gentlemen robbed the postboy, retired to read the letters at leisure, and commented on each letter or series of letters. All the letters and comments are given in full, with dates and salutations in most cases. Vol. I consists entirely of unconnected letters, each presenting a character or situation of interest. Vol. II consists of several series of letters, interspersed with miscellaneous unrelated letters. The series, most of which present a connected narrative or imply a narrative progression, are as follows:

A. Letters 1–13. A mysterious Asiatic traveler comments on his adventures (amatory and otherwise) in Spain.

B. Letters 15–24. Correspondence by and about Mrs. Broadhurst (probably authentic).

C. Letters 26–32. From a lady to her gallant.

D. Letters 33–41. To Mrs. ——. Answers to the above.

E. Letters 54–63. Lysander and Belvidera. A fictional or semifictional exchange.

F. Letters 70–71. "The Marchioness of Castel Rodorigo." Two letters, sent in a covering letter, tell the story of her adultery.

G. Letters 82–88. Lindamor and Clarinda. A love story in an exchange of letters, partly or wholly fiction.

FAMILIAR LETTERS: WRITTEN BY THE . . . EARL OF ROCHESTER (No. 57).

This two-volume work consists largely of the familiar letters of various Restoration wits. These, of course, were written partly as conscious literary productions. Tom Brown and Gildon doubtless revised them to some extent; some contain narratives and descriptions, and some of the love letters are so arranged as to indicate the progress of a courtship. Brown's own letters are semifictional, in the Nicholas Breton tradition. The contents:

Vol. 1 (edited by Brown)
    Letters from Rochester to various friends.
    Miscellaneous letters.
    Six letters of Otway. (Authentic letters to Mrs. Barry, but in the frantic vein of the Portuguese Nun.)

Translations of two letters of Boileau, burlesquing the styles of Balzac and Voiture.
Miscellaneous letters.
Letters of Katherine Philips.
Miscellaneous letters.
Letters by Tom Brown.

Vol. II (edited by Gildon)
Love letters of Rochester.
Miscellaneous letters.
Familiar letters of Etherege, Dennis, Wycherley.
Miscellaneous letters.
Letters of love and gallantry to Eugenia (by "Lysander").
A letter of Aeneas Sylvius.

FAMILIAR AND COURTLY LETTERS, WRITTEN BY MONSIEUR VOITURE (No. 65).

Although the issue of 1705 is called *The Works of Monsieur Voiture*, the second title page bears the old title.

Vol. I
A series of Voiture's letters, translated by Dryden, Brown, and others.
Twelve letters of Aristaenetus, translated by Brown.
Several letters of Pliny, translated by Brown.
Letters of Fontenelle, translated by Brown.
Original letters by Brown, some from earlier collections.
"Love-letters by gentlemen and ladies," including more by Brown and some of the correspondence of Mrs. Centlivre (known at the time as Mrs. Carroll).

Vol. II
A large collection of Voiture's letters, translated by various hands, mostly by Brown.
"A Pacquet from Will's" (see description of No. 70).
"Letters of Friendship and Several Other Occasions." (This is the correspondence of John Dennis with Dryden, Wycherley, and several other wits; it had appeared in print before.)

LETTERS OF WIT, POLITICKS, AND MORALITY (No. 68)

In this collection the semiformal familiar letter predominates, and most of the letters appear to be authentic, although some may be read as scandal material. The contents include:

Letters of Cardinal Bentivoglio.

Letters of Aristaenetus and Petronius. Each one gives a brief, vivid sketch, but there is no continued narrative.

Letters of Guevara.

Letters of Fontenelle and Latin authors. (These and succeeding letters probably also went into *Choice Letters French and English* (1707), on which Boyer and Brown were associated.)

Letters to and from Bussy-Rabutin and other French authors.

Miscellaneous letters by Boyer, Ayloffe, and others. Some of these are personal, some narrative, with satirical descriptions of English customs and places.

Miscellaneous letters "of love and friendship." These include the correspondence of Ayloffe and Mrs. Carroll (later Mrs. Centlivre) under the names of Astraea and Celadon. The correspondence is so arranged as to give the progress of their amorous intrigues, contains a good deal of plot, and might well be read as letter-fiction by one who did not know its source.

A PACQUET FROM WILL'S (No. 70)

This is a small miscellany, of only 80 octavo pages (which fact, together with the spicy nature of its contents, perhaps explains why it was sandwiched, wholly or in part, into several other miscellanies). It begins with a long letter by Ned Ward, in the manner of his *London Spy*, describing the vices and follies of the *beau monde* at Tunbridge Wells. Several more of Ward's letters follow. They are in the satirical or railing vein of the seventeenth-century English letter writer, either giving vivid little pictures of life in town and country, or hurling insults at a correspondent, as in "A Letter to a Crooked Lady." Some are decidedly bawdy. These are followed by two letters (doubtless authentic) from King Charles II and Queen Christina of Sweden, inserted for their value as "secret history," and a collection of miscellaneous letters and love letters including more of Mrs. Centlivre ("Madam C——ll") and Ayloffe ("Celadon").

THE WORKS OF MR. THOMAS BROWN (No. 88)

The edition of 1719–20, in four volumes, contains most of Brown's epistolary work, with the exception of what is printed in the *Remains* (discussed below). Contents:

Vol. I

A collection of original letters. Many of these had appeared in *A Collection of Miscellany Poems* ... (1699), and successively in the later volumes with which Brown was associated. Some reappeared in *Familiar Letters of Love* ... (discussed below). They include satirical letters of news, consolation, advice, travel, and love, and may be summarized as simultaneous satire on the vices of the age and on the conventional situations of the letter writer (such as the consolatory and "nuncupatory" letter).

A full collection of Brown's translations of Aristaenetus, Pliny, Cicero, and French authors, especially Balzac and Fontenelle (see under FAMILIAR AND COURTLY LETTERS).

Vol. II

This volume is composed of the collected *Letters from the Dead to the Living* (which had appeared in two separate parts), and *Certamen Epistolare*, a narrative *jeu d'esprit* in eight letters.

Vol. III

The epistolary portion of this volume is divided into two parts: "Letters Serious and Comical" and "Diverting Letters and Billet-Doux." The first part is made up of translations from the French and from the correspondence of Aeneas Sylvius. These contain facetious anecdotes, gossip, and satire. The "Diverting Letters" are imitations of Le Pays and Voiture, somewhat coarser than the originals. The "Billet-Doux" consist of witty correspondence with ladies, including Mrs. Centlivre's "Journey to Exon" (an imitation of Mrs. Manley), and a suitable reply to it composed by Brown.

Vol. IV

This volume contains a few letters of anecdote and satire. They are taken from earlier volumes; some went into *Familiar Letters of Love*.

FAMILIAR LETTERS OF LOVE, GALLANTRY, AND SEVERAL OCCASIONS (No. 112)

This two-volume work seems to represent an attempt on the part of the bookseller Samuel Briscoe, who had brought out four of the miscellanies discussed above, to present an anthology composed of the best and most popular epistolary material he could bring together. The collection contains verse, prose, authentic letters, and considerable fiction, nearly all of it in letter form. Most of the letters had stood the test of time, and if the edition of 1724 is indeed the sixth, as the title page states, they continued to be highly popular. Contents:

Vol. I

Hudibrastic letters in verse, by Butler.

Letters of Mrs. Behn. Three are authentic (two to Mrs. Price, and one to John Hoyle), and four (to "Philander," signed "A. B.," "A. Behn," and "Sylvia"), appear to be semifictional letters of passion in the Portuguese genre.

A collection of letters by Dennis and others. This includes Dennis's "Passion of Byblis" (a heroid), his travel letters, which had been published in 1694, and various other correspondence which is to be found in earlier volumes and in his *Works* of 1718.

Otway's letters, which had appeared in the *Familiar Letters of Rochester*.

Miscellaneous correspondence of Dennis and other wits. This had already appeared several times.

Correspondence of Charles II and others. Letters of Etherege.

"Memoirs of the fair Eloisa, a Nun, and Abelard, a Monk." This consists of the first letter of Heloise to Abelard. It differs from the translation of Hughes, and is said to be by L'Estrange. It had appeared earlier (see No. 45, Appendix A).

Miscellaneous letters of the wits, including Etherege and Flatman.

Vol. II

A selection of Voiture's letters, translated by Dryden, Dennis, and Brown.

"Original Letters from the Island of the New Atlantis." These are letters taken from Mrs. Manley's *Court Intrigues* or *Lady's Pacquet*. (Nos. 1, 2, 10, 34, 35, 36, 37, 38, 39, 40 in *Court Intrigues*.) Some of these, of course, have been identified as actual correspondence with Steele, the duke of Devonshire, and others, but some are scandal fiction.

"The Amours of Mrs. S." This long letter is the twenty-fourth of *Court Intrigues,* and is apparently a scandal story. It is an excellent piece of fictional writing.

"Olinda's Adventures: or the Amours of a Young Lady." This is an excellent domestic-sentimental novel in eight letters. It is said to be by Mrs. Trotter.

Miscellaneous love letters, including some of Farquhar and Mrs. Centlivre. (Some are satirical.)

Mrs. Centlivre's "Journey to Exon." See the *Works of Mr. Thomas Brown,* Vol. III.

A miscellany of satirical letters by Dr. Smith, John Savage, Ned Ward, and Farquhar.

Tom Brown's "remains." See No. 123.

THE POST-MAN ROBB'D OF HIS MAIL (No. 119)

It appears that Gildon, considering the success of his *Post-Boy Rob'd* in years gone by, decided to put together a mass of miscellaneous letters, parts of essays, and fictional fragments into a similar collection. Times had changed, however. The new volume is almost prudishly moral, compared to the old (for example, instead of robbing the mails themselves, the company of commentators find some mailbags which thieves have taken from the postman, and carefully send on the "letters of business"), and the whole book is dominated by the influence of the *Tatler* and *Spectator* in technique as well as in tone. The fictional content of the work varies from part to part: there is a letter novel, there are brief narratives in exchanges of letters, many of the letters contain anecdotes of "characters" and pictures of the times; some are merely essays with salutation and closing tacked on. The work is divided into five books, as follows:

Book I. Ten letters which are really loosely organized essays on popular topics.

Book II. Twelve essay letters from "Charles Dickson" to a noble lord, with projects for the advancement of the nation.

Book III. A fictional miscellany. A controversial exchange between a learned gardener and a pedantic schoolmaster, several humorous letters like the satirical ones of the *Spectator,* and *The Lover's Sighs.* This last is a novel in letters, depicting the emotions of the fair Stremunia when her royal lover forsook her. It shows considerable skill in characterization.

Book IV. Sixteen letters, mostly didactic.

Book V. Six critical essays in letter form and six letters from "Charles Dickson" proposing the establishment of a Royal Academy of Arts and Sciences.

MISCELLANEA AUREA (No. 122)

This collection of letters is rather innocuous in tone, and like Gildon's miscellany it relies heavily on the *Spectator* for moral and technical guidance. It is divided into seven sections:

"A Voyage to the Mountains of the Moon." A satire on contemporary literati.

Reproving letters to various aberrant persons with type names such as Lord Femmechace and Spondee Dactyl.

Essay-letters, including a "Vindication of Cardinal Alberoni."

"The Loves of Don *Alonzo* Duke of *Lerma*, and Donna *Olympia Di Bianchi*." A story in four letters.

Miscellaneous letters.

"The Garden of Adonis, or Love to no Purpose." Twenty love letters, single and in pairs.

Assorted letters and paradoxes.

THE REMAINS OF MR. THO. BROWN (No. 123)

Most of the contents of this work had appeared in *Familiar Letters of Love*, II. It contains a few items from earlier collections and may be considered as a supplement to the four volumes of the *Works*. Its contents are extremely miscellaneous, but include a number of new letters. The most interesting are:

A long letter descriptive of life in the country, followed by several others which are also in the *Works*. Pages 38–57.

"*Love-Letters* Written to Madam *Maintenon*, Stollen out of her Closet by one of her Servants." Pages 75–85.

Two satirical letters in a rather bawdy strain. Pages 140–41 and 332–38.

A List of Letter Fiction
in Periodicals

Though the periodicals of the early eighteenth century throve on political and foreign news and on advertising, their wares included innumerable pieces of brief fiction. Letter fiction was not the least of the varieties represented, and it ran the gamut from clearly fictional "letters to the editor," written by the perplexed, to miniature letter novels. Although the preceding pages have dealt almost entirely with letter fiction which appeared in books, it would be misleading to omit all mention of how much periodical fiction contributed both to the development of narrative in letters and to the cultivation of the reader's taste for it.

The following, highly selective list gives even in its brevity an indication of the great variety of fiction in letter form which the early eighteenth-century reader, though he might never read a novel, would have found in papers and journals. The entries are in chronological order.

1. *Athenian Mercury*, Jan. 12, 1691. Letters to the editor on dilemmas of love and passion, related circumstantially and at length.

2. *Tatler*, May 17, 1709. "Transcription" of a letter from Bath, giving an account of two ridiculous old coquettes who are rivals in social pretension.

3. *Tatler*, Oct. 18, 1709. Steele's well-known story of

the man who accidentally shot his bride on their wedding-day uses two letters to exhibit the hero's emotions.

4. *The Visions of Sir Heister Ryley*, Dec. 13, 1710. Sir Heister finds a cache of love letters which reveal a sentimental story; a young couple plan to steal a marriage.

5. *Spectator*, June 20, 1711. A footman relates his history in a letter, with considerable emphasis on emotion and sentiment.

6. *Spectator*, Aug. 17, 1711. Valets and maids write to give characters of their masters and mistresses.

7. *Spectator*, Aug. 27, 1711. A spark relates his amatory history in a letter.

8. *Spectator*, Oct. 8, 1711. Rebecca Nettletop writes an affecting account of how she was seduced and decoyed into a house of prostitution.

9. *Spectator*, Feb. 12, 1712. Sir John Enville relates how newly acquired wealth and marriage to a lady of quality have made him miserable.

10. *Spectator*, Mar. 10, 1712. A tiny letter novel. Octavia tells how she was secretly married, deserted, lost her marriage certificate by accident, and is now in a wretched state.

11. *Spectator*, May 10, 1712. By John Hughes, this story has been thought to be a source for *Pamela*. Three letters tell the tale; the plot is the same in essentials.

12. *Spectator*, Jun. 6, 1712. By Steele, a parody of epistolary affectations. In a miniature letter novel, Cynthio disengages himself from the affections of Flavia, in an exchange of nine brisk notes.

13. *Spectator*, Sept. 17, 1712. Two melancholy letters from men who are henpecked by their mistresses.

14. *Spectator*, Oct. 23, 1712. Sir Roger de Coverley's death described in a letter from his butler.

15. *Spectator*, Oct. 27, 1712. A bereaved husband tells of his wife's death, and his feelings when he thinks of her.

16. *Spectator*, Nov. 25, 1712. The Emperor of China, in a letter to the Pope, proposes that they unite their ecclesiastical establishments.

17. *British-Mercury*. Dec. 31, 1712—Jan. 28, 1713. "A Letter from Madrid" is a fictional piece in five installments. It was later sold as a threepenny pamphlet.

18. *The Lay-Monk*, Jan. 11, 1713. Two personal his-

tories with good characterization: one is from a girl who is to marry a blockhead in deference to her parents, the other from a woman married to a petty tyrant.

19. *Guardian*, May 8, 1713. "R. B." describes a country seat, his diversions, a pet owl, an abbey, and a barber who tells tedious stories.

20. *Spectator*, June 21, 1714. The ambassador of Bantam sends a "spy" letter to his sovereign, describing English morals and manners.

21. *News from the Dead*, Feb. 1715. Ramiel, a devil on business in London, tells his friend Arioc how much the metropolis resembles home.

22. *The St. James's Post*, Aug. 6, 1716. "News from the Dead; in a Letter from Tom Brown."

23. *Theatre*, Jan. 19, 1720. Leucippe, an Oxford girl, has been entrapped into a brothel by her perfidious lover and is now a noted strumpet; she laments her fallen state.

24. *British Journal*, Sept. 28, 1723. A letter, strongly reminiscent of Mrs. Manley's, describes a stagecoach journey, with incidents of the road, and several "characters," including a peevish lawyer.

25. *Universal Journal*, Dec. 26, 1723. The sentimental story of Leonora, in a letter.

26. *British Journal*, June 6, 1724. "Copy of a letter from Mrs. —— at Bath, to Lady Mary ——." A miniature scandal novel, with a lively "self-conscious narrator."

27. *Postmaster*, Mar. 26, 1725. "A faithful account of how a young lady was lately seduced and imposed upon, by an Abbot at Lisbon." A letter "in the natural and beautiful Style, in which it was writ by the ingenious Author."

28. *Universal Spectator*, Oct. 18, 1729. Clarissa relates the story of her life in a long letter.

29. *Universal Spectator*, Nov. 22, 1729. A retelling of the story of Lothario and Calista, in a letter from the repentant rake.

30. *Universal Spectator*, Jan. 24, 1730. A letter from Amelia; she repents of her rash marriage when her husband dies and her father disowns her.

31. *Universal Spectator*, Sept. 5, 1730. A long confessional letter from a man whose marriage for money resulted in the death of the girl to whom he had first been pledged.

32. *Universal Spectator*, Oct. 11–25, 1735. An account in installments of how a farm girl was ruined by a neighboring squire. It recalls *Pamela;* but the heroine's head had been so turned by novels and romances that her virtue was easily abandoned.

33. *Applebee's Original Weekly Journal*, Nov. 29, and Dec. 6, 1735. "The Effects of Love, or Reason Defeated. From the Portuguese."

34. *The Entertaining Correspondent; Or, Curious Relations*, 1739. "Digested into familiar letters and conversations, by George Smith."

35. *Universal Spectator*, May 24, 1740. The story of Honoria, with a theme similar to that of *Pamela.*

Index